POLITICS
AND THE
NOVEL

POLITICS
AND THE
NOVEL

Irving Howe

Columbia University Press
New York

Columbia University Press Morningside Edition
Columbia University Press
New York   Oxford

Morningside Edition with new preface
Copyright © 1992 Columbia University Press
Copyright © 1987 Irving Howe
Copyright © 1957 Irving Howe

Library of Congress Cataloging-in-Publication Data

Howe, Irving.
Politics and the novel / Irving Howe.
—Morningside ed., with new pref.   p.   cm.
First published in 1957.
Includes bibliographical references.
ISBN 0-231-07994-X (alk. paper) : —ISBN 0-231-07995-8
(pbk. : alk. paper) :
1. Politics in literature.   2. Political fiction—History and
criticism.   I. Title.
PN3448.P6H6   1992
809.3'9358—dc20   92-3255
CIP

∞
Casebound editions of Columbia University Press books are
Smyth-sewn and printed on permanent and durable acid-free paper.

Printed in the United States of America

c   10 9 8 7 6 5 4 3 2 1
p   10 9 8 7 6 5 4 3 2 1

ACKNOWLEDGMENTS

The chapter on Conrad first appeared in *Kenyon Review*, Autumn 1953 and Winter 1954 issues. The chapter on Turgenev appeared in *Hudson Review*, Winter 1956. Part of the chapter on Stendhal appeared in *The Avon Book of Modern Writing*, 1953. The chapter on James appeared in *Western Review*, Spring 1954. The chapter on Orwell appeared in *The American Scholar*, Spring 1956. The section on Silone appeared in *Dissent*, Winter 1956. The sections on Henry Adams and Hawthorne appeared in *The New Republic*, September 22, 1952 and September 5, 1955. Permission of the editors of these periodicals, who hold copyright on these respective items, is gratefully acknowledged.

The chapter on The Political Novel in America includes part of my introduction to the Modern Library edition of *The Bostonians* by Henry James, copyright 1956 by Random House Inc., whose permission is gratefully acknowledged.

CONTENTS

True tragedy arises "when the idea of 'justice' appears to be leading to the destruction of higher values."

—MAX SCHELER

PREFACE TO THE
MORNINGSIDE EDITION

To go back to the writings of one's younger years is an experience that is exhilarating and unsettling. Questions about identity trouble the mind. Who was the person who wrote this book? What relation do I now have to him? We bear the same name, there are perhaps some similarities between photographs of him and of me, and the quite modest royalties of his work have come down to me. But a gap of thirty-five years separates us, and the gap might be even larger than the mere number of years suggests. How could the earlier self whom I struggle to recall have written with such assurance about Dostoevsky's *The Possessed* or been so withholding in appreciation of Conrad's *The Secret Agent?*

One hopes, of course, for an organic development in life and thought, but the twentieth century has not been an ideal setting for that. In a time of blood, chaos, and ideology, the most one can hope for is a fragmented coherence, perhaps resting on the illusion that, notwithstanding the confusions of our time, one has lived and worked out of a firm center of belief. But who can be sure? In any case, let me turn to a few remarks about the circumstances in which this book was written.

In the early 1950s there was held each year at Princeton University, under the direction of the noted literary critic Richard Blackmur, a series of Christian Gauss seminars devoted to literature and ideas. Each seminar was led by an invited speaker who, several weeks in succession, would speak for about an hour and then respond to questions, comments and criticisms from a small group of literary people and intellectuals. The main speakers in 1952 were Edmund Wilson and Paul Tillich, two extremely formidable figures. And, since it was the custom to include one junior lecturer each year, Blackmur asked me to conduct the final seminar. Young and inexperienced, though not without ambition, I somewhat recklessly chose to give my talks on "the political novel," a category I readily acknowledged to be imprecise. As I would later argue in the opening chapter of this book, I did not discuss "the political novel" in order to set up still another subgenre. My intention was to try out a certain way of reading some, surely not most, novels. It was an idea that led me to say, as I remark in my first chapter, that by a political novel I meant "any novel I wished to treat as if it were a political novel, though clearly one would not wish to treat most novels in that way."

By the time I gave this seminar, I had written some literary criticism but was really still a beginner. Most of those who came to hear me were accordingly indulgent. For me this was a crucial, indeed a transforming experience. I approached my subject with a passionate interest, and some hobbling preconceptions, both deriving from my socialist youth and anti-Stalinist Marxism. A few years later, with additions and revisions, I published my lectures as the book you are now holding in your hands.

The perspective from which I wrote was hardly a popular one. The 1950s were a decade of conservatism, not quite as intellectually coarse or aggressive as the conservatism of the Reagan years, but with the advent of the Cold War, the blight of McCarthyism, and a kind of moral weariness that followed the end of the Second World War, conservative enough.

Whatever remained of the American left was breaking up internally or suffering assault. The once self-assured group of writers around the once-influential little magazine *Partisan Review* was disintegrating as most of its leading figures were no longer committed to the group's earlier effort to link cultural modernism with anti-Stalinist radicalism. By the 1950s it seemed to many American intellectuals that the posture of critical distance, or as it was sometimes called "alienation," had become outmoded. The blight of totalitarianism, now embodied in the rise of Stalinist Russia to a world power, seemed to be spreading across the globe, and the result was a turning away from any sort of radicalism, even liberalism.

A few of us, a very few, resisted this conservative mood which, at the time, was more a mood than an ideology and started the democratic-left magazine *Dissent* in 1953. We were a tiny and scorned group. Many literary people and many intellectuals came to be suspicious of all political schools and to accept, sometimes hesitantly or sometimes noisily, what was then called "the American celebration." So, while *Politics and the Novel* was not written in explicit opposition to this conservative mood or with any explicit polemical intent, it certainly came to be seen as a dissident work.

In the 1950s there was also a strong shift of literary opinion. The New Criticism was becoming the dominant literary tendency in the American academy. The customary outlook of cultivated literary people was now to insist that the poem or novel must be seen as a self-contained structure with its own norms and modes and free from the pressures or contaminations of history, society, and ideas. Indeed, the literary work was often seen as a kind of sanctuary against the vulgarities and corruptions of the outer world.

The mentors and models of the New Criticism were T. S. Eliot and I. A. Richards, literary figures of great distinction. The leading American practitioners of the New Criticism (though with many differences of opinion and stress among them) were John Crowe Ransom, Allen Tate, Austin Warren and Richard Blackmur. It is not hard to understand why sensitive people, in those troubled years, should have been drawn to the outlook of the New Criticism. These were extremely talented writers with a love for literature and keen gifts of analysis. They had developed a method which lent itself to close reading, something of genuine value in teaching literature. They spoke as ardent defenders of the great tradition of English literature against both dreary scholastics and cheap popularizers.

In those years, I counted myself as one of the minor antagonists of the New Criticism; however, I came to recognize that those of us who resisted its precepts and practises had probably the most to learn from it. For the New Criticism made even its antagonists, at least the serious ones, more sensitive to literary nuances, to inner properties of a work, and to the idea of literature as an autonomous realm. Finally, however, the New York critics around the *Partisan Review,* to which I had become an occasional contributor, wrote out of a persuasion that the historical and social approaches were, for them, all but second nature. Critics like Philip Rahv, Lionel Trilling, Harold Rosenberg, and a figure somewhat apart, Edmund Wilson, could not accept the esthetic of the New Criticism. They were too deeply engaged with social and moral questions of their moment, so that their approach to literature was necessarily, as opponents said, "impure." They felt that the formalist school of the New Criticism tended, in Lionel Abel's quip, to confine literature to mere literature.

The New Critics formed a vivid and generous group. I can testify to the generosity several of them showed to me, even though I clearly disagreed with them. After a time, relations between the New Critics and the New York critics grew warmer since both were hostile to what they regarded as the narrow academic historicism that prevailed in English departments at the time. They saw themselves as beleaguered defenders of high culture against the contaminations of middle-brow journalism and placed a distinct value on personal style in the composition of an essay. While the differences were real enough, both groups felt themselves to be "outsiders" in relation to academic life. This feeling would soon change in the 1950s as they would find positions in English departments. And both shared a proud belief that they were not just scholars or critics; they were, as poets, novelists or social commentators, *writers*. So again, while I did not deliberately set out in *Politics and the Novel* to confront the New Criticism or to engage in any explicit polemics, my book was generally taken to be a work in opposition to the then-dominant critical outlook.

There is a more personal aspect of this book's origins that requires a few words of description. *Politics and the Novel* was written at a moment when I was gradually drifting away from orthodox Marxism. By this statement I mean orthodox Marxism in its serious version or versions, not the corrupt authoritarian slogans of the Communist movement. Whoever cares about such matters can see that *Politics and the Novel* still bears the distinct signs of a Marxist outlook yet also, for good or bad, the distinct signs of a mind that is moving away from that outlook. When later scholars and bibliographers came to compile lists of critical writings in the Marxist tradition, they did not include my book—and they were right not to. I still hold firmly to the socialist ethos which partly inspired this book, but the ideology to which these essays occasionally return, both as a point of reference and as a point from which to diverge, no longer has for me the power it once had. Still, I can see that for the author of *Politics and the Novel* there were genuine advantages to be had from an involvement with Marxist categories. This involvement, it may be, makes for a fruitful tension between the outer world and the work considered.

It is an involvement that also leads to certain limitations of treatment. A pedantic title for this book might have been *Revolutionary Politics and the Modern Novel*, for it pays little attention to the kind of novel written by George Eliot, Meredith, and Trollope, which portray the political life of a settled society, that is, a society in which the usual interplay of group conflicts is regulated by democratic procedures. It may be that there were certain reasons for choosing to focus on fictions that deal with revolutionary crisis and apocalypse, not only because those were dominant in the imagination of serious people at the time I wrote but also because the novel, while closer to ordinary life than other literary genres, cannot hope to encompass all the happenings of ordinary life. Even in its occasional programmatic devotion to the commonplace, the novel still tests extreme situations, the drama of harsh and ultimate conflicts. Nevertheless, I find myself regretting that I didn't write about Trollope's Palliser novels, if only because that would have forced me to engage with situations and categories sharply different from those now dominating this book. Time is slipping away, but I still have some hope of writing about the Palliser series.

I notice still another difference between the author of *Politics and the Novel* and myself. Being young, he was clearly fond of epigrammatic sentences, tense verbal sequences, even occasional attempts at bravura. But now, especially at a time when critical writing is marked by jargon and obscurantism, my inclination is to care most about lucidity. The writer of expository prose, I now feel, should strive for that most difficult of styles: a prose so direct, so clear, so transparent that the act of reading comes to seem like looking through a glass.

Still, when all is said and done, I recognize certain advantages that followed from the conditions and atmospheres in which this book was written. The single greatest advantage is that this book is not a mere exercise, still another "study." It merges from an idea—what can occur in the meeting between the novel as form and politics as ideology—even as, I hope, it is not overwhelmed by a fixed thesis as to what "must" occur during that meeting. That is why I am still glad to see my name on its title page, together with that of the man who wrote this book.

PREFACE

This book is meant primarily as a study of the relation between literature and ideas, though a considerable part of it, I should say, consists of literary criticism. My interest was far less in literature as social evidence or testimony than in the literary problem of what happens to the novel when it is subjected to the pressures of politics and political ideology. In discussing nineteenth century writers I have employed more or less conventional methods of criticism, while in treating twentieth century writers I have found myself placing a greater stress upon politics and ideology as such; but this was not the result of any preconceived decision, it was a gradual shift in approach that seemed to be required by the nature of the novels themselves.

It is clear that, in addition to the books discussed in the following pages, there are a number of important novels that might profitably have been considered in the terms that I have here employed. Various friends suggested novels by Disraeli, Trollope, Meredith, Tolstoy, Pirandello and a great many contemporary writers. Some of these did not happen to interest me, others interested me too much. In any case, my intention was not to discuss every novel that might conceivably be treated as a "political novel"—nothing could be farther from my intention than a "definitive study"—but rather to bring to bear a certain approach upon those books where it would be most relevant.

Six of the chapters in this book were presented, in earlier form, as papers for the Christian Gauss Seminar at Princeton University; and to the directors for that seminar I wish to express my gratitude for enabling me to begin this project. The possibility for completing it I owe mainly to the editors of *Kenyon Review*, who awarded me a Kenyon Fellowship in Literary Criticism; and to them, too, I would here like to offer my thanks.

I owe many debts to friends who have read all or part of the manuscript, offered helpful suggestions, made acute criticisms, and provided continuous encouragement. Let me mention only a few of those friends: Meyer Schapiro, Lewis Coser, David Sachs, Rogers Albritton, and the late Louis Kronenberger and the late Philip Rahv.

Parts of this book have appeared, in somewhat different form, in *Kenyon Review*, *Hudson Review*, *The American Scholar*, *Dissent*, *The New Republic*, *The Western Review*, *The New International* and *The Avon Book of Modern Writing*. The section on *The Bostonians* forms part of an introduction to a Modern Library edition of that novel.

I.H.

PART ONE

CHAPTER ONE

THE IDEA OF THE POLITICAL NOVEL

"Politics in a work of literature," wrote Stendhal, "is like a pistol-shot in the middle of a concert, something loud and vulgar, and yet a thing to which it is not possible to refuse one's attention."

The remark is very shrewd, though one wishes that Stendhal, all of whose concerts are interrupted by bursts of gunfire, had troubled to say a little more. Once the pistol is fired, what happens to the music? Can the noise of the interruption ever become part of the performance? When is the interruption welcome and when is it resented?

To answer such questions one is tempted to turn directly to the concerts, anticipating those rude disharmonies—they will form our subject—which Stendhal hints at but does not describe. And in a moment we shall do that: we shall examine a number of major novels, each of them shaped and colored by a dominant variety of modern thought, to see what the violent intrusion of politics does to, and perhaps for, the literary imagination. But first, a few speculations.

Labels, categories, definitions—particularly with regard to so loose and baggy a monster as the novel—do not here concern me very much. Whether a novel may be called a political or a psychological novel—and it is seldom anything more than a matter of convenience—seems rather trivial beside the question, why does a particular critic, bringing to bear his own accumulation of experience, propose to use one or the other of these labels? What is it that his approach is to make us see more clearly? What mode of analysis does the critic employ, or what body of insights does he command, to persuade us to "grant" him his classification, in the sense perhaps that one "grants" a builder his scaffold?

When I speak in the following pages of the political novel, I have no ambition of setting up still another rigid category. I am concerned with perspectives of observation, not categories of classification. To be sure, distinctions of genre can be very useful in literary analysis: they train us to avoid false or irrelevant expectations and prepare us, within fluid limits, to entertain proper expectations; they teach us, if I may cite a familiar but still useful example, not to expect a lengthy narrative about the deeds of a hero when we read a lyric poem. But we are hardly speaking of genres at all when we employ such loose terms as the political or the psychological novel, since these do not mark any fundamental distinctions of literary form. At most, they point to a dominant emphasis, a significant stress in the writer's subject or in his attitude toward it. They may, that is, be convenient ways of talking about certain rather small groups of novels.

I stress this empirical approach—this commitment to practical criticism—because it has been my experience that a certain kind of mind, called, perhaps a little too easily, the academic mind, insists upon exhaustive rites of classification. I remember being asked once, after a lecture, whether *A Tale of Two Cities* could be considered a political novel. For a moment I was bewildered, since it had never occurred to me that this was a genuine problem: it was, I am now sure, the kind of problem one has to *look for*. I finally replied that one could think of it that way if one cared to, but that little benefit was likely to follow: the story of Sidney Carton was not a fruitful subject for the kind of inquiry I was suggesting.

Pressed a little harder, I then said—and this must have struck some of my listeners as outrageous—that I meant by a political novel any novel I wished to treat as if it were a political novel, though clearly one would not wish to treat most novels in that way. There was no reason to.

Perhaps it would be more useful to say that my subject is the relation between politics and literature, and that the term "political novel" is used here as a convenient shorthand to suggest the kind of novel in which this relation is interesting enough to warrant investigation. The relation between politics and literature is not, of course, always the same, and that too is part of my subject: to show the way in which politics increasingly controls a certain kind of novel, and to speculate on the reasons for this change. The chapters on Stendhal and Dostoevsky contain a far heavier stress upon the literary side of things than do the chapters on Koestler and Orwell. And, I think, with good reason. In a book like *1984* politics has achieved an almost total dominion, while such works as *The Possessed* and *The Charterhouse of Parma* cannot be understood without using traditional literary categories.

Having cast more than enough skepticism on the impulse to assign literary labels, I want now, in the hope that it will not seem a merely frivolous sequel, to suggest the way in which I shall here use the term "political novel." By a political novel I mean a novel in which political ideas play a dominant role or in which the political milieu is the dominant setting—though again a qualification is necessary, since the word "dominant" is more than a little questionable. Perhaps it would be better to say: a novel in which *we take to be dominant* political ideas or the political milieu, a novel which permits this assumption without thereby suffering any radical distortion and, it follows, with the possibility of some analytical profit.

Let us for the moment assume a vastly oversimplified schema for the genesis and growth of the novel. Several kinds of prose writing converge to form the novel as we know it, among them the picaresque tale, the pastoral idyll, the romance, the historical chronicle and the early newspaper report.

The most important of these is probably the picaresque tale, which flourished during the era in which the bourgeoisie was proving itself to be a vital class but was not yet able to take full political power. Largely good-natured in its moral tone, and often a lively sign of social health and energy, the picaresque novel, through the figure of the rogue-hero, obliquely suggested the new possibilities for social mobility. In acts of sly outrage the rogue-hero broke through the conventional class barriers while refraining from an explicit challenge to their moral propriety; his bravado thus came to seem a mocking anticipation of the regroupment of social strata which would soon take place in the nineteenth century. At the same time, however, the picaresque novel reflected the capacity of society to absorb the shocks of the bourgeois revolution. The atmosphere in which the rogue-hero moved was expansive and tolerant; society had room for his escapades and felt little reason to fear his assaults upon its decorum; in a curious, "underground" way he expressed the new appetite for experiment as a mode of life.

From the picaresque to the social novel of the nineteenth century there is a major shift in emphasis. Where the picaresque tale had reflected a gradual opening of society to individual action, the social novel marked the consolidation of that action into the political triumph of the merchant class; and where the rogue-hero had explored the various levels of society with a whimsical curiosity (for he was not yet committed to the idea of life *within* society), the typical hero of the nineteenth century novel was profoundly involved in testing himself, and thereby his values, against both the remnants of aristocratic resistance and the gross symbols of the new commercial world that offended his sensibility.

Once, however, bourgeois society began to lose some of its élan and cohesion, the social novel either declined into a sediment of conventional mediocrity (as, frequently, in Trollope) or it fractured in several directions. The most extreme and valuable of these directions were the novel of private sensibility, raised in our time to a glory of achievement and a peak of esteem that is without precedent, and the novel of public affairs and politics, which might be warranted in feeling a certain sibling rivalry . . .

The social novel has always presupposed a substantial amount of social stability. For the novelist to portray nuances of manners or realistically to "cut a slice of life," society must not be too restive under the knife; and only in England was this stability still significantly present during the first half of the nineteenth century.

The ideal social novel had been written by Jane Austen, a great artist who enjoyed the luxury of being able to take society for granted; it was *there*, and it seemed steady beneath her glass, Napoleon or no Napoleon. But soon it would not be steady beneath anyone's glass, and the novelist's attention had necessarily to shift from the gradations within society to the fate of society itself. It is at this point, roughly speaking, that the kind of book I have called the political novel comes to be written—the kind in which the *idea* of society, as distinct from the mere unquestioned workings of society, has penetrated the consciousness of the characters in all of its profoundly problematic aspects, so that there is to be observed in their behavior, and they are themselves often aware of, some coherent political loyalty or ideological identification. They now think in terms of supporting or opposing society as such; they rally to one or another embattled segment of society; and they do so in the name of, and under prompting from, an ideology.*

To see this most clearly we must turn to France where Stendhal, though he wrote only a few decades after Miss Austen, was already marking the death of an era. In France, which had known a bourgeois revolution both abrupt and violent, all social contradictions were sharper and the consciousness of them more acute than in England. Through his novels Sten-

* I am quite aware that in practice it would often be impossible or not very useful to draw a sharp line of distinction between the political and social novels as I have here described them. Many novels—for example, George Eliot's *Middlemarch*—would seem to straddle the two categories. But I think it is worthwhile making the distinction analytically even if one recognizes that there are few examples of the "pure" type.

dhal repeatedly declared that the hero, having been deprived of an arena for his talents and energies, must break his way into—and then through—society by sheer force of will. Decades before the world realized it, Stendhal's novels announced that the age of individual heroism was dying, the age of mass ideology beginning to appear.

The political novel—I have in mind its "ideal" form—is peculiarly a work of internal tensions. To be a novel at all, it must contain the usual representation of human behavior and feeling; yet it must also absorb into its stream of movement the hard and perhaps insoluble pellets of modern ideology. The novel deals with moral sentiments, with passions and emotions; it tries, above all, to capture the quality of concrete experience. Ideology, however, is abstract, as it must be, and therefore likely to be recalcitrant whenever an attempt is made to incorporate it into the novel's stream of sensuous impression. The conflict is inescapable: the novel tries to confront experience in its immediacy and closeness, while ideology is by its nature general and inclusive. Yet it is precisely from this conflict that the political novel gains its interest and takes on the aura of high drama. For merely to say that ideology is, in some sense, a burden or an impediment in a novel is not yet to specify its uses—is not yet to tell us whether the impediment may be valuable in forcing upon the novelist a concentration of those resources that are needed to overcome it.

It would be easy to slip into a mistake here, precisely the mistake that many American novelists make: the notion that abstract ideas invariably contaminate a work of art and should be kept at a safe distance from it. No doubt, when the armored columns of ideology troop in *en masse*, they do imperil a novel's life and liveliness, but ideas, be they in free isolation or hooped into formal systems, are indispensable to the serious novel. For in modern society ideas raise enormous charges of emotion, they involve us in our most feverish commitments and lead us to our most fearful betrayals. The political novelist may therefore have to take greater risks than most others, as must any artist who uses large quantities of "impure" matter; but his potential reward is accordingly all the greater. The novel, to be sure, is inconceivable without an effort to present and to penetrate human emotion in its most private, irreducible aspects; but the direction in which the emotion moves, the weight it exerts, the objects to which it attaches itself, are all conditioned, if not indeed controlled, by the pressures of abstract thought.

Like a nimble dialectician, the political novelist must be able to handle several ideas at once, to see them in their hostile yet interdependent relations and to grasp the way in which ideas *in the novel* are transformed into something other than the ideas of a political program. The ideas of actual life, which may have prompted the writer to compose his novel, must be left inviolate; the novelist has no business tampering with them in their own domain, nor does he generally have the qualifications for doing so. But once these ideas are set to work within the novel they cannot long remain mere lumps of abstraction. At its best, the political novel generates such intense heat that the ideas it appropriates are melted into its movement and fused with the emotions of its characters. George Eliot, in one of her letters, speaks of "the severe effort of trying to make certain ideas incarnate, as if they had revealed themselves to me first in the flesh." This is one of the great problems, but also one of the supreme challenges, for the political novelist: to make ideas or ideologies come to life, to endow them with the capacity for stirring characters into passionate gestures and sacrifices, and even more, to create the illusion that they have a kind of independent motion, so that they themselves—those abstract weights of idea or ideology—seem to become active characters in the political novel.

No matter how much the writer intends to celebrate or discredit a political ideology, no matter how didactic or polemical his purpose may be, his novel cannot finally rest on the idea "in itself." To the degree that he is really a novelist, a man seized by the passion to represent and to give order to experience, he must drive the politics of or behind his novel into a complex relation with the kinds of experience that resist reduction to formula—and this once done, supreme difficulty though it is, transforms his ideas astonishingly. His task is always to show the relation between theory and experience, between the ideology that has been preconceived and the tangle of feelings and relationships he is trying to present. This he does in a number of ways: diseased and intimate emotion twisting ideology into obsessional chimeras, as in Dostoevsky's *The Possessed;* ideology fortifying emotion for an heroic martyrdom, as in Malraux's *Man's Fate;* ideology pure and possessed strangling emotion pure and disinterested, as in Koestler's *Darkness at Noon;* and emotion fatally sapping the powers of ideological commitment, as in James' *The Princess Casamassima.*

The greatest of all political novels, *The Possessed,* was written with the explicit purpose of excommunicating all beliefs that find salvation anywhere but in the Christian God. "I mean to utter certain thoughts," wrote Dostoevsky, "whether all the artistic side of it goes to the dogs or not . . . even if it turns into a mere pamphlet, I shall say all that I have in my heart." Fortunately Dostoevsky could not suppress his "artistic side" and by the time his book reaches its end it has journeyed through places of the head and heart undreamed of in his original plan. But whatever else it does, *The Possessed* proves nothing of the kind that might be accessible to proof in "a mere pamphlet." For while a political novel can enrich our sense of human experience, while it can complicate and humanize our commitments, it is only very rarely that it will alter those commitments themselves. And when it does so, the political novel is engaged in a task of persuasion which is not really its central or distinctive purpose. I find it hard to imagine, say, a serious socialist being dissuaded from his belief by a reading of *The Possessed,* though I should like equally to think that the quality and nuance of that belief can never be quite as they were before he read *The Possessed.*

Because it exposes the impersonal claims of ideology to the pressures of private emotion, the political novel must always be in a state of internal warfare, always on the verge of becoming something other than itself. The political novelist—

the degree to which he is aware of this is another problem—establishes a complex system of intellectual movements, in which his own opinion is one of the most active yet not entirely dominating movers. Are we not close here to one of the "secrets" of the novel in general?—I mean the vast respect which the great novelist is ready to offer to the whole idea of *opposition,* the opposition he needs to allow for in his book against his own predispositions and yearnings and fantasies. He knows that his own momentum, his own intentions, can be set loose easily enough; but he senses, as well, that what matters most of all is to allow for those rocks against which his intentions may smash but, if he is lucky, they may merely bruise. Even as the great writer proudly affirms the autonomy of his imagination, even as he makes the most severe claims for his power of imposing his will upon the unformed materials his imagination has brought up to him, he yet acknowledges that he must pit himself against the imperious presence of the necessary. And in the political novel it is politics above all, politics as both temptation and impediment, that represents the necessary.

Abstraction, then, is confronted with the flux of experience, the monolith of program with the richness and diversity of motive, the purity of ideal with the contaminations of action. The political novel turns characteristically to an apolitical temptation: in *The Possessed* to the notion that redemption is possible only to sinners who have greatly suffered; in Conrad's *Nostromo* and *Under Western Eyes* to the resources of private affection and gentleness; in *Man's Fate* to the metaphysical allurements of heroism as they reveal themselves in a martyr's death; in Silone's *Bread and Wine* to the discovery of peasant simplicity as a foil to urban corruption; and in *Darkness at Noon* to the abandoned uses of the personal will, the *I* so long relegated to the category of a "grammatical fiction." This, so to say, is the "pastoral" element that is indispensable to the political novel, indispensable for providing it with polarity and tension; but it matters only if there is already present the public element, a sense of the rigors, necessities and attractions of political life.

The criteria for evaluating a political novel must finally be the same as those for any other novel: how much of our life does it illuminate? how ample a moral vision does it suggest? —but these questions occur to us in a special context, in that atmosphere of political struggle which dominates modern life. For both the writer and the reader, the political novel provides a particularly severe test: politics rakes our passions as nothing else, and whatever we may consent to overlook in reading a novel, we react with an almost demonic rapidity to a detested political opinion. For the writer the great test is, how much truth can he force through the sieve of his opinions? For the reader the great test is, how much of that truth can he accept though it jostle *his* opinions?

In the political novel, then, writer and reader enter an uneasy compact: to expose their opinions to a furious action, and as these melt into the movement of the novel, to find some common recognition, some supervening human bond above and beyond ideas. It is not surprising that the political novelist, even as he remains fascinated by politics, urges his claim for a moral order beyond ideology; nor that the receptive reader, even as he perseveres in his own commitment, assents to the novelist's ultimate order.

CHAPTER TWO

STENDHAL: THE POLITICS OF SURVIVAL

While Henry James was working on *The Princess Casamassima* he remarked in a letter that the English upper class "seems to me to be in many ways very much the same rotten and *collapsible* one as the French aristocracy before the revolution—minus the cleverness and conversation . . ." About the cleverness and conversation Stendhal might have had a caustic phrase, but he would certainly have accepted James' description of the English ruling class; as far back as 1819 he had written that he "hoped to have the joy of beholding a revolution in England." Stendhal was not, in any modern sense, a revolutionist or even a radical yet he instinctively placed himself in alliance with the revolutions of his day: they gave him joy.

He stands in the sharpest contrast to those novelists of the 19th century who turn, somewhat later, to political themes. When Dostoevsky, Conrad and James take revolutionary politics as their subject, they write partly in order to arouse the educated public to the dangers stirring beneath the "vast smug surface" (as James called it) of society. They do this in various ways: Dostoevsky by wrestling with political ideas, Conrad by forcing himself to confront the political milieu, James by divining certain problems of the political vocation. Involuntarily, they watch the coming-apart of the world to which they are emotionally bound. Antipathetic to radicalism, they lay bare the sources of its growing power. Alien to its style of life, they penetrate its central dilemmas in both experience and ideology. And even when their opinions spur them to vindictiveness or malice, they emerge as true witnesses.

Stendhal, however, is indifferent to their pieties. The Enlightenment that Dostoevsky abhors is for him the era to which one can return with most pleasure; the God for whom Dostoevsky yearns he treats as an hypothesis to be cheerfully dismissed; the stable and respectable morality toward which Conrad strives he spends a lifetime violating; the tone of massive solemnity James assumes in old age he mocks in his late writings even more than in his early. He is, in the best sense of the word, a dubious character.

And, one must quickly add, an enigmatic writer. No other modern novelist has so consistently approached political life in terms that so consistently evade political categories. Every page of his work is crowded with politics, but if you try to formulate his *position* you find that he has slipped past your fingers, as he slips past all his critics, and now stands at a disrespectful distance, thumbing his nose. Stendhal is not an ideologue in the manner of Dostoevsky nor even a novelist of ideas; nonetheless, ideology and ideas swarm through his books. Living at the time he does Stendhal cannot avoid them, short of risking irrelevance; he juggles political notions with the reckless good fortune of the gifted amateur; but in the end he proves to be a profoundly nonpolitical man. It need only be added that in the time in which he lives, as in the whole modern era, the nonpolitical temper implies a political choice: and what is more, Stendhal, unlike many writers who follow him, knows this.

I

Though mentioned only casually in his novels, and then in accents of ambiguous humor, as a bogey disturbing the sleep

of frightened monarchists, the French Revolution is the dominant force in Stendhal's novels. His adult life was spent in
the backwash of the revolution, at a time when the monarchists tried, with a conspicuous lack of conviction, to restore
what was forever gone and the republicans, exhausted by the
fury of their own regime, lacked the strength to claim their
historical privilege. The revolutionary leaders were dead, the
revolutionary wave had passed, the revolutionary ethos had
become corrupted; but the work of the revolution remained.
Politically, the bourgeoisie could be made to suffer temporary
defeat; socially, its rule was secure.

The modern hero, the man who forces society to accept him
as its agent—the hero by will rather than birth—now appears
for the first time: and he carries with him the disease of ambition, which flourishes among those who are most committed
to the doctrine of equality and spreads all the deeper as the
restored Bourbons try to suppress that doctrine. Before the
revolution men had been concerned with privileges, not expectations; now they dream of success, that is, of a self-willed
effort to lift oneself, through industry or chicanery, to a higher
social level. Life becomes an experiment in strategy, an adventure in plan, ruse and combat; the hero is not merely ambitious but sensitive to the point of paranoia, discovering and
imagining a constant assault upon his dignity; and Stendhal
carries this outlook to its extreme limit, perhaps even to
caricature, by applying it to affairs of love.

The great political problem of Stendhal's time is not really
how to be rid of the Bourbon restoration or Louis Philippe's
bourgeois monarchy; both are certain to fall of their own
rottenness, as the most acute minds of France, Stendhal in-
cluded, quickly realize. Rather is the problem one of finding
a viable order with which to replace these mediocre monarchs.
The ideology of liberalism, which had inspired the boldest
Frenchmen during the past half century, has now entered a
state of permanent crisis from which it cannot escape, except
by an act of self-transcendence. So long as the liberals had
been powerless, struggling in common peril to destroy the
ancien regime, liberalism could assume the appearance of

unity: it could seem to be, and indeed be, a great energizing force by which men could at last come into the open air of freedom. But once in power, liberalism must crumble into the conflicting purposes it has concealed; behind the exalted motto of Liberty, Fraternity, Equality there cross a great many less exalted social interests. The successive stages of the French Revolution represent less a curve of temperament or blood-thirst than a clash of view on how far to extend the revolution. This quarrel repeats itself in all later versions of liberalism, the original innocence of the Encyclopedists being quite beyond recovery; a temporary facade of unity may be erected in moments of danger but it is only temporary and only a facade; liberalism, even as it continues to speak for humanity as a whole, is now at war with itself.

In his little book on Stendhal, Léon Blum suggests a similar idea. Stendhal, he writes, "is the man of confused moments, social intermixtures, periods of disorder . . . Each time that, through natural historical developments, social classes find themselves mixed together at their surface but separated at their foundations, large groups of young people will be placed in the same equivocal position" as Stendhal's heroes. Stendhal, that is to say, is a writer of the moment when a great historical experience has reached its point of exhaustion.

Such a writer can no longer believe in the unity of society, neither the unity claimed by those in power, which is patently a fraud, nor the unity envisaged by those in opposition, which now seems distant and chimerical. In the novel he finds his most formidable means of criticism, for it is through the novel that the problem of society in conflict with the individual receives its fullest exploration. In all of Stendhal's novels the process of social division is shown to have gone very far, each character being highly conscious that his allegiance belongs less to society as such than to some embattled segment of it.

Nor can Stendhal place much hope in the unity of the people, certainly nothing like the hope felt during the revolution, for he sees the people—or as we would now say, the masses—in their phase of lassitude and despair. He does not harbor that mean contempt for the masses which will be expressed by Flaubert; he is not hostile, and when they stir to action, in the 1830 revolution, he becomes lyrical in his praise of their capacities ("The lowest rabble," he writes to Sutton Sharpe, "was heroic, and after the battle was full of the noblest generosity"); but the *mystique* of the plebes, the emotion of democracy seldom reached him in uncontrollable abundance. Like intellectuals of a later age Stendhal feels that the hope placed in the people has proved to be unwarranted; he hardly recognizes that this disappointment is itself a sign of how much the people, exhausted though they may now be, have changed the shape of history in the preceding decades.

Stendhal's cult of energy follows logically from his gradual loss of belief in the unity of society or the redemptive power of the people, yet it would be quite impossible without the immediate memory of the revolution. It is an energy he attributes to the exceptional man, the hero who surmounts history rather than the people who bear it. His political Bonapartism and his esthetic notion of "the happy few" are closely related to the cult of energy as well as to each other, all three involving an opposition to aristocracy *and* democracy, privilege *and* equality. Taken in political terms and perhaps not only in political terms, the cult of energy implies some motivating sense of desperation, a need to assert, rather too emphatically, the values of social and intellectual fluidity.

Stendhal, I have said, is not a systematic thinker, but in his appreciation of Napoleon he shows far greater insight than many historians. The common notion that he was a mere idolator of Napoleon is absurd; he attacks Napoleon for dickering with the Jesuits, and even more for becoming a despot. "In France," he writes, "the despotism of Napoleon was most poisonous; he feared the works and the memory of the republic, over which the people stood guard; he hated the old enthusiasm of the Jacobins." But Stendhal would have immediately rejected the view that Napoleon is the first of the modern totalitarian rulers, for he sensed that Napoleon had meaning in terms of the past rather than the future, as a glorious historical memory rather than a possible national revival. *The Red and the Black* constantly stresses the contrast between the loathesomeness of the society through which Julien Sorel must rise and the heroic spontaneity of the lost Napoleonic age. *The Charterhouse of Parma* opens with a quick reference to Napoleon's triumph in Italy—and critics have wondered what place this passage, as well as the long description of Fabrizio* at Waterloo, has in the novel. Both seem to me indispensable, for the book has as a central purpose to demonstrate the difficulty and tedium of trying to survive now that Napoleon is gone. The Waterloo episode, particularly Fabrizio's famous inability to decide whether he has been in battle, is marvellous not merely for its direct graphic power but also as a way of showing that the young hero can no longer connect with—can no longer find a place or a meaning in—the Napoleonic experience. Fabrizio's journey is a flight backward, into the radiant past; it does not succeed; its not succeeding is a condition for all that follows in the novel.

Stendhal realized that Napoleon took his meaning from the revolution: he betrayed its libertarian ethos and consolidated its property relations. But while criticizing Napoleon for becoming a despot, he also realized that under Napoleon there was still a chance for the ambitious young man, for the young man from the provinces whose father is a stuffy monarchist unwilling to allow his son a sufficient allowance for comfort in Paris. Napoleon perpetuates the bourgeois principle of social mobility: corporals do become marshals; and in the era of reaction that roughly parallels Stendhal's mature life, the loss of this principle seems very costly indeed. At the same time Stendhal betrays no hope whatever that Bonapartism can be revived; he senses that for France at least the age of bour-

* Since, in quoting passages from Stendhal, I shall be using the standard translation of Scott Moncrieff, I shall follow, for the sake of convenience and consistency, his rendering of the names of the characters, including the somewhat mystifying substitution of Fabrizio for Fabrice. In the other chapters dealing with continental authors, I shall also use the titles, names and references of the standard translations.

geois glory is at an end. "The shape of our civilization," he complains in 1831, "precludes great movements, or anything resembling passion." As a statement of the immediate condition this is entirely right, as a prediction it is remarkably wrong.

Stendhal ends with only the dimmest political hope or perspective. The idea of society, the memory of Napoleon, faith in the masses, the claims of liberalism—none will quite do. Nor does he know anything of the hopes that for a time will buoy later writers: the vision of socialism, the idea of a pure esthetic. "Born too late or too early," says Arnold Hauser, "Stendhal stands between the times, just as he stands between the classes."

Not above the classes, as his admirers sometimes like to suppose, but apart from them. And that may be why he finds it so desirable to identify himself with the Encyclopedists, who were hardly obliged to think of social classes at all. Stendhal's admiration for the Encyclopedists implies an effort to construct a *pure* liberalism, a liberalism not yet tarnished by history, a liberalism of concept to set off against the liberalism of practise, which he rightly finds both timid and absurd. (It is surely no accident that among the political movements of his day he feels closest to the Carbonari who, because they are still fighting to unify their nation, can with some justice retain the heroic tone of a unified and classless liberalism.) That Stendhal finally arrives at an intellectual impasse may follow from his occasional faint awareness that the political idea of liberalism, once put into practise, can hardly avoid social squalor and disintegration. His feeling for the Encyclopedists is consequently a romantic—a nostalgic—feeling, despite the fact that they were far from being romantics and he, as a literary craftsman, is an opponent of romanticism.

Stendhal's relationship to romanticism is extremely complicated and is made still more complicated by the ambiguity of the movement and the sheer contrariness of his own mind. Insofar as romanticism involves a celebration of the individual ego breaking past the previous limits of history, Stendhal is a romantic. Its rebellion against the "materialism" of

early capitalist society is also congenial to him, though he
does not seem to be aware that the assumptions behind this
rebellion are themselves grounded in the rise of capitalism.
But insofar as romanticism involves the idealizing of one or
another pre-capitalist society, Stendhal demurs; and when it
degenerates into a wilful inflation of language and emotion,
he stands firm by the Roman style of the republic and Napoleon.

If what I have been saying has any truth, it follows that
Stendhal occupies a central position in Western intellectual
history (not thought): he is one of the first creative writers to
look upon politics and society from the exclusive standpoint
of the intelligentsia, one of the first to measure history by its
effects on the intellectuals as a special, marginal and imperilled group. The dream of "the happy few"—which will
soon turn into the nightmare of the artist's alienation—remains the one indestructible buttress of his life. In many respects he is a déclassé; in the most honorable sense of the
word he is a dilettante; and in the absence of any large sus-
taining faith—for it is significant that in all his novels liberalism, gasping in defeat, is feared because of its past rather
than its power—he begins to speak, somewhat like Byron
though with greater seriousness, for those in the modern world
who feel themselves estranged and "homeless." The letters of
his final years are crowded with sentences such as one might
expect to find in the notebooks of twentieth century intellectuals. "Ideas," he writes, "are the bugaboos of people in
power." And "people in power hate people whose words get
printed." His last, unfinished novel *Lamiel*, far from being
the customary gesture of reconciliation by which writers are
expected to usher themselves out of the world, is the wildest
and most preposterous, indeed the most anarchistic, of his
books. In this fragment Stendhal recreates his typical situation in extreme terms: a hero is forced by a sluggish society
to break its bounds of decorum and law, only the hero proves
to be a heroine who discovers in a few quick pages the venality of official politics, the banality of official love, the pervasiveness of boredom and the possible pleasures of playing

the female castrator. Each of Stendhal's novels takes him further away from respectable society; his opinions mellow but his work toughens; his basic feeling is that for people like himself there is no longer any place: people, that is, who value ideas and conversation.

To the extent that they deal with politics, Stendhal's novels ask one question over and over again: how can we—we Europeans of cultivated tastes—survive in this era of cant and reaction? It is a question not entirely irrelevant to our time, and Stendhal's answer, insofar as he has one, may be summarized in a single word: ruse. Not hypocricy; not what is often and ignorantly meant by machiavellianism; but ruse, the strategy of having one's cake and eating it, being both a rebel and a *bon vivant,* deceiving society to undermine it and wooing society to enjoy it. Because of this complex and, at times, ambivalent point of view, Stendhal proves more satisfactory than most writers on that difficult political problem, the relation of ends to means: if nothing else, he abstains from moralizing. His books have been called devil's manuals for machiavellian rulers, but they are nothing of the sort: they are really devil's manuals for men in revolt at a time when there is no possibility of revolt. Stendhal had only a limited sense of society but he had a superb sense of history and an especially superb sense of his particular moment; he measured with the greatest realism the extent of European reaction during his time; and what some critics call his "silly mystifications," those strategems by which he tried to outwit Metternich's police, may have been, at least in motive, not quite so silly. He knew that in this age the great problem for men of intelligence was simply to survive, and to survive without becoming fanatics or flunkeys. Only now, from the distance of a century, can we fully credit the seriousness behind the silliness.

What complicates Stendhal's politics still further, and his novels as well, is that he recognizes no precise boundary between political and private categories, he allows each to dissolve into the other but not to destroy one another. Unable to solve the crisis of liberalism, he evades it by abstracting from the liberal position a code, a style of life, a vision of joyousness—it is one of the most glorious evasions in literary history, though his belief in the possibility of such an evasion marks Stendhal as a man of the pre-totalitarian age. Liberalism is elevated from a politics into a personal strategy, a way of outwitting the dullards who control things; rationalism is flipped onto its back and made to proclaim a recognition of its own limits, of the presence in human life of phenomena that hardly conform to its orderly procedures. Against the stabilized hypocrisy of society Stendhal exalts the insubordinate freedom of the person, what he calls *espagnolisme*, the vitality of instinct and emotion which creates a valid order of its own, brushing aside both morality and convention. To trick society you must employ ruse, but the energy that makes ruse possible comes from *espagnolisme*. Stendhal thinks of it primarily as a private endowment, but in all his novels it plays a political role: it motivates the rebellion of the favored characters and still more important, it defeats their rebellion, upsets their plans, renders their ruse unsuccessful. *Espagnolisme* in Stendhal's novels represents the triumph of emotion over ideology, of humane impulse over calculated cleverness. Stendhal's heroes are always advised to calculate and he himself seems always to concur in this advice; yet his greatest joy is in seeing calculations undone, even those of which he approves, the calculations of his insurgent heroes.

It is characteristic of Stendhal that even his praise of spontaneity should be highly calculated—though, by way of further bedevilment, one must add that his machiavellian ruses are often disarmingly playful and innocent. No writer who admires elegance as much as Stendhal does, can be long content with spontaneity as a principle of existence. His very admiration for elegance, however, reveals his political predicament, for elegance is a quality likely to be most admired in a static society: neither Danton nor Napoleon was elegant. Stendhal is one of the first modern writers to raise elegance to a political virtue and yet remain—it is the mixture of the two that one finds so impressive—quite free from the usual kinds of snobbism. Stendhal does not suppose that elegance and cultivation are confined to any social class and he is quite certain that they are largely absent from the class in which they are supposed to bulk largest; but he fears that these qualities must, in the nature of things, be limited to a marginal élite, "the happy few"—and this anticipation of the artist's loneliness in a mass society becomes all the sharper as Stendhal learns to accept his situation as a great writer barely recognized in his time. His books are full of ambiguous and frequently funny references to America: he greatly admires the democratic statesmen, particularly Jefferson, yet feels he could not live here: imagine, a country without culture or conversation! His criticism of America, often similar to De Tocqueville's, deserves to be taken seriously, but it should not be assumed that Stendhal was serious each time he made it. He admires the liberal idea but shrinks from democratic fraternity; the warmth he feels for the people is genuine but he would just as soon feel it from a distance; all of his liberal impulses are modified and complicated by the extent to which he retains deep attachments to the French past. His liberalism, in short, is that of a man who is the product of an old society. When Lucien Leuwen says, "I need the pleasures provided by an ancient civilization," he speaks for Stendhal.

The very patterns of Stendhal's prose seem emblematic of his political situation. In all of his novels there frequently occurs a sentence structure that Stendhal has made his own: it begins with a limited statement and after an intervening colon or semi-colon proceeds to a second statement that is not so much a development from the first as an oblique or ironic comment on it. Ordinarily the colon is a bridge, here it is a chasm. Stendhal's construction controverts his claim to spontaneity, it is perfectly adapted to his passion for "the sublime unexpected," which also means, to his position as a cultivated and skeptical liberal. The assertions of Rousseauian liberalism have here been transformed into a complex but still subversive wit.

Stendhal is a unique intellectual figure and a unique novelist. His vision of the good life is essentially Nietzsche's —minus the philosopher's neurotic swagger; both hope for an intellectual "superman"—though Stendhal is free of the confusions that attach themselves to Nietzsche's use of the phrase; their ideas as to style, though not their styles, are very similar; and the interplay of Dionysian and Apollonian elements Nietzsche was later to call for is already achieved in Stendhal's work. Above all, the Nietzschian conception of the Good European—the man of superior cultivation, liberal tastes and disinterested humaneness—is anticipated in Stendhal. Summed up in a phrase, Stendhal's politics are the politics of the Good European.

II

The Red and the Black is a novel about politics in an era which makes politics impossible. Though felt throughout the book as a directing energy, politics is seldom directly visible, except in the chapter where the nobles scheme to cauterize their country by entrusting it to English mercies. The society of *The Red and the Black* is not totalitarian, it enforces conformity through pressures rather than terrors. It is a society of pall even more than of fear, though its fear of the immediate past, of that free play of politics it has dedicated itself to suppress, is more than acute. In the absence of freedom, the political impulse takes the shape of ambition or hatred or banditry: all three stir in Julien Sorel. The book suggests, among other things, the price that must be paid when politics is eliminated from the surface of social life, and as such might be read with belated profit by those literary people who fancy themselves above the "dirt" of politics.

Stendhal shows politics incarnated in non-political behavior, the struggle of the classes at a time when they lay dormant, crushed into a stupor of reconciliation. Nothing can appear directly in the world of this novel, nothing can be said openly: politics must break through in the guise of appetites, manners and sex. Julien Sorel is a man conducting a secret war against society, and a war that confuses him so much, for he has no firm base in principle, that he spends half his time conducting it against his mistresses and himself; he represents the militant phase of Stendhal's policy of ruse, but a militancy that has lost its meaning with the defeat of the Jacobins. He is, as Stendhal says, "an unhappy man at war with all of society" but he cannot make proper distinctions among the various elements of society. He tells himself, "I will not follow the bourgeois, middle-of-the-road way of life, I seek rather some revolutionary exaltation," but this very exaltation, coming as it does in an age of social retreat, tempts him into crime. (Stendhal would have agreed with Oscar Wilde's remark that in the 19th century only the lower classes retain enough energy for crime.) Julien is the stranger in a hostile world but the stranger who no longer knows what he wants, who lacks, as Stendhal says, "the courage to be sincere." He is visited by libertarian emotions, he has moments of genuine compassion, but his major complaint against society is that it cramps him: he is bitter, above all, because it will not allow him to abandon, and perhaps betray, his own class.

The world as it presents itself to Julien Sorel is a battlefield: the battle has been fought and lost. Yet the image of warfare is crucial, for in no other 19th century novel is there such a formulated awareness that society has broken into warring classes. Every character in the book identifies himself with a special interest. "Between the liberty of the press and our existence as gentlemen," says M. de La Mole, spokesman for the nobles, "there is war to the knife." M. Renal, the rising bourgeois, cannot tolerate the thought that his rival has purchased two horses, and he finds relief only by hiring a tutor. That is the arithmetic of the bourgeois: two horses equals one tutor. And Julien himself, who thinks like a strange blend of Byron and Marx, begins his final speech to the jury almost— this seems to me a key to the novel—as if he were a *political* prisoner: "Gentlemen, I have not the honor to belong to your class . . ." If Julien could be transported to the Russia of a half century later, he would be a terrorist; given the necessity for living in Restoration France, which he can neither accept nor resist, he is hero, madman, clown. At the end he submits to his death in the consciousness, again like a political martyr, that he has already become a symbol.

The suppressed politics of *The Red and the Black* breaks out as hatred, class hatred; and while *Lucien Leuwen* is not nearly so fierce a book, there too the hardening of classes is a major theme. "In the provinces," writes Stendhal in that uncompleted novel, "there is no longer the slightest communication between hostile classes." But the theme of class relations does not receive so harmonious a rendering in *Lucien Leuwen* as in the two great novels. The first volume of *Lucein Leuwen* lists too heavily toward a Stendhalian romance, the second is overweighted with political detail, and the fusion of these two elements, actually the two sides of Stendhal's creative activity, is never quite achieved.

The novel returns, though at a lower pitch of intensity, to Stendhal's theme: "the quarrel that afflicts the Nineteenth Century [is] the resentment of rank against merit." But the social disintegration portrayed in *The Red and the Black* has here gone much further: under Louis Philippe's bourgeois monarchy neither royalists nor republicans are happy, government has passed into the hands of finance, the reactionaries have become grotesque and the radicals impotent. Money reigns; passion dies. Stendhal's contempt for this epoch is remarkably similar to that of Marx in his little book, *Class Struggles in France*, except that Marx writes with sarcasm and Stendhal in the tone of opéra-bouffe. Society has become a farce; nothing deserves to be taken seriously by men of intelligence. Stendhal is drawing further and further away from the society of his day, despite his expert verisimilitude in mirroring its surface; and the greater his distance the more he relies on comedy.

Those scenes in the second volume which detail the political corruption of the bourgeois monarchy, while vivid in themselves, lack the support from the rest of the novel that such scenes must have. Stendhal's sense of class relations operates primarily on the political level, while a novel like *Lucien Leuwen*, which ventures a tour of the social orders, needs a range of material that can be had only by plunging below the political level and into the recesses of the city. For this Stendhal, whether or not he had the gift, clearly lacked the patience; the social novel, in the sense that Balzac's may be so described, is not his forte; he prefers to hurry across the surface of society rather than break through it. Instinctively, Stendhal suspects Balzac's strategy of composition, just as he would have suspected, had he known it, Marx's sociology; for both Balzac and Marx, being committed to the 19th century in a way Stendhal is not, employ, as he cannot, the method of penetration in depth. Yet *Lucien Leuwen*, by reason of its structure, requires precisely this kind of penetration in depth —in any case: Stendhal will not make this mistake again.

III

The Charterhouse of Parma signifies Stendhal's most complete removal from the contemporary scene and his most complete triumph over it; the novel is the fullest expression of his alienation from the age—and of his refusal to be crippled by that alienation. Parma belongs neither to the 19th century nor, as some critics have argued, to the era of Machiavelli; it is an abstraction from time and place, a small-scale model of autocratic government; here politics, by a paradox that lies at the heart of Stendhal's greatness, takes on both the representative directness of a parable and the stylized extravagance of an opera.

Most novelists who turn to politics—I think especially of Conrad—tend to look upon it as an obstacle the world throws across the path of happiness. Stendhal too sees politics in this way, but his view and his manner of reaching it are far more complex. Politics keeps Count Mosca and the Duchess Sanseverina from the happiness within their immediate reach, it keeps Fabrizio from running off with his dear little Clélia; politics is that force of the world which distracts men from their most decent instincts; but it is also something else which only Stendhal and Dostoevsky among the 19th century novelists quite realize: it is an outlet for the very passions it suppresses, it is not merely an obstacle to the will but also a challenge, not merely the occasion for meanness but, sometimes, for heroism.

The range of political behavior in Parma is narrow: there are no real parties, ideas are suspect, the people are dumb, and the monarch, while not an absolute ruler, has enough power so that his whim can shape the daily lives of his ministers and his court. It is symptomatic of Stendhal's growing disenchantment with the world of affairs—*The Charterhouse* occupies a place in his literary development somewhat similar to that of *The Tempest* in Shakespeare's—that throughout the novel he treats power in its aspect of pettiness, as a craven absurdity on the part of those who employ it, a constant threat to intelligent men, and a certain corruption for weak ones. Power is something one must learn to evade or soften, to escape from or make a truce with. Repeatedly the major characters concern themselves with the problem that was to absorb Stendhal throughout his later years: how to gull one's rulers. Stendhal's attitude toward power is not that of the man at the top of the social heap or at the bottom of it, but rather of the man on its margin.

The three central figures represent three possible attitudes toward, and distances from, social power. Mosca manipulates it while privately holding it to be a farce; Sanseverina tolerates it but is always ready to oppose it with the full force of her personal desires; Fabrizio bends to it with the bow of the courtier and cleric but remains fundamentally indifferent to its claims. Stendhal shares in all these attitudes, but in none exclusively.

Mosca is a man who believes in the durability, if not the wisdom, of the social world. In his youth he had fought with Napoleon's armies, now "I dress up like an actor in a farce to win a great social position and a few thousand francs a year." The key word is "farce," which Mosca repeatedly uses in speaking of the events at Parma—a clue, seldom taken up, that Stendhal offers his readers. Mosca has had to accommodate himself to the world but he does not accept its cant. He knows that when he conducts the nightly search for assassins beneath the bed of Ernesto IV, not only is the monarch ridiculous but he too is ridiculous. The burdens of power do not rest easily upon him: he finds it grueling simply to keep his face pitched at the proper solemnity; and he knows that the continual prudence his political position requires from him must sap his energy both as public figure and private person. He is brave but not heroic, intelligent but not creative. He has no illusion that he is covering himself with glory or goodness, and like many men who are not very cynical yet feel obliged to accept tasks they intensely dislike, he affects a pose of cynicism by means of which he can anticipate, overstate and disarm the criticism that may be brought against him. For he knows the ways of the world: when Fabrizio suggests that he be tried by "magistrates judging according to their conscience," Mosca replies with devastating mildness, "You would oblige me greatly . . . if you would give me the addresses of such magistrates; I shall write to them before I go to bed."

Mosca has high standards of personal honor and he knows that in his trade, as in his world, they can not very well remain unbruised; but his great difficulty—it is this which almost ruins him—is that having lost the liberal élan of his youth he now thinks about the mechanics of government rather than the purpose of government. He is not power-drunk, he does not wish to hurt or humiliate anyone, he exerts himself to keep Ernesto IV from outraging his office, but he acts from stray impulse rather than moral conviction. Mosca is a good man, but a good man without belief. He can never resist the temptation—it is the *professional's* temptation—of showing the monarch he despises how best to carry out his despicable policies; he tells Ernesto IV, for example, that the problem of the insurgent Carbonari can be met either by slaughtering ten thousand rebels or by making popular concessions. The advice is intelligent, we are quite sure which of these two courses Mosca prefers, and it seems likely that he has exaggerated the number of necessary victims in order to persuade Ernesto IV toward leniency; but the trouble is that Mosca thinks purely in terms of "statecraft," banishing from his line of vision those more fundamental problems of value which would require him to start from a *judgment* of the Carbonari. Mosca's theory of governing, like Machiavelli's theory of government from which it derives, works well enough in periods of social equilibrium, when class relations are relatively stable, the masses are politically dormant and politics can therefore be narrowed to the art of maneuver and arrangement. Mosca does not realize, though Stendhal sometimes does, that all of his delicate calculations can be destroyed, on the one side, by the explosion of personal passions and, on the other, by the intervention of class movements. It is a mistake characteristic of those who like to think of administrative politics as a "science."

Numerous critics have said that in Mosca Stendhal was embodying a machiavellian vision of politics; Arnold Hauser, one of the best social critics of our time, writes that Stendhal's novels are "courses of instruction in political amoralism" and cites with approval Balzac's remark that *The Charterhouse* is the novel Machiavelli would have written had he lived in, and been banished from, the Italy of the 19th century. There is such an odd mixture of truth and error in these statements that it may be worth a brief digression to glance at Machiavelli himself, who is indeed, though not in the way usually supposed, an ancestor of Stendhal.

Like Stendhal, Machiavelli was a liberal at a time when liberalism was in rout. He believed that the best form of government was a republic, and in his *Discourses on Livy,* a far more important book than *The Prince,* he formulated ideas about democratic government that remain valuable to this day. "In every republic," he writes, "there are two parties, that of the nobles and that of the people; and all the laws that are favorable to liberty result from the opposition of these parties to each other." Still more impressive: "Nothing renders a republic more firm and stable than to organize it in such a way that the excitement of the ill-humors that agitate a state may have a way prescribed by law for venting itself." At the same time Machiavelli, as a patriot, passionately desired the unification of Italy; otherwise, his beloved Florence would remain helpless before assaults from the north. He believed that Italy could be unified only under a prince, and his famous book is a guide, mainly serious but not without irony, for that prince.

Machiavelli recognized that in politics there can be no easy correspondence between ends and means, and much of *The Prince* is occupied with saying: *If* you wish to achieve this end, you must use these means; but this does not mean that Machiavelli was "amoral," it merely indicates that he was honest enough to face the difficulty of adjusting political behavior to moral precepts. When he writes that "to use deceit in any action is detestable, nevertheless in conducting war it is praiseworthy and glorious," he irks us, first, because of the possibility that he is being ironic at our expense and second, because he is telling a kind of truth. Given war, deceit is necessary; given politics, which is often a mild form of war, intrigue is likely. Those who righteously condemn Machiavelli usually dislike him for preaching what they practise, and more, for describing what they practise.

Nonetheless, there *is* a difficulty in making out Machiavelli's thought, I mean in reconciling his two sides, the *Discourses on Livy* and *The Prince,* the republican and the hardboiled analyst. Partly, this is the difference between normative and descriptive treatments of politics, a difference made all the more acute by the fact that Machiavelli is one of the first political writers to set himself the task of describing what is rather than what should be. But the difference can be seen in another way: it symbolizes the problem of the liberal who, in a moment of social helplessness, retains his vision of the desirable society yet feels intransigeance to be futile and therefore tries to adapt himself to the realities of power. Because of this effort, Machiavelli's political thought is not finally a unified system, as Stendhal's political insights do not quite add up to a unified vision. Stendhal, and particularly that part of him reflected in Mosca, is also troubled by the difficulty of reconciling what he believes or would like to believe with what he must do or supposes he must do. (In *The Red and the Black* Julien Sorel had already asked: "Who knows what one goes through on the way to a great deed?") It is this problem, more than any specific doctrine, that makes Machiavelli so "modern" a thinker and Stendhal so "modern" a novelist

If, as has generally been done, we identify Machiavelli with *The Prince*, *The Charterhouse* is far from being completely machiavellian in spirit. For it is essential to the novel that Mosca never has the last word on any important matter, that he is continually bested, as he knows and indeed wishes, by both Sanseverina and Fabrizio. Mosca's advice to Fabrizio is not too far from Machiavelli's to his prince: both provide a manual on how to rise in the world, if one must. When Mosca fails, it is precisely because he lives too closely by his own precepts, by his inured political habits. It is he who in behalf of Ernesto IV omits the phrase "unjust proceedings" from the paper Sanseverina dictates to him, and it is this omission that allows Ernesto IV to throw Fabrizio into jail. Sanseverina rightly describes Mosca's behavior as that of a "miserable fawning . . . courtier"; she jabs him at his weakest point— the weakest point of all professional politicians and parliamentarians—when she says, "He always imagines that to resign is the greatest sacrifice a Prime Minister can make." On the other hand, Mosca's triumph, that is, his transcendence of his public self, comes when he breaks from the machiavellian system and allows his passion for Sanseverina to imperil his career and perhaps his life. It is then that he becomes a truly magnificent figure, a man capable of every precaution yet discarding all, a man for whom love is the means of recovering Fortune. In moving away from the Machiavelli of *The Prince*, Mosca approaches the other Machiavelli, the one who wrote that Fortune favors the young and impetuous: "like a woman she is a lover of the young because they are less respectful, more ferocious and with greater audacity command her."

Sanseverina, that superb woman for whom literary critics have been ready to sacrifice everything, also meddles in the politics of Parma, but there is never any question, in her mind or anyone else's, about the value she assigns to her meddling. She is interested in politics not as a means of regulating social tensions or of slaking thirsts for power, but as a form of action that brings into highest relief the contours of human character. She judges Ernesto IV as a man rather than a monarch (it does him no good), she takes advantage of Archbishop

Landriani's plebeian awe before titles, she is enchanted with Ferrante Palla's Robin Hood liberalism, she measures with admirable accuracy Fabrizio's distance from the world. In all of her responses she immediately breaks through to the personal core: she is one of the least snobbish figures in all literature. Sanseverina is a romantic who personifies the Napoleonic principle in personal relations, or at least that principle as understood and elevated by Stendhal. The great passion of her life is her feeling for Fabrizio, which is more than, though it certainly includes, an incestuous love, for it involves the desire to establish a kind of spiritual stake in another person and thereby to shape life again. Through the power of another being, she would return to the condition of youth, not to dominate Fabrizio but to share in him. She admires generosity, impetuousness, gaiety, passion—and a certain ruthlessness in reaching for them. At the end of the book she accepts her fate, which is to marry Mosca and relinquish Fabrizio. As Stendhal beautifully puts it, "she combined all the outward appearances of happiness."

Sanseverina dominating Mosca represents the victory of *espagnolisme* over calculated ruse, the power of desire to elbow aside the restraints of caution. In drawing her with an affection seldom matched in literature, Stendhal suggests that wherever passion is vital and full, morality must suffer some consequence. Sanseverina seems frequently to move beyond the margin of morality, though one is less inclined to suppose that she has achieved a Nietzschian transvaluation of values than that she is impervious, like some majestic natural force, to moral argument.

Fabrizio stands still a step further, a long step, from the political world. Not that he lacks political opinions: Stendhal sees to it that he is properly provisioned. But Fabrizio is not really concerned with politics, the world claims him far less than it does Julien Sorel. Unlike Julien, he is usually a passive figure, and passive despite his fighting at Waterloo and escaping from the tower. He begins to exert his will only when it is a question of winning Clélia—that is, of abandoning the world of Mosca and Sanseverina, the world of politics and af-

fairs. Like *The Red and the Black*, *The Charterhouse* ends
with a strange ritual of sacrilege in which there is nonetheless
a powerful if suppressed strain of religious feeling. Fabrizio's
sermons are violently false, they are *black* sermons, for he is
not a religious man; but they do express a genuine emotional
compulsion, an obscure but authentic need for purity and
exaltation, a desire to preach though he really has no message,
for himself or his listeners, beyond the expression of that
desire.

Psychologically, Fabrizio suffers from an extreme case of
self-alienation: he frequently seems divorced from his own
activity, as if he were assuming a series of roles from which
his inner self is quite detached. Socially, he is even more of an
outcast than Julien Sorel, for while Julien is tormented by an
inability to reach his place in the world, Fabrizio doubts that
one's place is worth having. Fabrizio is a youth in whom there
lies dormant a germ of moral aspiration which another age
might stir to growth; that he finally becomes a cleric, making
his life into a mockery of faith, is hardly an accident, for in
however distorted a form he does possess the religious vocation. Though not dreamy, Fabrizio is devoted to dreams—to
escape, back into the self, deep into the cocoon of childhood
and innocence. Perhaps his greatest scene, and certainly one
of the greatest in the novel, is that in which he returns to the
chestnut tree where he had played as a child and now acts
out a ceremony of reinvigoration, thereby expressing his need
to declare not merely his manliness, about which, like his creator, he is never entirely certain, but also the profound piety
he feels toward his childhood and its still visible relics.

Taken together, Mosca, Sanseverina and Fabrizio embody a
remarkable interplay of values: worldliness, personal passion
and a kind of distracted innocence. They are people who have
been stranded in a hostile world, people who are conscious
that little is left for them to believe in except their desire to
snatch some fragment of happiness for themselves and for
each other. As Martin Turnell perceptively remarks, they form
"an immensely civilized aristocratic elite and they stake everything on a single chance—happiness through personal rela-

tionships . . . They are tragic figures precisely because 'they do not believe in anything.' For we cannot say that they 'believe in' personal relationships; they are passionately attached to them, but they are profoundly conscious of the absence of a *mystique* and of the precariousness of their way of life when it is pitted against despotism."

We are back, then, where we started: the debacle of liberalism and the problem of how intelligence can survive in an age of cant. Stendhal's characters do not make a long face about this, at least not for very long; they believe that if one cannot live heroically one can still live happily, provided one uses one's wits. Stendhal has not reached the feeling of Flaubert, that one cannot live heroically or happily, nor the feeling of Malraux, that happiness has become irrelevant but heroism, at whatever cost, mandatory.

Stendhal, it seems to me, was entirely conscious of the political dimension in his work. Surely it was only a man of the very highest political intelligence who could have conceived the idea of having the official leader of the Liberal party serve as the governor of the Citadel, reporting weekly to Ernesto IV on his measures for keeping the liberals locked in their cages. No denunciation of the moral cowardice that has so often characterized modern liberalism has ever had the conclusive power of the image Stendhal constructed, as it were, in passing: General Fabio Conti, leader of the opposition, flunkey of the king, warden of his prison.

Still more brilliant is Stendhal's conception of Ferante Palla, a character who deserves all the praise Balzac lavished upon him. To make the only effective liberal of Parma a somewhat mad poet and a highway robber as well, a Robin Hood completely cut off from the people yet staunch in their behalf—this is political wit of the highest order. When all the conventional liberals fail or sell out, the crazy artist remains in opposition. Wild, impetuous, extravagant, he throws up everything for love (love and liberalism are all the same in his eyes), writes great sonnets and, alone in the world of Parma, is actually a happy man (perhaps, suggests Stendhal rather slyly, because he is a little mad.) Partly, he is what

Stendhal would have liked to be, the man who remains in principled opposition no matter how absurd it makes him seem, had there not been the reality of a pot belly and the temptations of the opera and the salon to distract him. Comic though he seems, Palla is also a stirring figure, a call to resistance; he is the only man whose recklessness matches that of Sanseverina, and it is symptomatic of Stendhal's meaning that it is the prime minister rather than the outlaw who wins the Duchess. In order to maintain his liberal intransigeance, Palla must become a ridiculous, even a farcical figure, yet precisely his readiness to accept the costume of farce endows him with a redeeming dignity. In the world of Parma, heroism appears in the mask of self-parody.

It is this blend of seriousness and farce that makes *The Charterhouse* seem so enigmatic a novel, particularly the fact that the seriousness is not solemn and the farce not frivolous. Forever vivacious and subversive, Stendhal will not settle into one attitude long enough for our tired eyes to focus upon him steadily, he does not allow us the luxury of becoming dull; which leads us to suspect, of course, that he suffers from an unstable personality.

Stendhal is a difficult writer. There are some novelists who present only the difficulty of finding out what is happening in their books, and then it all becomes clear, even too clear. But in Stendhal the carpet is well-brushed, neat and clean; the figure is sharply outlined, without mystery—only the meaning, the relationship of parts, proves elusive. I think this is largely due to Stendhal's mixture of tones. That a writer's characteristic accent should be ironic, does not disturb us; these days we insist upon it with a monumental lack of irony. Nor are we too disturbed when the characters, who have every right to be as clever as their creator, are habitually ironic about each other and themselves; though this does tend to complicate the tone of the novel rather more than we find comfortable—and it is consistency of tone rather than plot or characterization that allows us to fall into that comfortable drowse we call "getting used" to a book. But what makes for Stendhal's special quality, his mixture of dialectical speed and aloof coolness, is that he will frequently be ironic about the irony of his characters. Mosca pokes fun at Fabrizio and with good reason, yet Stendhal, if by no more than a syntactical flip, makes sure that Mosca too does not get off scot-free. In a sense, Stendhal is very much the omniscient author who does not hesitate to show that the characters are of his manufacture; but once created they are treated by him with complete equality, as if they were old friends whose faults he knew perfectly well and whom he loved nonetheless. Irony here becomes a password admitting the favored characters into the charmed circle, the happy few.

The range of tone in *The Charterhouse* is, of course, wider still. In a few places, as if to strike a quiet contrast to the prevailing bustle and worldliness of the novel, Stendhal comes close to a touch of pastoral, a yearning for "the natural," of which all his characters, like Stendhal himself, are utterly incapable. Fabrizio returns to his tree but must soon leave it; Mosca speaks wistfully of having at his disposal "Petrarch's old house on that fine slope in the middle of the forest, near the Po" to which they may retire as if to some sacred retreat of poetry and love. But such notes come at rare intervals; most of *The Charterhouse* is outright farce, even burlesque, particularly those parts in which Fabrizio's outward conduct most closely approximates that of a Byronic hero. Fabrizio breaking out of the tower, engaging in duels that bore him and pursuing women he does not want to love—this is the farce of the antiheroic novel, the inversion of romantic modes in order to assert, finally, romantic values. Sanseverina going through the idiotic motions of court intrigue, in fact, the whole treatment of love in terms of petty politics; Mosca living in fear because he has been so indiscreet as to refer to Ernesto V as "that boy"; Rassi, that great clown of a scoundrel, telling Ernesto IV precisely why he cannot do without him, for where else could he find so accomplished a scoundrel—all this is done in the colors of farce. At times the novel takes on the quality, half burlesque and half thriller, of a wild movie, what with signals flashing from tower to tower, heroes refusing to escape from prison because they love the jailer's daughter, duchesses poisoning monarchs and inciting crazy poets to open the dams.

The style in which all this is communicated has best been described by Nietzsche when he speaks of the author who "cannot help presenting the most serious events in a boisterous *allegrissimo,* perhaps not without a malicious artistic sense of the contrast he ventures to present—long, heavy, difficult, dangerous thoughts and a *tempo* of the gallop, and of the best, wantonest humor." The description fits exactly, though Nietzsche happened to be talking about Machiavelli; it establishes the true line of descent from the Italian to the Frenchman.

All the while, however, Stendhal is fundamentally serious in his meanings and intentions. The seriousness of the book is to be measured only if one fully apprehends the degree to which the action is farce; the tragedy of the book consists in the fact that these marvellously intelligent people must behave as if it should all be taken seriously and that if they do not, the consequences for them will be serious indeed. This is the political significance of their behavior, a behavior forced upon them by the politics of defeat. They live now as if they had read in advance Nietzsche's great maxim for rebels in an unrebellious age: "Objection, evasion, joyous distrust, and love of irony are signs of health; everything absolute belongs to pathology."

CHAPTER THREE

DOSTOEVSKY: THE POLITICS OF SALVATION

In 19th century Russia the usual categories of discourse tend to break down. Politics, religion, literature, philosophy—these do not fall into neat departments of the mind. Pressed together by the Tzarist censorship, ideas acquire an extraordinary concentration; the novel, which in the West is generally regarded as a means of portraying human behavior, acquires the tone and manner of prophetic passion. Not till the rise of the Symbolists at the end of the century does the cult of estheticism, with its tacit belief in a fragmenting of experience, prosper in Russia; for the most part Russian thought is seized by that "mania for totality" which is to become characteristic of our time. Where ideas cannot be modulated through practise, they keep their original purity; where intellectuals cannot test themselves in experience, they must remain intransigeant or surrender completely. For the subtler kinds of opportunism, such a society offers little provision. The seriousness we all admire in Russian literature is thus partly the result of a social impasse: energies elsewhere absorbed by one or another field of thought are here poured into the novel. "Literature in Russia," writes the critic Chernyshevsky, "constitutes almost the sum-total of our intellectual life." And that is why, in dealing with the Russian novel, one is obliged to take religion as a branch of politics and politics as a form of religion. The school of criticism which treats the novel mainly in terms of social manners will consequently face grave difficulties when confronted with a writer like Dostoevsky, for whom the act of creation invariably means an act of prophecy.

During Dostoevsky's lifetime the intelligentsia multiplies at an astonishing rate. A belated seepage from Western thought, the frail beginnings of capitalist production in the cities, the decay of both serfdom and communal peasant holdings in the countryside—these are but a few of the reasons. It is an intelligentsia of a kind found only in "backward" countries: ablaze with activity yet brutally confined in its power to communicate, brimming with the boldest ideas yet without a tradition of freedom, aspiring to independence yet reduced to an appendage of the city poor.

The problem which more than any other obsesses the Russian intellectuals is their relationship to the people, the dark unsounded mass of peasants on top of whom has formed a skim of proletarians only yesterday peasants. One may read 19th century Russian history as a series of attempts by the intellectuals, frequently desperate and always pathetic, to make contact with the people. That fashionable disdain for the masses which in the latter part of the century arises among Western literary men is virtually unknown in Russia, for there the intellectuals, deprived of even a marginal independence, sense that their fate is bound up with the fate of the people. Political discussions repeatedly focus on the question: how can we awaken the peasants? And so long as this question remains unanswered, there will always be some who despair of answering it and decide to do the job themselves —to force history by sacrifice and terror.

Dostoevsky once wrote that Russian literature was "a literature of landowners." Despite its touch of malice, his remark is extremely acute. A great many Russian writers, from Griboyedov to Turgenev, are disaffected noblemen. Both Tolstoy and Turgenev owe a large debt to Aksakov, an author whose pastoral chronicles flow with the evenness and fullness of the Russian seasons. Some of the loveliest passages in Tolstoy and Turgenev are nostalgic in tone, romantic turnings to 18th century manorial life which seems to them, at least from a distance, relatively stable and free from modern troubles. Dostoevsky shares their tendency to romanticize the peasant, but like Gogol before him and Leskov beside him, he represents a decisive break from the literature of landowners; he is a creature of the city, his writing beats with the rhythms of urban life, his greatest achievement is to penetrate the problematic moods and ideas of homeless intellectuals.

Only superficially does it seem odd that the rise of an urban intelligentsia should coincide with the flourishing of Slavophile ideas. Though themselves men of the city, the Slavophiles placed their faith in the Russian peasants; they believed that Russia could and should avoid the path of the West; and from their vantage-point in the social rear they were able to see the terrifying consequences of the atomistic individualism that had sprung up in the West—though in their disdain of the liberal ideal they were far less perceptive. Their faith in the peasants is a sign of their distance from the peasants, their belief in a special Russian destiny a sign of their helplessness before the problems of Russia.

Popular opinion often assumes that the Slavophiles were a gang of reactionaries brewing fantastic theories about the Russian soul, but while such Slavophiles no doubt existed, it would be a mistake to suppose the movement to have been consistent and homogeneous. One can find traces of its influence in the thought of almost every Russian writer and thinker of the time, including such "Westernizers" as Herzen and Turgenev, who wished to copy from the West but were repelled when they looked too closely at their models. *Narodnikism* (from *Narod*, folk or peasant), a populist movement aiming for a non-industrial socialism based on the *mir* (peasant commune), bears the Slavophile stamp. And so does Bolshevism—for while desiring an industrialized Russia, the Bolsheviks did not suppose that it had to retrace each step of Western history. Slavophilism may therefore be divided into at least three main tendencies: the pan-Slavists who provide a rationale for Tzarist imperialism; a middle group which fluctuates between its desire to retain Russian distinctiveness and its desire to reform Russian society within the framework of a constitutional monarchy; and the radicals who aspire toward a peasant democracy. Now the key—at least one key—to Dostoevsky is that he managed, with varying degrees of emphasis and clarity, to hold all three perspectives at once.

The dominant formal theme in his work is a conception of Russian destiny. Everything characteristically Russian, he wrote, "everything that is ours, preeminently national (and therefore, everything genuinely artistic)—is unintelligible to Europe." For Dostoevsky Russia was inseparable from the Orthodox Church, the unsullied vessel of Christianity in which alone was preserved "the Divine image of Christ." But Russia was also a world power with imperial ambitions, and Dostoevsky shouted: "Sooner or later Constantinople will be ours."

A disturbing though not unusual paradox: the writer whose most sacred image is that of Christ turning the other cheek demands the conquest of Constantinople, the almost craven apostle of humility exalts the use of brute power. Part of the truth about Dostoevsky is that this extraodinarily sensitive man who trembles for the slightest creature can also be a coarse and brutal reactionary.

For there *was* something coarse and brutal in Dostoevsky. He knew it perfectly well, hence his desperate straining for love and humility. The love-seeker or God-seeker is particularly vulnerable to self-torment if he inwardly believes that he seldom experiences true love and that instead of embracing God he merely celebrates his own ego. This is a central ambivalence of neurotic character—one is almost tempted to say of modern character; and it is nowhere more spectacularly illustrated than in Dostoevsky, whose spiritual imago is Alyosha Karamazov, but whose life is tainted by the lust of Dmitri, the skepticism of Ivan, the emotional torpor of Stavrogin.

At least in part, Dostoevsky's politics is a function of his psychology, that is, of his struggle to heal his moral fissure and of his horrified recoil from the sickness he finds in all men. Dostoevsky dreaded the autonomous intellect, the faithless drifting he had himself experienced and was later to portray in Ivan Karamazov; he feared that the intellectual, loosed from the controls of Christianity and alienated from the heart-warmth of the Russian people, would feel free to commit the most monstrous acts to quench his vanity. Once man is free from responsibility to God, what limit can there be to his presumption?—an argument that might be more convincing if there were evidence that believers as a group have been less arrogant than skeptics. Together, it should be noticed, with the messianic strain in his religion, there is an element of coarse "pragmatism": God as celestial overseer.

Though a tendentious moralist, Dostoevsky was an entirely honest novelist, and in his novels he could not but show that while the will to faith is strong in some modern intellectuals, it seldom leads them to the peace of faith. His God-seekers, like Shatov in *The Possessed*, are men peculiarly driven by anguish: the more serious their desire for God, the more must they acknowledge the distance separating them from Him—and the more they are tempted, in the manner of the radical Slavophiles, to assimilate God to the people. Since the quest of such characters is partly motivated by an intense dislike for commercial civilization, they often find themselves in unexpected conflict with society. Their ideas, it is true, have little in common with socialist doctrine, but their values lead them to an uneasy kinship with socialism as a critical activity.

Yet they cannot accept socialism. Dostoevsky despised it as "scientific," a bastard of the Enlightenment and the twin of rationalist atheism; he rejected it, also, because he feared that man might barter freedom for bread. No political system which located salvation in the secular world could have been acceptable to him, and in a sense R. P. Blackmur is right when he says that Dostoevsky's politics were those of a man "whose way of dealing with life rested on a fundamental belief that a true rebirth, a great conversion, can come only after a great sin." It is even profitable to think of Dostoevsky's novels as rituals of rebirth, with a series of plebeian heroes (in *The Possessed*, it is Shatov) reenacting the drama of the Resurrection. But Blackmur's observation is not complete, a counter-term is needed.

Dostoevsky's politics were indeed, as Blackmur says, "non-social" and hence apocalyptic, but they were also colored by an intense fascination for the social politics of his time. Though he despised the ideas of the revolutionary intellectuals, he had been soaked in the atmospheres that nourished them, and as a result, his intellectual divergence signified less than his temperamental affinities. He "translated" the political radicalism of the 1840's, the radicalism of fraternity and utopia, into Christian terms—highly unorthodox and closer in spirit to primitive Christianity than to any church of his or our day. At times he verged on the heresy—I am not enough of a theologian to identify it—that every man is or can be Christ. This heresy, which may involve a rejection of the Last Judgment except insofar as it occurs every day, is in radical opposition to Catholicism, since it denies the Church, and in milder opposition to Protestantism, since it depreciates the Word; it is closer to Rousseau than to Paul. In his brilliant study of *The Possessed*, Philip Rahv is entirely right in saying that Dostoevsky's idea of salvation comes to "little more than an anarcho-Christian version of that 'religion of humanity' which continued to inspire the intelligentsia throughout the nineteenth century and by which Dostoevsky himself was inspired in his youth, when . . . he took for his guides and mentors such heretical lovers of mankind as Rousseau, Fourier, Saint-Simon and Georges Sand."

Repelled by the present, distrustful of those who claimed the future, Dostoevsky had but one recourse—to construct an ideal society based on an idyllic version of the Russian past. (In *A Raw Youth* the major character Versillov has a dream of "A Golden Age," which is to be "the earthly paradise of man. . . The Golden Age is the most unlikely of all the dreams that have been, but for it men have given up their life and all their strength, for the sake of it prophets have died and been slain, without it the peoples will not live and cannot die. . .”). The idyllic past was the communal life of the Russian peasant, whose greatness of soul, wrote Dostoevsky, was revealed in a “craving for suffering, perpetual and unquenchable suffering.” Ignorant and debased though the peasant may be, he is superior to the intellectual in that he knows, at least, from whom to beg forgiveness. That Dostoevsky himself was entirely urban in habit and psychology, merely widened the gap between his experience and his ideas. Everything in his work implies an exalted vision of the peasants yet he is one of the few Russian masters who barely touches on their life.

Now it should be recognized that Dostoevsky’s peasant was as much an idealized figure as the proletarian of the cruder Marxists, that his ideal Russia had about the same relation to the actual Russia as T. S. Eliot’s “idea of a Christian society” to the existing Christian states. And his celebration of the peasant’s desire for suffering, apart from its dubious accuracy, must be related to the fact that in his own life he could not always distinguish between ecstacy and humiliation. Dostoevsky’s ideal Russia was a “projection backwards,” in which the bureaucracy of the Orthodox Church was made to enclose the utopian dreams of his youth. For the novelist such a “projection backwards” is both advantage and danger: it stimulates the most powerful criticism of the present but also tempts him into confusing reality and desire.

II

The Possessed is drenched in buffoonery. This itself is a major reason for the atmosphere of violent negation which hangs over the book. Dostoevsky’s buffoonery means that while he takes seriously the problems raised in his novel he cannot do as much for the people who must face them; unwittingly, his book becomes a vote of no-confidence in society, both the seething Russian underworld and the stiffening overworld. Not one character is spared his ridicule, which seems more corrosive than Swift’s because more local, intimate and viciously jolly. A novelist who proclaims himself the partisan of order and then mocks and lacerates everyone within his reach, is entirely subversive in effect. By the time he came to write *The Possessed*, at the age of 50, Dostoevsky's opinions had turned reactionary but his temperament remained thoroughly revolutionary.

Buffoonery is appropriate to *The Possessed* because the characters are mainly pretenders. Stepan Trofimovitch is a liberal pretending to heroism, a liberal who trembles before his shadow and is so lost in rhetoric that he cannot separate what he says from what he thinks. Stavrogin is called Ivan the Tsarevitch, the false Tsar who will reign once the nihilists have triumphed. This description is provided by Pyotr Verhovensky, himself a pretender who speaks in the name of socialism yet admits he is a fraud with no call to speak in the name of anything. The upper strata of the novel—Lembke, the brackish Governor; his wife Yulia, a prototype of the wealthy woman who dabbles in the causes of interesting young men; Karmazinov, the famous writer who toadies before the revolutionaries because he wishes to be praised by everyone—these too are pretenders. And so are Shatov and Kirillov, the most serious people in the book, for they pretend to a clarity and resoluteness they seldom enjoy, and must therefore struggle with the unrealizable images they have constructed of themselves. Every character is a mockery of his own claims, a refutation of his own ideas; all are self-alienated in conduct and feverishly erratic in thought: even the saintly Father Tihon suffers, suggestively, from a nervous tic.

A tone of buffoonery, a cast of pretenders—and a setting of provincial meanness. Though Dostoevsky despised Turgenev and in the character of Karmazinov assaulted him with the utmost ferocity, his view of Russian manners is quite similar to that which Turgenev will express a few years later in his most Westernized novel *Smoke*. Dostoevsky's provincial town becomes emblematic of the smugness and ignorance, the moral coarseness which Turgenev's Potugin charges against all Russia. The society of *The Possessed* is a society gone stale from lack of freedom, seedy from lack of cultivation. Dostoevsky hammers at this theme throughout the book, scoffing, for example, at the Russian "men of science" who have "done nothing at all"—though, he wryly adds, "that's very often the case . . . with men of science among us in Russia." When Pyotr Verhovensky, in the midst of preparing to murder Shatov, stops at a cafe and calmly devours a raw beefsteak, his grossness seems completely typical of the Russian milieu. And still more revealing is the passage in which the clerk Lyamshin, who plays the jester to Stepan Trofimovitch's enlightened circle, improvises on the piano a musical duel between The Marseillaise and Mein Lieber Augustin, with the "vulgar waltz" obliterating the French hymn. Lyamshin intends this as a parody of the Franco-Prussian war but one feels that it is also a parody of all the Lyamshins, that Dostoevsky means to say: this is what happens to our provincial Russia, we start with the pretensions of The Marseillaise and end with the sloth of Mein Lieber Augustin.

Tone, character, setting—all depend on Dostoevsky's conception of the book. "I mean to utter certain thoughts," he wrote, "whether all the artistic side of it goes to the dogs or not. . . . Even if it turns into a mere pamphlet, I shall say all that I have in my heart." Fortunately the "artistic side of it" could not be suppressed and the book takes us through areas of experience never accessible to pamphleteers. Dostoevsky begins by wishing to sound a warning, he will rouse the educated public to the dangers of Western radicalism and atheism. But this wish so disturbs him, it raises such ambiguous memories and feelings that he can never decide what—other than a fiery incarnation of the anti-Christ—the enemy really is. On one level of action radicalism seems a poison rushing through the veins of society, on another level a mere schoolboy prank, a rude fabrication without social basis or intellectual content. This uncertainty of response is typical of Dostoevsky, himself split between God-seeking and God-denying, pan-Slavic reaction and Western radicalism; and it is responsible, as well, for the violent changes which his central idea—the idea of salvation—undergoes in *The Possessed.* Even as he warns against radicalism and scorns liberalism, they repeatedly penetrate his thought; the problem of ideology, which other writers objectify in an imaginary action, is for him a personal torment.

Some critics have used the politics of *The Possessed* to point lessons and draw analogies; to these I shall return shortly; but here I would remark that to read Dostoevsky primarily as a religious or political prophet—and one with a formulated prophecy—is invariably to rob him of those tensions which are the bone and blood of his art. Other critics complain that his treatment of radicals is malicious, a caricature of the facts. This is quite correct, and Dostoevsky has brought such complaints upon himself by writing Alexander III that *The Possessed* was an historical study of Russian radicalism. But while correct, such criticism is of secondary interest; a caricature of the facts may reveal truth, and it is precisely as caricature—what I have called buffoonery—that the book must be read.

Revolutionists cannot help being tainted by the societies they would overthrow. The followers of Pyotr Verhovensky are exactly what one might expect to find in the airless depths of autocratic Russia: they are petty bureaucrats turned inside out, provincial louts in need of fresh ideas and clean linen. And even at his most malicious Dostoevsky knows this; knows that the Stavrogins, Shigalovs and Verhovenskys are an integral part of the Russia he exalts. The sores are on *his* back.

Dostoevsky's conception of the Russian radicals is clearly limited: he knows next to nothing about the populist-terrorists of the *Narodnaya Volya* or about the incipient Marxists just beginning to appear in Russia at the time he wrote his book. But in however distorted a way, he does draw upon Russian history and his personal experience for the circle of plotters in *The Possessed.*

In his youth Dostoevsky had belonged to a St. Petersburg discussion group, called after its leader the Petrashevsky Circle, which met to consider utopian schemes for the regeneration of society. Dostoevsky was more deeply involved in these conversations than is generally supposed, and when several members of the Circle formed a secret revolutionary society he joined it. Everyone knows the sequel: police arrests, humiliating sham executions, years in Siberia. Upon his return to St. Petersburg ten years later Dostoevsky, his spiritual features lacerated and transformed, was no longer a radical, though neither was he the vitriolic reactionary of his last years. From his acquaintance with the "Petrashevskyists" he drew first an acute sense of the distance between grand talk and social impotence: in *The Possessed* he is always teasing the radicals with this; and secondly an insight into the monomania which afflicts or fringes every political movement: few things in the novel are funnier or more pathetic than the rosy-cheeked girl forever ready, whether at a radical meeting or the Governor's fete, with her set speech: "Ladies and gentlemen, I've come to call attention to the sufferings of the poor students. . ."

After the Petrashevsky affair Russia became an intellectual graveyard, and not until the 1860's did active political opposition appear. Inevitably, part of this opposition, weighed down by a sense of its futility, turned to terror. The most extraordinary figure of this period is Sergei Nechayev, a déclassé intellectual of plebeian descent. Insignificant as a socialist or anarchist theoretician, Nechayev made his mark by taking for his own the ethics of the Tsarist police, together with a few flourishes from Machiavelli and Loyola; his famous *Catechism of the Revolutionist* is a classical exposition of amorality as a method of politics. It begins with the striking sentence, "The revolutionist is a doomed man," and continues with a list of tactics he must employ: terror, arson, duplicity, spying on comrades. A belated Jacobin who has neither roots nor confidence in the people and is utterly scornful of "the gentlemen playing at liberalism," Nechayev elevates despair into an ideology. But he is also a man of great courage, and his life is filled with remarkable escapes, frauds and sacrifices, climaxed by ten years of solitary imprisonment during which he never once breaks down.

In 1869, while forming some revolutionary groups, Nechayev found that one of his disciples, Ivanov, doubted his claim to be the Russian representative of a revolutionary Secret Committee. Ivanov was right, Nechayev was shamming in order to give himself an air of authority; but it cost the doubter his life. To dispose of Ivanov and bind the other followers with a chain of guilt, Nechayev arranged for the murder of Ivanov. This is the incident which stirred Dostoevsky to compose the political part of *The Possessed*. Pyotr Verhovensky is Nechayev's double, a double in whom monstrous courage has been deflated into farce.

And indeed, as long as Russia remained both autocratic and isolated, what could it produce but Nechayevs? Russian rebellion had always been cut from the cloth of despair. Even in the Decembrist revolt of 1825, a movement among officers and nobles to prod the Tsar into granting a constitution, there had appeared an extreme wing called the Southern Society which in some respects anticipated Nechayev. Its leader Pestel had developed a program calling for a military dictatorship to replace the Tsar, and had planned his organization as a strict hierarchy with three classes of members, ranging from top conspirators to obedient drones.

These incidents of Russian history became particularly important for Dostoevsky by the time he wrote *The Possessed*, for he believed they illustrated that fatal isolation from the people which drove intellectuals to the error of socialism. Yet it would be false to say that his early radicalism was replaced by reaction. He did not change his ideas as much as add onto them; the radicalism did not disappear, it became encrusted with layers of reaction. Entirely plebeian in outlook, instinctively sympathetic to the complaints of the *lumpen* intelligentsia, Dostoevsky could never become a dull conservative. He still knew what it meant to be hungry and homeless, miserable and lonely; and if he could not always distinguish between alienation from other men and alienation from God, he never forgot that in whatever form alienation is a curse. He was the political opposite of Stendhal, for where Stendhal was a liberal but not a democrat, he was a democrat but not a liberal. Behind his radical Christianity and his mystic populism there is always a sense of being one with the insulted and the injured. The whole of *The Possessed* seems evidence of this, but perhaps it will be more useful to look at an incidental passage:

Stavrogin stands with Captain Lebyadkin, his brother-in-law and the most buffoonish of Dostoevsky's buffoons. It is raining. Stavrogin offers Lebyadkin an umbrella. In an over-sweet voice Lebyadkin asks, "Am I worth it?" Stavrogin replies, "Anyone is worthy of an umbrella." And then Lebyadkin suddenly pours out: "At one stroke you define the minimum of human rights. . ." Such a passage, deepening buffoonery into tragic statement, is the unique mark of Dostoevsky, possible only to the writer who had once said, "Man is a crook—and a crook is he who says so."

III

Stavrogin is the source of the chaos that streams through the characters; he possesses them but is not himself possessed. In the first part of the novel, where Dostoevsky plants several clues to his meaning, Stavrogin is likened to Petchorin, the Byronic protagonist of Lermontov's *A Hero of Our Time* who has lost the capacity for identifying or acting upon his emotions. Like Petchorin, Stavrogin seeks excitement because nothing excites him, experiments in sensuality because he wishes to *become* sensual. His tragedy is that he can replace the sense of cosmic fear only with the sense of cosmic void: the awareness of human limits which Dostoevsky regards as essential to life he entirely lacks. A "subtle serpent" who is one of the Devil's party, though from metaphysical despair rather than a Faustian bargain, and a typically modern personality haunted by the "demon of irony," Stavrogin suffers from *acedia,* that torpor of the spirit which provides the greatest resistance to God because it lacks the power to resist anything. Repeatedly Dostoevsky declares the atheist only a step from the perfect believer:

the atheist, unlike Stavrogin, exercises moral choice and thereby demonstrates, whether he means to or not, the freedom of his will.

Stavrogin lives below, not beyond, good and evil; naturally so, for in the absence of desire, morality can hardly matter. The Nietzschean vision of "beyond good and evil" implies a harmonious resolution of desires to the point where moral regulation becomes superfluous; Stavrogin, by contrast, is on *this* side of morality. Yet it is no mere perversity on the part of his friends that they look upon him with awe, for in his wasted energies they see the potential of a Russia equally disordered and distraught. People expect Stavrogin to lead, he himself "seeks a burden." Though he never attends the fete, it becomes an occasion for the full display of his chaos; the intellectual saturnalia that occurs there, from "the women who were the embodiment of the women question" to Lebyadkin's vulgar verses and the rumor that Karmazinov will recite in the costume of a governess, is a public release of all that Stavrogin represents. Yet he is never so far gone as Pyotr Verhovensky, for there are a few moments when he judges himself by standards implicitly Christian. Because he still thinks of his fate in "ultimate" terms, he moves within the orbit of Christian metaphysics. But even from a secular standpoint the distance between the two men is very large: Stavrogin cannot tolerate his condition while Verhovensky relishes his; Verhovensky is a *reductio ad absurdum* of rootless individualism, while Stavrogin would immediately understand Bakunin's typically Russian cry, "I do not want to be I, I want to be We."

In a sense he is We: all but one of the major characters are his doubles. Pyotr is his social double, Liza the Byroness his emotional double, and Marya, the cripple he has married, his double in derangement. Fedka the peasant murderer is a double through the link of the intellectual Kirillov, while Lebyadkin and Liputin are doubles in the dress of burlesque. The most important doubles are Kirillov and Shatov, who act out the two sides of Stavrogin's metaphysical problem. There is a significant political reason, though Dostoevsky would not accept it as a basic one, for the impasse in which these two find themselves. They have tried radicalism and recoiled, Shatov into hostility and Kirillov into indifference. Together they have journeyed to America, symbol of the new capitalism, and have left it in hatred. Now they return to what Dostoevsky regards as philosophical bed-rock: Shatov to the problem of God, Kirillov to the problem of man. But this very turn may itself be seen as a token of political despair: when the problems of the social world seem insoluble, as they did in Dostoevsky's Russia, men feel an insidious temptation to "transcend" them.

Though at opposite poles ideologically, Shatov and Kirillov are in close emotional dependence, functioning as the split halves of an hypothetical self. Living in the same house yet tacitly avoiding each other, they represent in extreme form the issues thrown up by Stavrogin and debased by Verhovensky. Both are appalled by their intellectual isolation, Shatov developing a Christian heresy to overcome his and Kirillov lapsing into a gentle indifference to escape from his. Shatov believes in a God who is a man, Kirillov in a man who will be God. Both revere Christ, but Shatov is not sure he believes in God and Kirillov thinks it unworthy to believe in God. Shatov hungrily pursues God, Kirillov admits that "God has pursued me all my life." A man of pride, Shatov worships humility; a man of humility, Kirillov develops an ethic of pride. Both yearn for sacrifice, Shatov through immersion in the Russian people, Kirillov through immersion in a neutral universe. Neither can tolerate the conditions of existence, Shatov despairing over his distance from God, Kirillov protesting against the edict of Nature which keeps men in the certainty of death. Shatov desires a second reformation to cleanse Christianity of its bourgeois defilement, Kirillov yearns to become the Christ of atheism, sacrificing himself to assert man's freedom and to destroy a God who is nothing but "the pain of the fear of death." To Shatov is assigned Dostoevsky's most cherished idea, to Kirillov his most intimate sickness. Shatov suffers from an excess of self, Kirillov from ideas that can only destroy the self. The two are bound together by a thousand dialectical ties, neither has meaning without the other; Dostoevsky's image of the ideal man implies a unity of Shatov and Kirillov, followed by an act of heroic self-transcendence.

For a moment—it is one of the most exalted in all literature—this unity is almost realized. When Shatov's wife returns to have her baby, he begins to glow with a beautiful, a holy excitement, to which even Kirillov responds. The two men are quickly reconciled, Shatov telling Kirillov that if only he were rid of his atheistic ravings "what a man you'd be," and Kirillov replying with his native sweetness, "Go to your wife, I'll stay here and think about you and your wife." Under the stress of a great experience, ideology is brushed aside and the two men stand together, merely and completely two men—though it is a mark of Dostoevsky's greatness that the purer response is not assigned to his *alter ego* Shatov.

Kirillov is one of Dostoevsky's most brilliant ideological projections but not, I think, an entirely satisfactory one. Is it really true, as Dostoevsky seems to assert, that the highest expression of the will is suicide? One would suppose that a higher heroism of the will might be a choice to live, a choice made with full awareness of the knowledge Kirillov has reached. In any case, Kirillov, having spontaneously helped Shatov, has lost his "right" to commit suicide, for by his act of help he has recognized a human obligation: he is no longer alone, he has acknowledged a "thou," he has granted the world a claim upon his life. And surely a man with his intellectual acuteness would recognize this. Still more troublesome is his readiness to take responsibility for the murder of Shatov. No doubt, Dostoevsky meant to suggest here that Kirillov's ideas make him indifferent to the fate of his friends and indeed of all men, but Dostoevsky himself has shown us otherwise: he could not help presenting Kirillov as a good man. For once—it does not happen very often—Dostoevsky the novelist has been tripped up by Dostoevsky the ideologue.

Shatov is conceived with greater consistency and depth. As

he tells his wife, he is a Slavophile because he cannot be a Russian—which is another of Dostoevsky's marvelous intuitions, this one lighting up the whole problem of the intellectual's estrangement and the strategies of compensation by which he tries to overcome it. When Stavrogin presses him, Shatov stammers his faith in Russia, in her orthodoxy, in the body of Christ—and in God? "I . . . I will believe in God," which is to say: I do not yet believe. Shatov defines God as "the synthetic personality of the whole people," and when Stavrogin justly charges him with reducing deity "to a simple attribute of nationality," he replies with still another heresy: "On the contrary I raise the people to God. . . The people is the body of God." Whichever it may be, Shatov cannot accept —he cannot even face—man's distance from God; in Kierkegaard's dictum that "between God and man there is an infinite, yawning, qualitative difference," he would have found a dreadful confirmation of the lovelessness, the "Christlessness" of Protestantism.

In Shatov's mind, as in Dostoevsky's, God figures as a national protector rather than a universal mover, Christianity is seen as a radical morality committed equally to the extremes of ecstasy and suffering, and paradise, being realizable on earth, approaches the prescription Nietzsche offered for the good life. Before Nietzsche wrote, "What is done out of love always takes place beyond good and evil," Dostoevsky had written, "There is no good and bad." When Shatov declares the people to be the body of God, he offers a refracted version of 19th century utopianism with its dream of a human fraternity that will dispense with the yardsticks of moral measurement. Together with this utopian faith, which cannot easily be reconciled with most versions of Christianity, Dostoevsky had a strong sense of the conservative and authoritarian uses of organized religion. (Pyotr Verhovensky tells an anecdote which slyly reinforces the story of the Grand Inquisitor: A group of liberal army officers "were discussing atheism and I need hardly say they made short work of God. . . One grizzled old stager of a captain sat mum, not saying a word. All at once he stands up in the middle of the room and says aloud, as though speaking to himself: 'If there's no God, how can I be a captain then?'") In only one respect is the anarcho-Christian vision of Dostoevsky incomplete: like most primitive Christians he cannot find a means of translating his radical impulses into a concrete politics.

Politics is left to Pyotr Verhovensky, whose role in the book, as a Nechayev turned buffoon, is to bring the fantasies and fanaticisms of the Russian intelligentsia into visible motion. He reduces Kirillov's metaphysical speculations to petty problems of power, acts upon Stavrogin's nihilism by spreading confusion through all levels of society, and deflates the liberal rhetoric of his father, Stepan Trofimovitch, to mere political maneuver. Under Verhovensky's grotesque guidance, politics becomes a catalyst speeding the moral break-up of Russia; it is a sign of the national derangement, chaos made manifest, the force which sets into motion those latent energies of destruction which Dostoevsky finds beneath the surface of Russian life ("every Russian," he bitterly remarks, "is inordinately delighted at any public scandal and disorder").

Simply as a character in a novel, Verhovensky is somewhat nebulous. What does he believe? Does he believe anything at all? Which of the many motives suggested for him are we to credit? How much sincerity, how much guile, can we allow him? Is he a revolutionist, a police spy or both? Twice he describes himself as "a scoundrel of course and not a socialist"—which is to imply that a socialist is something other than he, something other than a scoundrel. One would suppose that Verhovensky has begun as a vague, muddled revolutionist, become entangled with the police and now continues on his own, deceiving the secret service, his comrades and himself. Though Dostoevsky is often most remarkable for the life-like fluidity of his characterization, Verhovensky is allowed to become too fluid, perhaps because Dostoevsky was never quite sure what to make of him. Certainly as a thinker Verhovensky is absurd, and the implication that he "represents" Russian radicalism is vicious.

Yet once noted, these strictures may be put somewhat to

the side. For we have learned to know political types at least as ambiguous as Verhovensky, men so confused in belief, so devious in affiliation, so infatuated with intrigue that they themselves could hardly say which cause, if any at all, they served. Verhovensky is not merely the *agent provocateur* to the provocation born, he also foreshadows the adventurers who will soon spring up in the unswept corners of all political movements, ready to capitalize on victories and betray in defeat.

Toward the wretched little circle of plotters which revolves about Pyotr Verhovensky, Dostoevsky shows no sympathy: *he does not need to*, he is their spiritual brother, his is the revilement of intimacy. Mocking and tormenting them with fraternal violence, Dostoevsky places each of the radicals exactly: Liputin, a cesspool of a man, frothing with gossip and slander yet sincere in his reforming zeal; Virginsky, a pure enthusiast whom the latest apostle of the most advanced ideas will always be able to lead by the nose; Erkel, a fanatical youth searching for a master to worship and finding him in Verhovensky; and Shigalov, a superb caricature of the doctrinaire. As portraits of radical personality, all of these are malicious, slanderous, unjust—and rich with truth about human beings, particularly human beings in politics. The "old Nechayevist" Dostoevsky—so he called himself and he did not lie—knew them all like the fingers of his own hand: they *were* the fingers of his own hand. Dostoevsky could have said, to paraphrase a remark of Henry James: "Where extremism is, there am I." *

* Dostoevsky has never received the critical attention from Russian Marxists that Tolstoy has, but in the early years of the revolution, before it was strangled by Stalinism, his genius was often appreciated. Lenin is said to have called *The Possessed* "repulsive but great," and Lunacharsky, the first Commissar of Culture, praised him as "the most enthralling" of Russian writers. In a memorial published in 1920 for the hundredth anniversary of Dostoevsky's birth there appears this generous tribute: "Today we read *The Possessed*, which has become reality, living it and suffering with it; we create the novel afresh in union with the author. We see a dream realized, and we marvel at the visionary clairvoyance of the dreamer who cast the spell of Revolution on Russia . . ."

Still, we should be wary of those critics who claim a neat correspondence between Verhovensky's followers and recent political movements, if only because all efforts to find real-life models for characters in a work of art are inherently dubious. To identify Verhovensky with, say, the Leninist personality is to shed the most uncertain light on either *The Possessed* or the Russian Revolution. Between Verhovensky and the Leninist type there is the difference between intellectual chaos and a rigorous, perhaps too rigorous ideology; conscious cynicism and an idealism that frequently spills over into fanaticism; contempt for the plebes and an almost mystical faith in them. Given the continuity of Russian history from Alexander II to Nicholas II, there are of course bound to be certain similarities: Verhovensky, for example, anticipates the dangerous Leninist notion of a "transitional generation," one which molds its conduct from a belief that it is certain to be sacrificed in a revolutionary maelstrom. And Shigalov personifies those traits of dogmatism to be found among the Russian radicals, indeed, among most Russian intellectuals, who were forced by their intolerable position to drive all opinions to extremes. But even these similarities, while real enough, should not be pressed too hard.

Somewhat more plausible, though also limited in value, is the comparison frequently made with the Stalinists. Verhovensky's vision of a society in which all men spy on one another and "only the necessary is necessary" has largely been realized in Stalinist Russia, but his "movement," in both its political bewilderment and intellectual flux, bears little resemblance to Stalinism. Dostoevsky's characters are profoundly related to reality, but they exist only in Dostoevsky's novels. His radicals are men of wildness, creatures of extreme individuality, largely cut off from social intercourse; the Stalinist functionary, by contrast, is a machine-man, trained to servility, and rooted in a powerful state. Verhovensky himself would not last a week in a Stalinist party, he would immediately prove too erratic and unreliable.

"Starting from unlimited freedom," says Shigalov, "I arrive at unlimited despotism. I will add, however, that there can be no solution of the social problem but mine." Familiar as this sounds, it is not quite the blinding anticipation of totalitarian psychology some critics suppose. For Dostoevsky has failed to recognize that side of ideology, in our time the most important one, which consists of unwitting self-deception, sincere masquerade; his scoundrels not only know they are scoundrels, they take pleasure in announcing it to anyone who will listen. In his eagerness to get at the root of things, Dostoevsky has confused the objective meaning of "Shigalovism" with Shigalov's subjective mode of thought. For surely a Shigalov would insist, in accents of utmost earnestness, that he starts with unlimited freedom and, no matter how bumpy the road, ends with a still higher conception of freedom. Between Shigalov's naive frankness and the torturous workings of the totalitarian mind there has intervened a whole epoch of political complication.

Dostoevsky's truly profound insight into politics appears elsewhere, and cannot be appropriated by any political group, for it has to do with ideology in general. From *any* coherent point of view, Dostoevsky's politics are a web of confusion—few fears now seem more absurd than his fear that Rome and socialism would band together against the Orthodox Church; yet he is unequalled in modern literature for showing the muddle that may lie beneath the order and precision of ideology. Himself the most ideological of novelists, which may be half of his secret, he also fears and resists ideology, which may be the other half. In our time ideology cannot be avoided: there is hardly a choice: even the most airy-minded liberal must live with it. Dostoevsky knew this, and would have mocked those cultivated souls who yearn for a life "above mere ideas." But ideology is also a great sickness of our time—and this is true despite one's suspicion of most of the people who say so. In all of his novels Dostoevsky shows how ideology can cripple human impulses, blind men to simple facts, make them monsters by tempting them into that fatal habit which anthropologists call "reifying" ideas. No other novelist has dramatized so powerfully the values and dangers, the uses and corruptions of systematized thought.

And few passages are as remarkable in this respect as the one toward the end of *The Possessed* in which Shigalov refuses to participate in the murder of Shatov. Here, one hopes, here at last is one man who will not lend himself to this shameful act. But in a moment it becomes clear that Shigalov has left, not because he is revolted by the act itself but because the murder is not required by his scheme. In a sense, he is worse than Pyotr Verhovensky, for he is neither hot nor cold; for him the man Shatov does not exist; the only reality he acknowledges is the reality of his doctrine. He has become the ideological man in his ultimate, most terrible form.

IV

I have said that all but one of the major characters is a double of Stavrogin, and that exception is, of course, Stepan Trofimovitch, the liberal with heroic memories. Toward him Dostoevsky is least merciful of all; he stalks him with a deadly aim; he humiliates him, badgers him, taunts him, and finally shatters him—and yet: he loves him.

For all that Stepan Trofimovitch fancies himself a "progressive patriot," a "picturesque public character" living in "exile," he depends upon the patronage of Varvara Petrovna, an eccentric landowner. In the relationship between these two quarrelsome yet loving creatures—I am aware of the dangers of allegorizing—Dostoevsky seems to suggest the relationship between matriarchal Russia and her errant liberalism. Stepan Trofimovitch is Varvara Petrovna's "invention," her "day-dream," but Dostoevsky is too honest not to add that "in turn she exacted a great deal from him, sometimes even slavishness." And in one of his moments of sudden self-awareness, Stepan Trofimovitch acknowledges, though not without an edge of bravado, the condition of liberalism: *"Je suis un simple dependent et rien de plus. Mais r-r-rien de plus."*

Though he preens himself on being advanced, he has only a childish notion of social realities: the liberal has been protected too long, he does not realize how much his comfort depends on the indulgence of authority. Stepan Trofimovitch really believes he will be arrested for his imaginary political heresies, and each night he hides under his mattress a letter of self-defense concerning a poem several decades old and read by no one at all. In the presence of his friends he becomes boastful and eloquent when recalling his youth, but the thought of the police sets him trembling. When a peasant riot breaks out in the province, he is among the first to call for stern measures: "He cried out at the club that more troops were needed. . ." And indeed, precisely its half-heartedness and cowardice is one of Dostoevsky's major complaints against liberalism.

By making Stepan Trofimovitch the protégé of Varvara Petrovna, Dostoevsky destroys the liberal's claim to intellectual independence; by making him the parent of Pyotr, he implies that nihilism is the necessary outcome of liberalism. Yet in both relationships Stepan Trofimovitch shows considerable resources. He gratifies Varvara Petrovna's hunger for new ideas, for scraps of Western thought with which to relieve the dullness of Russia, and not least of all, for a consistent if erratic display of affection. Toward Pyotr he behaves with impressive and unexpected dignity. "She [Varvara Petrovna] was a capitalist," sneers the son, "and you were a sentimental buffoon in her service." It is true, it strikes to the heart of the old man's situation, and yet it is not the whole truth, just as the generalized form of Pyotr's indictment is not the whole truth about liberalism.

In his portrait of Stepan Trofimovitch, Dostoevsky incorporated every criticism Marx or Nietzsche or Carlyle would make of classical liberalism; and then he transcended them all, for Stepan Trofimovitch in his ridiculous and hysterical way is a sentient human being whom one grows to love and long for, so that the actual man seems more important than anything that may be said about him. As the book progresses, Stepan Trofimovitch moves through a number of mutations: the liberal as dependent, the liberal as infant, the liberal as fool (in both senses), the liberal as dandy, the liberal who

tries to assert his independence, the liberal as spoiled darling
of the radicals, as *agent provocateur*, as provincial, as bohemian, as bootlicker of authority, and the liberal as philosopher.
(Which are more important, he asks the young radicals,
Shakespeare or boots, Raphael or petroleum?) In each of
these roles or phases, Stepan Trofimovitch demonstrates the
truth of Dostoevsky's remark that "The higher liberalism and
the higher liberal, that is a liberal without any definite aim,
is possible only in Russia."

Yet it is Stepan Trofimovitch who is allowed the most
honorable and heroic end. Driven to hysteria by the behavior
of his son, his patroness and himself, he sets out in his old
age on a mad pilgrimage, taking to the road, he knows not
where, "to seek for Russia." Since for Dostoevksy salvation
comes only from extreme suffering, Stepan Trofimovitch
begins to rise, to gather to himself the scattered energies of
the book, after having been completely broken at the fete.
Some two hundred pages earlier, this ending has already been
anticipated: "I will end like a knight," says Stepan Trofimovitch, "faithful to my lady." His phantasmagorical wander-
ings inevitably recall Don Quixote, and indeed he becomes
a Russian Quixote seeking Russia, truth, love and reality.
These are troublesome words, perhaps it would be best to turn
once more to a small passage. On the road Stepan Trofimovitch meets Lise; he rants in his most melodramatic fashion, falls to his knees, weeps, pities himself extravagantly—
and then, as the rain continues to fall, he rises "feeling that
his knees too were soaked by the wet earth." The "wet earth"
is reality, the reality he has begun to find in his quixotic
way; his talk is fantastic but his knees are soaked by the wet
Russian earth. It is the reward he wins for having remained
beyond Stavrogin's grasp, for clinging to a faith, even if it
be the hollow faith of old-fashioned liberalism rather than
the faith of Christianity. Together, the earth and the faith
make possible his redemption.

But another character has also found his redemption:
Shatov, in the Christ-like love that has flooded him upon the
return of his wife and the birth of her child. Is this not

suggestive of the political ambivalence of the book: that the character with whom Dostoevsky identifies most closely and the character he attacks most violently should both come to a kind of apotheosis? And does this not imply the possibility of some ultimate reconciliation? It has not yet occurred, Dostoevsky will not falsify, the two characters stand apart —but Shatov and Stepan Trofimovitch, symbolically placed at opposite poles, are now, for the first time, ready for each other.

If we ask ourselves, what is the source of Dostoevsky's greatness, there can of course be no single answer. But surely part of the answer is that no character is allowed undisputed domination of the novel, all are checked and broken when they become too eager in the assertion of their truths. Once Stavrogin has asked Shatov the terrible question, "And in God?", Shatov can never control the book, and even after Stepan Trofimovitch has soared to a kind of quixotic grandeur he is pulled down to reality by his old patroness who tells a priest: "You will have to confess him again in another hour! That's the sort of man he is."

Dostoevsky is the greatest of all ideological novelists because he always distributes his feelings of identification among all his characters—though putting it this way makes it seem too much an act of the will, while in reality it far transcends the will. "What decides the world view of a writer," says Arnold Hauser, "is not so much whose side he supports, as through whose eyes he looks at the world." And Dostoevsky looks at the world through the eyes of all his people: Stavrogin and Father Tihon, Stepan Trofimovitch and Shatov, even Lebyadkin and Pyotr Verhovensky. He *exhausts* his characters, scours all the possibilities of their being. None escapes humiliation and shame, none is left free from attack. In the world of Dostoevsky, no one is spared, but there is a supreme consolation: no one is excluded.

CHAPTER FOUR

CONRAD: ORDER AND ANARCHY

By temper and discipline Joseph Conrad was hostile to the life of politics. He could not identify with a cause or idea, in the manner of Dostoevsky; he did not live by the glow of an exalted historical moment, as did Stendhal; he would have shuddered at Disraeli's fondness for the mechanics of intrigue; and it is difficult to imagine him trapped, as was Turgenev, in a barrage of polemic. The grime of routine maneuver disgusted him, and the politics of a more intense, ideological kind he found peculiarly open to the sin of righteousness. A man of carefully tended austerity, Conrad disliked the whole "modern" atmosphere, with its wild fluctuations of belief, its feverish introspection, its impatience before traditional duties. Yet, by some curious paradox of his creative life, he repeatedly abandoned his established subjects and turned, with a visible shudder of distaste, to the world of London anarchists, Russian émigrés, Latin revolutionaries.

The two writers who mattered most in Conrad's life were Dostoevsky and James, and not merely as literary influences but as symbols of two paths of dedication, polar responses to the possibilities available to the modern artist. Dostoevsky, whom he called "a grimacing and haunted creature," Conrad hated with a dull fury which goes far beyond the range of literary taste. Dostoevsky meant a nagging memory, a sardonic challenge, an unsubdued pressure of rejected energies. Dostoevsky was his Smerdyakov.

One of Conrad's friends, Richard Curle, has written that "Dostoevsky to Conrad represented the ultimate forces of confusion and insanity . . . He did not despise him as one despises a nonentity, he hated him as one might hate Lucifer and the forces of darkness." Conrad wrote of *The Brothers Karamazov* that it was "an impossible lump of valuable matter. It's terrifically bad and impressive and exasperating. Moreover, I don't know what Dostoevsky stands for or reveals, but I do know that he is too Russian for me. It sounds to me like some fierce mouthings from prehistoric ages." These "prehistoric ages," I would suggest, are a projection of Conrad's own past, the years of his youth which he may well have wished to consign to the blackness of the prehistoric. The meaning of Dostoevsky, far from being "too Russian," was immediately and profoundly accessible to Conrad, as *Under Western Eyes* so dramatically shows. The truth is, Conrad did not wish to understand Dostoevsky.

He did not wish to because in the novels of that "grimacing and haunted creature" were recreated not the events but what was far more terrifying, the atmospheres and emotional patterns of the youth he had escaped. Conrad's father, Apollo Korzeniouwski, had been a leader of the extremist wing of Polish nationalism, which believed in direct, violent action. Despite Conrad's embarrassed claim that his father was merely "a patriot," Korzeniouwski was a revolutionist on the model of Garibaldi, struggling to create a free and unified homeland. The flavor of revolutionary nationalism is unique and certainly different from that of revolutionary socialism; it is romantic rather than analytical, it exalts the *mystique* of the nation rather than the war of the classes, it creates an ambience of blurred fraternity rather than of social antagonism. And because it was a movement doomed to defeat,

Polish nationalism took on a mood of desperate and quixotic melancholia.

After the collapse of the Polish rebellion in 1863 Korzeniouwwski was exiled to a distant province in Russia, together with his wife and five-year-old son Joseph. The scar of this experience, as it throbbed in Conrad's later memories, was to recall both glory and humiliation. When the children of revolutionaries revolt, it is against revolution: Conrad as a young man escaped from the world of both his father and those who had persecuted his father. But few things short of an actual return to Poland or Russia could have recalled this world as vividly as Dostoevsky's novels. For in those novels were mirrored the two sides of his memory: the hated oligarchy of Tzarism and the rebels against this oligarchy who, for all that Dostoevsky wrenched them into ugliness and caricature, might still stir in Conrad the dimmed fires of his political past.

Part of what I have been saying is a modified version of Gustav Morf's thesis that Conrad lived his life in the shadow of his Polish heritage and that many of his novels are efforts, by symbolic indirection, to justify or expiate his "desertion" from the national cause. Like most original minds, Morf went too far; he strained for connections between Conrad's life and work that are unnecessary to his thesis. But he was right in suggesting that when Conrad left Poland he cut himself off from the support of his native setting and thereafter remained a stranger, a wanderer at sea and an alien on land. Few writers—few men—have ever had their lives so sharply fractured: oppressed Poland, the maritime service, literary England. It was a bewildering journey and each step must have exacted a psychic price.

At the time Conrad came to England, the writer was still regarded as a gentleman: and a gentleman was what Conrad passionately wished to be. Once he began to publish, the best literary men of his day—James, Galsworthy, Garnett—accepted him as colleague and peer, and this acceptance kept him afloat through some difficult years. James is the crucial figure here, though not quite as the literary mentor he is sometimes said to have been; for while Conrad admired his novels, he seems to have thought of James, above all, as an examplar of the Western literary man, the writer dedicated to craft yet secure in the social world, the writer as moral spokesman in a free society. And perhaps—the ways of identification being what they are—Conrad fastened upon James as his model of the literary man because James, for all that he seemed so consummate a gentleman, was still, like himself, a foreigner.

This need to be at least as English as the English has been shrewdly noticed by Ford Madox Ford and J. H. Retinger, a Pole in Conrad's circle. Ford writes that Conrad's "ambition was to be taken for—to be!—an English country gentleman of the time of Lord Palmerston," and Retinger that "there was always a certain touch of snobbishness in [Conrad's] assumed English outlook . . ." Snobbishness is not quite the word. Far more was at stake—Conrad's profound yearning for security, recognition and tranquility. Conrad was one of the first of those modern writers who react against the "nonsense" of bohemia by adopting a way of life that is notable for its gray bourgeois prudence.

Conrad's conservatism, which is at least as much a psychological reflex as a formulated opinion, reached its full bloom in England. It is not an aggressive conservatism, Conrad being, for one thing, anti-imperialist in an age of imperialism; his rather querulous political mood came closest to that of the "Little Englanders," those who wished to freeze history at the point where England had been a prosperous mercantile nation but not yet a world power, and where the English gentleman and his country house had seemed indestructible monuments to an eternal order of virtue. This is a politics of defense: a desire to remain untouched by the fearful effects of industrialism, to be let alone by history, to retain privileges and values that are slipping away.

To connect this conservatism with Conrad's famous "philosophy" may help clear aside the murk that usually accompanies that philosophy. For the philosphy of his novels is of a piece with his political conservatism: genuinely felt, fervently clung to, but not finally organic to the work. They represent Conrad's public face—by which I do not mean that they are insincere or insignificant but that they exert their force mainly on the surface, through the cautions of the will. At every critical moment in his books, or in rare moments of relaxation, long repressed and discordant materials break through this surface. Or in hyperbole: the Jamesian Conrad directs, the Dostoevskian Conrad erupts.

The stoical attitude is compatible with almost any politics: twist it one way and it becomes a sanction for quietism, another way and it becomes the mask of revolution. But the prolonged emphasis in Conrad's novels upon order and responsibility, restraint and decorum, fortitude and endurance, is strongly congenial to an unspectacular conservatism, the politics of a class losing self-confidence yet still determined to keep its power. Such a class has a good many ideological resources, but none more soothing and few more useful than an appeal to pluck and the tried virtues. So that if one can imagine Conrad in any political setting at all, it is perhaps as a second-rank dignitary of the later Roman republic, sternly holding to the values of simplicity and restraint as they suffer attack from tyrants and mobs.

Conrad's motto certifying fidelity as the basic human obligation and his remark that because the universe cannot be regarded as ethical one must suppose the aim of creation to be purely spectacular, fit in well enough with his insecure stoicism. Yet the claim sometimes made for Conrad, that these attitudes lead to a redeeming vision of human solidarity, must be sharply discounted. Conrad reaches for such a vision and believes in its necessity, but it is almost never found, and in his political novels, those terrible surveys of desolation, it never is found. For Dostoevsky human life is always drenched with terror, yet men turn to each other for comfort and support; in Conrad the terror is also there, but each man must face it alone and the only solidarity is a solidarity of isolated victims.

We cannot stop at this point of formal statement, much as Conrad might wish us to; for beneath the controlled stiffness of Conrad's stoicism, as beneath his conservatism, there flows a bleak and terrible disbelief, a radical skepticism that corrodes the underside of everything he values. Christianity, he wrote to Garnett, he had "disliked" since the age of fourteen; politics, and particularly the rationalist liberalism of his day, he found at least as distasteful; and he was too serious and morally self-conscious a man to console himself with the cult of estheticism. His stoical mask served him well, but not continuously. For his every tribute to fortitude there is also in his work an image of desolation, of the terror that is left when belief crumbles. Conrad cannot share Dostoevsky's faith in universal salvation nor can he accept Stendhal's minimal solidarity with "the happy few"; he finds comfort neither in the future nor the present, the heavenly seat of judgment nor a mundane circle of devotees. There remains to be sure, his famous "job sense," the satisfactions he found in the discipline of the maritime service and to which he repeatedly returned in his novels, if not in his life. But the "job sense," whatever its modest returns, is a security *faute de mieux:*—because there is nothing better by which to live, you fall back on your way of earning a living. It is a useful crutch, but little more. In the end Conrad is alone, unmoored, perhaps sunk. Long before Hemingway began to look for a clean well-lighted place, Conrad knew the meaning of *nada.*

The stoical attitude has been described as a mixture of sternness, simplicity and an absolutely untheatrical feeling for life. The first two Conrad had, the last not quite. And it is here that his romanticism crops up—in a fondness for the theatrical, which in his case usually means the exotic. The romantic impulse in his fiction, and particularly in the sea stories, works as a *controlled* release from the stoical burden. Security of a kind is found at sea, its very terrors being predictable and at their worst demanding nothing more than resistance and resignation, while the land is crowded with dangers, class intrigues, perplexing social mechanisms. In the contrast between what Marlow says and what he tells, lies the distance Conrad can allow between the stoical norm and the romantic deviation. Which is to say: between the desire to cling to moral formulae and the recognition that modern life cannot be lived by them, between the demands of social conscience and the freed fantasies of the idyllic or the dangerous, between the commandments of one's fathers and the quandaries of exile.

In only one important way is Conrad anti-romantic: he violently resists the demonic and the sensual. By straining his will, he suppresses the chaos within him; but it breaks past his guard in the shape of a free-floating anxiety, a sense that the universe is—not actively malicious, which might even be consoling, but—permanently treacherous and ominous. Conrad is finally unable to sustain either commitment or skepticism: what remains is the honorable debris of failure.

I am aware that this reading, to gain full credence, requires psychological support, but this is not the occasion, nor am I the person, to supply it. Suffice it to remark that in Conrad the sense of repression is persistently acute: in his agonies of composition, his style of baroque wariness, his inability to imagine living women, and above all, his persistent need to maintain a safe distance, through narrator or manner, from his own work.

If these remarks have any value, they should help explain why Conrad's philosophical soulfulness is often so irritating, why his addiction to adjectives of ultimacy in, say, *The Heart of Darkness* strikes one as a straining for some unavailable significance. For isn't *The Heart of Darkness* itself a kind of parable about Conrad the writer, a marvellously colored and dramatized quest for something "unspeakable," which proves to be merely unspecified?

Conrad's conservatism, his hatred of the anarchists, his suppressed residue of nationalism must now seem more equivocal than at first sight. The anarchism he attacks is a political movement, and if we are to read his novels with a minimum of objectivity we cannot forget that; but it is also something else, a projection of an unrevealed self, of the desolation a modern ego fears to find beneath its domesticated surface. Conrad is entirely serious in his warnings against social disorder, which he mistakes for a state of anarchy, but his seriousness is shaped and then mis-shaped by an exorbitant need for personal order. His fascination with the informer as a psychological type is partly the token of guilt over his removal from the Polish cause that Morf takes it to be, but more fundamentally it is a recognition by an up-rooted European that the world of political realities is far less settled than the world of political appearances. Perhaps, too, there is another sort of identification: The informer who serves the established world by prying into the world beneath it, may he not be seen as a projection of the writer who pries, not without guilt, into the depths of motive? The informer informs on his comrades, the writer on himself.

Nationalism, though minor in Conrad's mature thought, is the seed-bed of his politics. And even of his tone. The posturing that sometimes disfigures his work has a strong resemblance to the romantic melancholia of a nationalism that could not hope for success. (Wrote Conrad to an English friend: "You forget that we [Poles] have been used to go to battle without illusions. It's you Britishers that 'go in to win' only.")

The politics Conrad accepts and the politics he rejects are both rooted in Polish nationalism. By its nature, nationalism has no invariable social content: its role has been to create an independent nation in which the suppressed problems of capitalism can belatedly come into free play. In Poland, squeezed between Prussians and Tzars, nationalism tended to be aristocratic (the aristocracy of petty nobles) and reactionary (the reaction of a country not quite ventilated by the Enlightenment). Conrad's conservatism thus has some roots in the militant nationalism of his fathers.

So too does his uneasy interest in the anarchists. Nineteenth century anarchism and nationalism share many features, more than either does with Marxian socialism. Both are impelled by despair and romantic in mood, both solicit individual heroism rather than mass activity, both resort to violence against personalities taken to be symbols of oppression, and both appeal to a unitary consciousness in the people which socialists say does not or should not exist. The scent of anarchism as it rises from Conrad's novels is a recollection, though not entirely a faithful one, of the scent of Polish nationalism. His fascination with the smoky plots of the anarchists is a sign that the experience of childhood survives; his antipathy, a sign that he would prefer to destroy this memory.

Even conservatism and anarchism, which now seem to be emerging as the polar forces of Conrad's politics, are not quite so distant as might be supposed. Conservatism is the anarchism of the fortunate, anarchism the conservatism of the deprived. Against the omnivorous state, conservatism and anarchism equally urge resistance by the individual. Both conservative and anarchist—here they diverge, along parallel lines, from the socialist—find industrial society odious and indulge, if only by way of willed nostalgia, in a rural bias. Both try to improvise a moral shelter in the crevices of this society, the conservative in his cultivated circle, the anarchist in utopian communities shivering on the rim of great cities. And both see the ideal society as one in which men stand at a measurable distance from each other, free to enter direct relationships without the mediation of the state. What the anarchist anticipates, the conservative has won for himself; what the conservative feels to be the limited good of an achieved reality, the anarchist would distribute, after rites of purification, among humanity at large.

This kinship of apparent opposites may explain why Conrad kept returning to the dark corners of anarchist conspiracy. It is not, of course, the only reason: Conrad meant to sound a warning against the enemies of social peace and to disparage the codes and motives of the radicals. But his acute knowledge of their life—acute when not blocked by malice—would have been impossible without the fervor of his Polish past and the ambiguousness of his conservative present. Had his thoughts been harmoniously settled he would have been a "Tory anarchist"; as it was, and happily for his work, he was a Tory with repressed affinities for anarchism.

Upon this reading I would now bring to bear one of Conrad's lesser stories, "The Informer." The narrator, a timid art collector, confronts X, a revolutionary of mild appearance but ferocious history. With some discomfort the narrator examines the similarities between X and himself: "He was alive and European; he had the manners of good society, wore a coat and hat like mine, and had pretty near the same taste in cooking. *It was too frightful to think of.*" But the logical space between these sentences is too wide, something has been omitted—perhaps the final pair in the series of similarities, which alone could make it "too frightful to think of."

X the revolutionary tells the art collector of an incident in which an anarchist group was plagued by an informer. By a ruse the traitor was discovered to be a seemingly devoted leader. At this revelation a wealthy young woman, an "amateur of the emotions" who had been flirting with both anarchism and its leader, was so appalled that she retired to a convent. "Gestures! Gestures! Mere gestures of her class!" sneers X. Somewhat later a neutral character remarks to the narrator that X "likes to have his little joke sometimes." To which the narrator, in the final sentence of the story, adds: "I have been utterly unable to discover where in all this the joke comes in."

Where *does* it come in? Would it seem too far-fetched to suggest that X has been pulling the narrator's leg? That X has manufactured the melodramatic incident as a sly way of mocking the narrator's fears and curiosities about anarchism? Gestures, mere gestures of your class!, the revolutionary may thus be saying with regard to the art collector's polite inquiries into radical life. The shocked lady in the anecdote would then stand in relation to the anarchists as the narrator to X; and the narrator to X as the two sides of Conrad's temperament, the esthetic self and the political "other." If there be any truth to this surmise, Conrad's final sentence becomes a marvellously ironic thrust at himself.

II

In both *Under Western Eyes* and *The Secret Agent* Dostoevsky is everywhere to be seen, though more as a force to resist than an influence to absorb. Dostoevsky had wrestled with ideas, the problems of *The Possessed* were defiantly his; Conrad cultivated an acquired distaste for ideology. For him there was no danger of being caught up in the Dostoevskian effort to define salvation, there was only the danger of being enticed into that airless world, that madhouse of intellectuals and prophets, where the effort takes place. To Conrad the Dostoevskian milieu seemed barbaric, lawless, Eastern, an enemy of the "sanity and method" he clung to; and yet, perhaps because he sensed that in this milieu was to be found the most highly charged experience of his time, he could not turn his back upon it.

The plot of *Under Western Eyes* is inconceivable without Dostoevsky—the betrayal of the student revolutionary and political assassin Haldin, by another student, Razumov, and the ensuing service of Razumov as a Russian government agent among the radical émigrés; the analysis of Razumov's suffering when he turns in Haldin and of his isolation when, as a spy pretending to be Haldin's comrade, he must associate with the radicals he detests ("All sincerity was an imprudence. Yet one could not renounce truth altogether . . ."); the maliciously satiric portrait of the émigrés, particularly of their leader Peter Ivanovich. But what is quite alien to Dostoevsky is the tone of cool detachment—of willed detachment—in which most of *Under Western Eyes* is composed. Dostoevsky looks at the political world as a reactionary, Conrad as a conservative. The advantage is largely with Dostoevsky: precisely because he does not accept the status quo, because he cannot delude himself with day-dreams about "sanity and order," the reactionary enjoys a keener scent for political realities than the conservative. Conrad shares Dostoevsky's contempt for radicals, but he also indulges a condescension toward them that would be impossible to Dostoevsky. These differences go beyond opinion: Conrad distrusts abstract ideas as such, he grows uneasy before the furies of controversy, while Dostoevsky embraces them with the insatiable excitement of an addict. Conrad writes about politics to reject, Dostoevsky to transform.

The political strength of *Under Western Eyes*—as also its literary merit—is largely felt in the first 100 pages, that sweeping overture of terror which, from the moment Haldin bursts into Razumov's room, rises steadily in pitch and volume. Politics enters the narrative in several forms: as environment and character, fetter and goad, "the monumental abode of misery" which is absolutist Russia and the frantic rebellion of isolated intellectuals. In this section of the novel as in few other parts of his work, Conrad permits himself a complete absorption in his subject, feeling no need, whether from panic or caution, to fall away from what he has created, to smother it with irony or box it in with skepticism.

Where freedom is absent, politics is fate. This encompassing fact of modern life Conrad dramatizes with incomparable intensity in the "overture" of *Under Western Eyes*. By allowing Haldin some autonomy, Conrad shows a restraint unusual in his treatment of revolutionists. A terrorist prepared for death, entirely disinterested in motive yet naively unaware of the complications that attend his idealism, Haldin emerges with a fine political exactitude. His declaration, "The modern civilization is false, but a new revelation shall come out of Russia," is typical of the pre-Marxist Russian radicals, populists by conviction and terrorists by despair. Terrorism in Europe having often been the work of intellectuals without support or steadying from a mass movement, it is entirely right for Conrad to see Haldin as a student who lacks political roots or experience. For in a country like Russia, how can enthusiasm be expressed but in the language of desperation? Nor does it matter that Haldin never emerges as a fully developed character, for his only role in the novel, and that he performs efficiently, is to implicate Razumov, to make "normal life" forever impossible for that unhappy victim. To Razumov, Haldin is the face of Nemesis, the Nemesis which haunts Russia; and having looked at it long and squarely, he does not care whether it bears the features of guilt or justice, he wants only to be rid of it.

The characterization of Razumov is a triumph secured by Conrad's decision to shape each action affecting him from a political design. Razumov is the ideal functionary, the man for whom the world has little use because he is so entirely useful. Without a past, tied to nothing in the present, he is an anonymous stranger who yet claims Russia for his home. No one thinks of him as an individual with sorrows and desires of his own: to Haldin he means shelter, to the peasant Ziemianitch fated brutality, to Prince K—— embarrassment, and to Councillor Mikulin a likely recruit for the secret service. Each of these responses is molded by the pressures of Russian politics and society; the very Razumov who wishes only for the obscure solace of a career is shattered by the politics of oppressor and oppressed. He is the man in the middle, and he pays the price. Neither disturbingly good nor conspicuously bad, he betrays Haldin with full knowledge that he is doing wrong yet with some reason to resent Haldin's fatuous assumption that he would prove hospitable to a revolutionary terrorist. It is a tremendous stroke of irony: that Razumov's mediocre silence should lead Haldin to suppose him a secret rebel, that his appalling anonymity should set off his destruction by the political world.

Having betrayed Haldin, Razumov utters his great and redeeming sentence: "I have walked over his chest." To his credit he does not say, as with some justice he might, "State and revolution have forced me to walk over his chest." He yearns to confess, to beg forgiveness, but no one will hear him, no one cares: to the world it does not matter. So great is his loneliness, he could not find peace even if the world were to forget him. Nothing can save him now, he is sure prey for Mikulin, the bureaucrat who displays his power by neglecting to finish his sentences. As they are brought together in muted climax, Razumov tells Mikulin that he wishes to withdraw from the whole affair, simply to "retire":

> An unhurried voice said—
> "Kirylo Sidorovitch."

Razumov at the door turned his head.

"To retire," he repeated.

"Where to?" asked Councillor Mikulin.

This question cannot be answered, not by Razumov and not by us. The whole first part of the novel, shaped and deepened by its brilliant ending, is a dramatic statement of Conrad's realization that in the modern world politics is total: it will create all or destroy all, it provides no exemptions, permits no mercy, offers no haven.

What follows in *Under Western Eyes*, for all its frequent richness, has neither the political nor dramatic authority of the first part. The trouble is usually laid to the fumbling narrator, an old Englishman thrust into accidental relations with the refugees, who is accused of breaking the integument of the fiction. It would be a mistake, however, to suppose his tedious prominence a mere technical slip. The narrator is not simply an awkward intrusion: he signifies a wish on Conrad's part to dissociate himself from his own imagination. The pontifical teacher gratifies Conrad's need to be aligned with the orderly West, to be insulated from all that Russia implies—a Russia that has been transformed into a passion for confronting those problems of society which the sanguine 19th century would as soon have avoided and which Conrad tried to avoid because he was so entirely unsanguine. But this Russia cannot be avoided: it is a bloated image of our world. That the novel was written at all shows that Concord knew this; that the English narrator so often blocks our view of things shows how deeply he needed to resist his knowledge. The mere presence of this academic *raisoneur*, inflating his timidity into a virtue of liberalism, is enough to suggest a disharmony between the ideology and the action of the book. The narrator expresses Conrad's opinions, the narrative incarnates Conrad's vision.

In a moment of intensity the Englishman declares what must have been Conrad's own bias:

A violent revolution falls into the hands of narrow-minded fanatics and of tyrannical hypocrites at first. Afterwards comes the turn of all the pretentious intellectual failures of the time

. . . The scrupulous and the just, the noble, humane and devoted natures; the unselfish and the intelligent may begin a
movement—but it passess away from them. They are not the
leaders of a revolution. They are its victims . . . Hopes gro-
tesquely betrayed, ideals caricatured—that is the definition of
revolutionary success.

Though praised in our time as prophecy, this famous
passage will not resist critical examination. It reduces history to a cycle of enforced repetition and frees us, con-
veniently, from the need to study either specific revolutions
or their complex consequences. "All revolutions," wrote
George Orwell, "are failures, but they are not all the same
failure." Some, I might add, have even been successful, the
French Revolution, despite the Terror and Napoleon, having
opened Europe to political freedom. Conrad's formula suggests the complacence of a man who fails to see that at times
political revolt is the only honorable choice and the skepticism of a man who urges the gesture of moral heroism yet
insists that it is ultimately meaningless.

Were Conrad merely indulging a stray reflection it would
be pointless to worry this matter; but the passage is his
political signature, it controls the narrator's point of view.
And it leads, for one thing, to a serious failure in judgment:
an equation of rulers and ruled, both of whom Conrad finds
to be stained by "the cynicism of oppression and revolt." To
assimilate the behavior of a Haldin to the behavior of a
Tzarist functionary is to indulge the middle-class smugness
which afflicts Conrad whenever he decides to place his drama
under western eyes.

It is a smugness which frequently blots the later pages of
the novel. By failing to restrain his antipathy toward the
émigrés and by casting most of them as knaves or fools,
Conrad undermines the dramatic integrity of his book. Like
all political novels, it needs a dialectic of opinion that will at
least *seem* free from the author's motivating prejudices, a
force of resistance that will clash with the author's dominant
energies and convictions. But these it often lacks. In his
treatment of radicals Conrad often commands great shrewd-

ness, certainly more shrewdness than can be expected from the English narrator on whom he relies. (A Greek proverb has it: *a man can't hide behind his finger*.) More rarely, there flickers through his disgust a light of sympathy and understanding. With Sophia Antonovna, that familiar female radical whose impressive selflessness has been purchased by a destruction of the self, Conrad is superb. ("Life, not to be vile," she says, "must be a revolt—a pitiless revolt —all the time." And even more striking: "You have either to rot or to burn.") Though hardly treated with gentleness, Sophia Antonovna is "there," created, tangible. So too, if not as unambiguously, is the peacock leader of the émigrés, Peter Ivanovitch. Malice enters Conrad's view of him, but at least on the political side he is done full justice. Given to strutting and self-condolence, a flunkey before those he needs and petty tyrant before those he uses, Peter Ivanovitch is yet capable of so remarkable and so Russian a thought (Russian in that it can move toward either a populist or Bolshevik sequel) as this:

For us at this moment there yawns a chasm between the past and the future. It can never be bridged by foreign liberalism. All attempts at it are either folly or cheating. Bridged it can never be. It has to be filled up!

The writer able to imagine this speech is not quite so alien to the politics of the East as he would have us believe. Yet his radicals do not exert the force they might and should exert: he does not let them. Mocked and scorned, alternately infantile and sinister, fanatical but even worse, foolishly fanatical, the revolutionists are too much what the English narrator—and by proxy Conrad himself—wants them to be, too much a reassuring index of Western expectation. Conrad has failed to accept the challenge of his own book: to confront the revolutionists in their strength and not merely in their weakness, to pit Razumov against men of serious if wrong-headed commitment rather than merely against "apes of a sinister jungle," as in his preface he so fatally calls them.

Because of this failure, a whole side of the novel remains static: Razumov's line of action develops but the subsidiary motions that should be whirling about and against him do not. In the end one wonders why Razumov should wish to confess before these counterfeit revolutionaries, for if they are indeed as contemptible as he supposes he can hardly believe them the proper agents of either Haldin's heritage or revenge. In what sense can he be said to owe them a debt? and how can he, or anyone else, suppose them worthy to hear his *mea culpa*? Here, I would suggest, is a critical instance of the way bias run wild can damage a political novel. By refusing to extend his radicals the necessary credit, if only later to call it in, Conrad fails to establish the dramatic ground for his denouement.

At the end Conrad strives, as do most political novelists, for a non-political resolution of his political theme. The final stress of the book is a blank hostility to politics, on one level, a westerner's rejection of the extremism he supposes unique to Russia ("senseless desperation provoked by senseless tyranny"—though neither tyranny nor desperation was quite senseless), and on a much profounder level, a passionate outcry against the hardening and narrowing of character that is enforced by political life. The diseases of dogma, the corruptions of power, the impoverishment of fanaticism—these, for Conrad, are the very marrow of politics. Against the falseness of public life he stakes his hope in the private virtues represented by Natalie Haldin.

I believe [she says] that the future will be merciful to all. Revolutionist and reactionary, victim and executioner, betrayer and betrayed, they shall all be pitied when the light breaks on our black sky at last. Pitied and forgotten; for without that there can be no union and no love.

These words are moving, but more so in isolation than in context; for the vision of an ultimate harmony—and no political novel would be tolerable without it—can gain our full assent only after the existing disharmonies have been fully explored. As Conrad himself admitted, Natalie Haldin, his figure of reconciliation, "does not move" perhaps because, like the radicals she is meant to set off, she seems the creature of Conrad's political will rather than of his free imagination.

III

In *Under Western Eyes* the recommendation to charity is heeded on occasion, in *The Secret Agent* hardly at all. The secret agent is Mr. Verloc, employed by the Czarist embassy to spy upon a group of harmless, aimless and witless London anarchists. To gain a life of comfort Mr. Verloc has chosen the profession of informer and despite the revolutionary phrases he must mouth, comfort is all he wants. He is entirely respectable in his social impulses, he would no more think of violating the prevalent norms than of submitting to heavy labor, and his scorn for the anarchist chatterboxes with whom he must associate is proper enough to satisfy the most exacting philistine. But Mr. Verloc's ease comes to an abrupt stop when his employer prods him to commit an outrage meant to force the British government into abandoning its tolerance of refugee radicals. Cursing the fate—he cannot distinguish between indolence and destiny—that has led him to gamble his life on borrowed rhetoric, Mr. Verloc stumbles into a nightmare of calamities and then, a squalid death. As with so many other characters in Conrad, his destruction follows from his desire—the desire of a moderate man—to insulate himself from the complications of the great world.

The very conception of Mr. Verloc is brilliantly original, a fine example of Conrad's gift for noticing the threads of the ridiculous as they weave their way through political life. (A gift that is likely to be cultivated by people who look with discomfort upon their political past.) "There isn't a murdering plot for the last eleven years," wails Mr. Verloc in the voice of a clerk suddenly cashiered, "that I haven't had my finger in at the risk of my life. There's scores of these revolutionists I've sent off with bombs in their blamed pockets to get themselves caught on the frontier." For even as he acts the informer, that most lonely of vocations and until recently the least honored, Mr. Verloc remains a dull-minded complying Englishman, a beef-and-ale patriot whose ordinariness has served, by a wild curve of irony, to place him beyond the limits of ordinary society.

Nothing in the novel is equal to this opening invention, but there are moments which show Conrad's corrosive genius at something very close to its best. *The Secret Agent* is a work of enormous possibilities, far from fully realized but realized just enough to enable us to see how Conrad thwarts and denies his own gifts. At times his ability to make the life of humanity seem a thing of shame reaches an appalling completeness—as, most strikingly, in the conversation between Mr. Verloc and his wife the moment before she plunges a knife into his ribs. Reading such passages—it is they that prompt me to speak of Conrad's genius as "corrosive"—one feels overwhelmed before the power that sheer fatuousness can exert upon man's destiny. But Conrad pushes too hard. The final meeting between Mr. Verloc and his wife, dazzling *tour de force* though it may be, shatters the structure of the novel; Conrad's insistence upon squeezing the last ounce of sordid absurdity from their relationship is in conflict with the narrative rhythm of the book. He lacks the talent for self-resistance that is indispensable to a novelist for whom irony has been transformed from a tactic into a total perspective.

Few things in the novel, or in all of Conrad, are more gloomily impressive than the care with which he demonstrates that every part of society is implicated in Mr. Verloc's fate and responsible for Stevie's death. Since *The Secret Agent* is a novel in which the sense of nausea is at least as powerful as the claims of indignation or even pity, there is no unavoidable obligation to regard it as an indictment of anything; but if there is an indictment, it is total. The anarchists and the Russians—their guilt is obvious enough, and in Conrad perilously close to the banal; but the English too are implicated, their moderation, before which Conrad so frequently abandons all critical judgment, now being seen as a form of obtuseness as well as a quality of civilization.

Thomas Mann, who regards *The Secret Agent* as an expression of Conrad's uneasy Anglophilism, finds in the novel "the whole conflict between the British and the Russian political ideology." He is right, but only up to a point.

Frightened and appalled by everything he regards as distinctively "European," Conrad repeatedly hurries back to the comforts of English moderation; but in the end even the English do not come off very well, for if they are not guilty of the crimes committed by the Russians and the anarchists, they are guilty of a stupidity and complacence which renders them accessories to these crimes. Inspector Heat, having made a good thing out of Mr. Verloc, hates to see his man endangered: one must think of one's career, and for the careers of policemen secret agents are indispensable. The Inspector's outlook, which is simply that of the official mind, is magnified and parodied in the great elder statesman Sir Ethelred. When this living monument to the genius of England is told by the Assistant Commissioner that

"This is an imperfect world—"
The deep-voiced presence on the hearthrug, motionless, with big elbows stuck out, said hastily:
"Be lucid, please."

Against the English Conrad's half-affectionate complaint is that they are too stolid, too untrained in the imagination of disaster, to understand the dangers that are threatening the civilized world. It is a familiar complaint.

The Secret Agent is the work of a man who looks upon the political spectacle—as, a little too often, the whole of life—from a great and chilling distance, and who needs to keep that distance in order to survive. Conrad's growing alienation from the modes and assumptions of modern society, which has nothing in common with literary fashion but is an utterly serious response, seems to me profoundly impressive; too often, however, the impressiveness has more to do with sociological and ethical statement than literary value. Conrad's critical distance, the sense he communicates of writing as a man who has *cut himself off*, may win our sympathy, but it has unhappy consequences for the novel. He tends to become stiff, even rigid, in his rejections, and the novel resembles, at times, a relentless mill in which character after character is being ground to dust. The sense of a *They* —whatever in the outer world imperils and destroys human life—is overwhelming; the sense of a *We*—whatever in ourselves can resist this enemy—is extremely faint. And I say this not primarily on moral grounds, though that would not seem to me at all irrelevant, but out of a consideration of the local needs of the novel. What one misses in *The Secret Agent* is some dramatic principle of contradiction, some force of resistance; in a word, a moral positive to serve literary ends. Conrad's ironic tone suffuses every sentence, nagging at our attention to the point where one yearns for the relief of direct statement almost as if it were an ethical good.

And this is true even for Conrad's development of the theme that the most deviant political figures are driven to destruction by their desire, shared with the vast sluggish mass of men, for normal and domestic convenience. That the very motives which lead one man to a suburb can entangle another in a conspiracy, that the extremists of politics can be as mediocre in their personal standards as those who find safety in the cant of political moderation—this is a brilliant insight. And yet in its very brilliance, it disfigures the novel. *The Secret Agent* is surrounded by a thick fog of irony which steadily eats away at the features, the energies, the very vitals of its major characters. What the English narrator does in *Under Western Eyes*, Conrad's style overdoes in *The Secret Agent*. It is one thing for a novelist gradually to deprive his characters of their pretensions or illusions, another thing to deny them the mildest claims to dignity and redemption. The novel forces one to conclude either that Conrad's fable is not worth troubling about, which I take to be manifestly untrue, or that his irony has turned in upon itself, becoming facile through its pervasiveness and lack of grading. The qualifications required by irony are present in abundance, but it is difficult to determine *what* is being qualified, which standard of behavior is being singled out for attack or defense. So peevish an irony must have its source less in zeal or anger than in some deep distemper.

Only one character escapes this heavy irony, and that is Stevie the idiot boy, a literary cousin of Dostoevsky's Myshkin. But unlike Myshkin, poor Stevie cannot support the weight of suffering thrust upon him, for where Dostoevsky's idiot grazes the sublime Conrad's never emerges from the pitiable. Stevie's history is acutely worked in, but he figures merely as a prepared victim, the irony which drenches all the others never so much as touching him. He is meant to convey a purity of pathos and to represent the humanitarian impulse in its most vulnerable form; but a character for whom one feels nothing but pity can hardly command the emotion Conrad intends.

Where Conrad presumes to render the London anarchists in their characteristic haunts and accents, he drops to a coarse-spirited burlesque. That the anarchists whom the Tzarist embassy fears should prove to be inept and impotent is part of Conrad's ironic intent, and for purposes of the novel an entirely acceptable intent; but the burlesque is too vindictive, the malice too cruel. Seldom did Conrad miscalculate so badly as in his view of the bomb-laden "Professor." To Cunningham-Grahame he wrote that the Professor was not meant to be "despicable . . . I wanted to give him a note of perfect sincerity"; yet it is difficult to regard this grimy lunatic as anything but a cartoon. The defect, as Conrad was later to say about another revolutionary in *The Rover*, "is, alas, in the treatment, which instead of half-pathetic makes him half-grotesque."

Anarchists, wrote Conrad, are motivated by a "dislike of all kinds of recognized labor." One need hardly be a partisan of the anarchist movement to grant that with regard to such of its leaders as Kropotkin and Bakunin this estimate is a fabulous vulgarity. Not only does Conrad fail to account for the fascination they obviously hold for him, he removes any reasonable ground for the fear they also arouse in him. For if it be irony to portray them as garrulous fools, a stricter irony would allow fools a hidden strength.*

* In *The Great Tradition* F. R. Leavis reports that "Q" once told him Henry James "didn't know the right people." A fair point, concedes Mr. Leavis: "after all, the admirable types, the public spirit and serious culture . . . were characteristic products of the England of 'the best families' of James' time. Why does he seem to know nothing about this real and most impressive best?" A chap-

From Conrad's letters one gathers that some of his friends questioned him about his treatment of radical characters. To Cunningham-Grahame he replied: "I don't think I've been satirizing the revolutionary world. All these people are not revolutionists—they are mere shams." And to John Galsworthy: "The whole thing is superficial and but a tale. I had no idea to consider Anarchism politically or to treat it in its philosophical aspect; as a manifestation of human nature in its discontent and imbecility."

These disclaimers do not satisfy. To plead that the anarchists of *The Secret Agent* are mere shams and therefore no reflection on the radical world, is to evade the question: why does Conrad habitually populate that world with shams? and even more important, doesn't his association of anarchist and sham deprive him of access to the complexities of the radical mind? Conrad's "esthetic" defense, that he was merely writing a piece of fiction, would have been scorned by Dostoevsky, as by most great writers; Dostoevsky would surely have insisted that his novels, far from being mere tales, were expressions of fundamental truth.

These remarks bring us, unavoidably, to the slippery problem of the relation between a novel and actuality. In our fiercely partisan age it is difficult to read books like *Under Western Eyes* or *The Secret Agent* without fiercely partisan emotions. No matter what their authors intend, such novels serve rhetorical ends, persuading toward one or another point of view. In practice it is hard to make the Aristotelian distinction between the imaginative and the rhetorical, since an author's vision, or imaginative quality, depends partly on his beliefs, or rhetorical ends. And the critic too had better acknowledge that he comes to the political novel with an eye that is partial and perhaps inflamed.

---

ter later Mr. Leavis notes, without a tremor of disturbance, Conrad's opinion that the anarchists were inspired mainly by laziness. It is interesting that a critic ready to chastise James for harshness toward the landowning class should not also wonder whether Conrad neglected "the real and most impressive best" among the 19th century anarchists.

That a novel includes an accurate report of an historical event is not necessarily a point in its favor. What would be a point in its favor is the presence of that quality we loosely call "true to life," or here more pertinently, true to the moral complexities of political behavior. This quality may be had by modelling a novel on actual events, but if that is so it merely explains how good novels are sometimes written, not why they are good. A causal explanation should not be taken as a ground for valuation.

But if a close adherence to actual events is sometimes necessary for writing a good novel, the mere accurate transcription of those events is not a sufficient condition for declaring it good (thus we say, "he has the facts right but misses the spirit completely.") Still, when a critic praises a novel for giving an accurate picture of the 19th century anarchist movement he may be making, through ellipsis or clumsiness, a valid point in its behalf, namely, that it does communicate a sense of the moral complexities of political behavior.

A person without any knowledge of the anarchists might come to see that Conrad's treatment of them is warped or at least dubious. But even here his experience would shape his judgment, he would be testing the life of the novel by his sense of life. As critics we may claim to be interested only in the life that is *in* the novel, but we cannot engage in this formal apprehension except as we bring to our reading some mature sense of what is living and what is dead. And this holds true, though in a more complicated way, for fantasy, surrealism and other non-realistic modes.

Since the novel is concerned with what "really happens," with the essential or the probable, it must have some correspondence to what *has* happened. So to say that a novel which contains characters called "anarchists" and is set in "the 19th century" does not give an accurate picture of 19th century anarchism, *may* be a way of making, elliptically, a judgment against the novel. It may be a way of saying that the events in the novel, partly because they are too different from what has happened in such circumstances, are not sufficiently like what "really happens" in those circumstances.

As a novelist Conrad is under no obligation to admire the anarchists or accept their doctrine; he need not give a faithful report of their history, and he may even, without excessive jeopardy, distort some of the facts about them. But he cannot, short of damaging his book, violate our sense of what "really happens" in the kind of world that is summoned by the world "anarchist."

IV

With *Nostromo* we come to a work of the first rank, much wider in social scope and more delicately balanced in point of view than either *The Secret Agent* or *Under Western Eyes.* *Nostromo* lacks—it does not strive for—the virtuoso flashes of *The Secret Agent,* and except for the haunting night scene in the Placid Gulf, it cannot equal the intensity of the first 100 pages of *Under Western Eyes.* But if *Nostromo* leans heavily on the panoramic method for presenting its subject, that is because the subject is so large and ambitious; the accompanying advantage is that *Nostromo* is one of the few Conrad novels against which it cannot be charged that its moral theme unfolds in an exotic vacuum, at too great a distance from familiar life. Like Forster's *A Passage to India* it may be read as a fictional study of imperialism, an area in which the two novels seem lonely, towering peaks. Conrad's novel is not bruised by anger as often as Forster's, and while far from impartial toward the conflict in Costaguana Conrad manages a composure which would have been impossible, perhaps even deceitful, for Forster to attempt. By sublimating his political anxieties in the melodrama of a Latin republic, Conrad gained what was indispensable to him as a writer: the protection of distance.

Political ideas are seldom expressed directly in *Nostromo,* and when they are they generally seem banal; Conrad lacks Dostoevsky's intellectual range or Stendhal's intellectual audacity. But it hardly matters, for the ideas of the book are thoroughly absorbed by its personal drama, with problems of morality and problems of politics coming to seem very much the same. Only in Martin Decoud, the dilettante who perishes in the Costaguanan civil war, do we find a direct reflection of Conrad's own attitude: skepticism softened by humane impulse.

If *Nostromo* rarely displays a Dostoevskian flair for "entering" ideas, it is superb at dramatizing them. Because Conrad does not hurl himself so violently into his book as Dostoevsky, he can present a coherent social world from the outside, a world in which all the relevant political tendencies are finely balanced, one against the other. The political action occurs in the rearground, as a shadow-play behind the personal action; but to grasp the book entire one must move into its shadows.

Though Conrad would have been alarmed to hear this, *Nostromo* verifies, in the limited way a novel can verify anything, Leon Trotsky's theory of the "permanent revolu= tion," a theory which sketches the problems of a backward country in an industrialized world. The semi-colonial nation, writes Trotsky, suffers from a sickly blend of primitivism and sophistication, a severance from its indigenous past and a crippling distance from the industrial present. It must compete with the advanced countries yet cannot; it desperately needs their capital yet strives to resist the domination that is the price of capital. What Trotsky calls "the tasks of the bourgeois revolution"—the setting up of a stable republic, the division of the land among the peasants, the achievement of both political and economic independence—cannot be completed by a native ruling class which depends on foreign capital for its survival. Hence, he concludes, the leadership of the nation falls to the young and rising proletariat which performs the tasks once assigned to the bourgeoisie; and thereby the two revolutions, bourgeois and socialist, are telescoped into one.

Trotsky's prognosis need not here concern us, though we may note that it has been seriously challenged by recent events in Asia. His analysis, however, I take to be valid, forming a paradigm of what happens in *Nostromo*—but to demonstrate this I shall have to reconstruct Costaguana's political history.

It starts with the dictator Guzman Bento, for whom "the power of supreme government has become . . . an object of strange worship, as if it were some sort of cruel deity." Bento rules in the dawn of free Latin America, shortly after Bolivar has swept the Spaniards from the continent and his generals have begun to nurture tyrannical ambitions of their own. Supported by the white and near-white *Hidalgo* land-owners who form an alien ruling class, the Bento dictatorship aims to contain those popular excitements which had to be stirred in order to win the war of independence; in its methods, however, it is entirely "old-fashioned," neither seeking mass support nor trying to assemble an ideology. We sense here a peculiarly "Spanish" atmosphere, the atmosphere of a government closer to barbaric autocracy than to streamlined totalitarianism. Conrad has struck exactly upon the note of fanatical solemnity which is to vibrate through the bloody comedies of Latin American politics; and by lingering on the Bento cruelties he has begun to develop the profound theme that in countries which exhaust themselves to achieve independence, the victorious generals will often mimic the oppressors they have expelled: there is no other model.

An interval of chaos follows. The dormant Indians begin to stir, the middle class is bled white by political thieves, a thin crust of proletarians appears. So harassing and so expensive is this period of lawlessness that the landowners, through the Blanco party, and the San Tomé mine, by a policy of sedate bribery, sponsor a conservative democratic revolt. A new regime is installed. Headed by the scrupulous and colorless professor, Don Vincente Ribiera, it hopes to limit corruption to a decent regularity, maintain social peace —and above all, pay foreign debts.

But Ribiera, like all moderate politicians in immoderate countries, takes little hold of the popular imagination. In fact, remarks Conrad with his dry shrewdness, it is "the tacit approval [of Holroyd, the American millionaire backing the San Tomé mine] that made the strength of the Ribierist movement." Like all comprador governments, the Ribiera administration can neither satisfy the needs of the poor, which would require radical measures distasteful to its domestic supporters, nor engage the sentiments of Costaguanan nationalism, which would require radical measures distasteful to its foreign supporters. The Blancos, writes Conrad with a touch of slyness, were "cultivated men, men to whom the conditions of civilized business were not unknown." Men, that is, whom Charles Gould, the manager of the San Tomé mine, could expect to find entirely reasonable.

Ribiera falls. In the name of national honor, his minister of War, General Montero, leads a revolt of the barracks. And it is here, in his treatment of Montero, the Bonaparte of the Campo, that Conrad soars to astonishing political insight, in its unsystematic way quite as magnificent as Marx's analysis of Bonapartism in *The 18th Brumaire of Louis Napoleon.*

In Europe Bonapartism arises from a fairly equal balance of antagonistic classes: the rulers cannot rule, the ruled cannot displace them. Into this crisis of the nation there leaps the military man raising the banner of social order and harmony. As the dictator who speaks in the name of the people as a whole, he will rise above "petty" parties and transcend "sordid" interests; actually, he preserves the familiar relations of power at the price of ruffling the sensibilities of the dominant class. For this political phenomenon Trotsky, in his *History of the Russian Revolution,* offers a striking image: "The idea of a master of destiny, rising above all classes, is nothing but Bonapartism. If you stick two forks into a cork symmetrically, it will, under very great oscillations from side to side, keep its balance even on a pin point: that is the mechanical model of the Bonapartist super-arbiter."

In Latin America, however, Bonapartism emerges not from an equilibrium of strength but from the mutual lassitude of exploiters and exploited. A country where semifeudal relations still prevail, where the middle-class is too weak to become the bulwark of property it has elsewhere become, and the entire economy rests upon an extractive industry controlled from abroad—such a country can reach neither stability nor democracy. Proclaiming himself a strong man who will lift his people to glory, the *Caudillo* proves to be a pigmy whose bombast reflects the vanity and frustration of a nation left behind by history.

To take power the *Hidalgo* landowners and their Blanco friends must use General Montero: it is a law of politics, those who lack the people turn to the officers. And this proves their undoing. The democratic interval, because it does not rest upon an articulate and educated people, soon collapses in futility; the politician falls prey to the general, the constitution is pushed aside by a miniature Caesar. Crudely sensitive to the moods of the masses, Montero rallies behind him every fraction of discontent; he charges the Ribiera government with slavish compliance to the "demands of the European powers" and raises the eternal chant of the colonial world: "Death to the Foreigners!" Nor is it entirely fabrication when Pedrito Montero, the aspiring Duc de Morny to his brother's Napoleon, describes the Blancos as "Gothic remnants, sinister mummies, who plotted with foreigners for the surrender of the lands and the slavery of the people." For Montero is not so pliant before the San Tomé mine as were his predecessors; when Martin Decoud asks Antonia Auellanos why the usual effort was not made to buy him off, she replies that it was impossible. Decoud immediately grasps the reality: "He wanted the whole lot? What?"

As his troops converge on Sulaco, the last Blanco stronghold, Montero can expect—and this is another fine political touch on Conrad's part—some considerable support from within the town, from those plebeian and declassed elements Conrad so unkindly calls the rabble. "Rooted in the political immaturity of the people, in the indolence of the upper classes and the mental darkness of the lower," the Monterist revolt, through its primitive "radical" demagogy, becomes a threat to every established power in Costaguana: to the haughty landowners, to the constitutional liberals led by the idealist Avellanos, and to the mine which Charles Gould defends with a superb talent for identifying private interest with moral ideal. And just as Gould has his "material interests" to defend, so does Don Justé Lopez, the practical leader of the Blancos who has led a timid opposition to Montero but now is ready to make peace with the upstart general. On what are you deliberating?, asks Avellanos as he comes upon the remnant of the Provincial Assembly. "On the preservation of life and property," is the chorused reply. "Till the new officials arrive," adds Don Justé with the solemn side of his face. Though he holds no illusions about Montero, the respectable Don Justé plans to honor him with a declaration of loyalty "in order to save the form at least of parliamentary institutions." *

In its ending *Nostromo* again reveals the controlling presence of a subtle political mind. The Monterist rebellion, aimed at setting up "an imperial rule based upon the direct popular vote," is defeated, yet the country finds no peace, the mine on which Gould had staked his hope for security and order becomes a focus of hatred among the country's workers, and the idealistic dreams of Avellanos, like his

* Through his extraordinary insight, Conrad came upon a basic pattern of Latin American politics. Montero is Peron, Batista, he is a hundred other President-Dictators. The comparison with Cuba is particularly striking: In the early 'thirties the brutal regime of Machado (Guzman Bento) employed gangs of gunmen to terrorize opponents. In 1933 a popular revolution brought to power Professor Ramon San Grau Martin (Professor Ribiera), with the military aid of Sergeant, later Colonel Fulgencio Batista (General Montero). Mildly democratic and moderately corrupt, the San Grau Martin government proved helpless before the domestic and foreign problems of Cuba. Meanwhile, Batista accumulated power, acquiring both a veneer of culture and real estate in Florida. A series of governments followed which were merely variations on San Grau Martin. In 1951 Batista, capitalizing on the accumulated disgust and desperation of the country, openly seized power. "I am a dictator," he said, "with the people . . . It is my destiny to make bloodless revolutions . . . The only blood spilled will be that of those who oppose us."

Batista's speeches were of course written by Pedrito Montero.

manuscript pages of Costaguana's *Fifty Years of Misrule,* are buried in dust. The fatuous Captain Mitchell bewails the rise of socialism among the Italian immigrants and the native laborers; Dr. Monygham, one of the choral figures in the book, makes his famous speech declaring "material interests . . . inhuman . . . without rectitude, without the continuity and force that can be found only in a moral principle"; and Mrs. Gould suffers her terrible vision, a vision of nothing less than capitalism itself: "She saw the San Tomé mountain hanging over the Campo, over the whole land, feared, hated, wealthy, more soulless than any tyrant, more pitiless and autocratic than the worst government, ready to crush innumerable lives in the expansion of its greatness."

A fruitful disagreement as to the ending of *Nostromo* has arisen between two of Conrad's critics, Albert Guerard Jr. and Robert Penn Warren. Guerard writes that finally the mine "corrupts Sulaco, bringing civil war rather than progress," while Warren argues that this is "far too simple. There has been a civil war, but the forces of 'progress'—i.e., the San Tomé mine and the capitalistic order—have won. And we must admit that the society at the end of the book is preferable to that of the beginning." Both critics seem to me right: the civil war brings capitalism and capitalism will bring civil war, progress *has* come out of chaos but it is the kind of progress that is likely to end in chaos.

Perhaps the central political point of *Nostromo* is that imperialism does indeed bring order, but a false order, an order imposed, an order which destroys the rhythms of native life and gives rise to the fumes of nationalism. Even Decoud, for all his skepticism, is infected by the nationalist contagion: "The whole land," he cries, "is like a treasure-house, and all these people are breaking into it, while we are cutting each other's throats . . . We are a wonderful people but it has always been our fate to be"—he does not say "robbed," but adds after a pause—"exploited."

Not only does Conrad observe the finest shades of the relationship between Costaguana and the foreign investors, he also charts the gradual shift in power among the imperialists, the slow displacement of British capital by American. It is not yet so radical a displacement as to prevent him from treating the matter with a somewhat wicked humor. Once Gould has exhausted his effort to find European backing for the mine, he can turn only to Holroyd, a broadly conceived yet not very harsh caricature of the American millionaire. "We," declares Holroyd, "shall run the world's business whether the world likes it or not. The world can't help it— and neither can we, I guess." A man endowed with "the temperament of a Puritan and an insatiable imagination," Holroyd is an exquisite blend of piety and ambition, spreading the "purer forms of Christianity" in a profusion symmetrical with his investments.

From this interweaving of political claims and passions there finally appears a stark and dominant image: the martyrdom of a land which will suffer from the deeds of its conquerors decades, perhaps centuries, after they have been driven away. "The heavy stone-work of bridges and churches left by the conquerors proclaimed the disregard of human labor, the tribute-labor of vanished nations." But the nations have not vanished, their groans echo through Costaguana; in politics as elsewhere it is the weight of the past, the evil of generations, which forms the heaviest tribute-labor man must bear.

Striking in their own right, as images of individual behavior, the characters also take on symbolic political meanings: personal and public roles merge, each enriching the other. The polar forces of the novel are politics and loneliness, social vortex and private desolation. For Conrad politics is a realm of illusion, resting in vanity and hatred, while the reality is a loneliness so intolerable as to drive men to seek comfort in illusion. In no other work does Conrad realize with such profundity his great theme that isolation destroys those who covet it, for in no other work is this theme so thoroughly defined in social terms. The deepest loneliness is not, as one might suppose from Conrad's lesser novels, a consequence of being cut off physically or branded morally for some transgression; it is normal and common-place, affecting none more than those committed to the affairs of the world. Between one man and another falls the silver shadow of the San Tomé mine, the symbol of the inhuman in human society. The haze of mystery surround-ing the mine, its staggering greatness of potential, tempt all who come within its radius to surrender to its power. Each incident, whether surveyed from a distance or scrutinized in close-up, is twisted by the magnetic power of the mine. Becoming a symbol as large and inclusive as Zola's mine, it forces the reader to see private drama as public struggle, to recognize that not the least tragic aspect of individual life is the fatality with which it melts away in the stream of history.

Nostromo, as he staggers under the weight of his secret and the loneliness which is its price, develops what he never before knew or needed: a political awareness. As soon as he touches the contaminated silver, the Cargardor who had once been a small-scale comprador loses his place in the scheme of things, his mysterious power over the people. But once forced into reflection, a man like Nostromo is helpless; Nostre Uomo, the one man the Blancos could count their own, turns into an accomplice of the malcontents, abandoning his role of the magnificent Capataz de Cargardores who could bend the workers to his will. His history anticipates those fissures of consciousness that will soon work their way through the masses, his estrangement represents the dawning realization of distinct class interests and sharpening class antagonisms. With consciousness there also comes loneliness, and with loneliness ambition. Ambi-tion, we are told, can blind a man, but to Nostromo it brings a painful lucidity, the lucidity he finds in the black-ness of his night on the Placid Gulf; it wakes him from the drowse of vanity and leaves him with the "bewildered con-viction of having been betrayed." Guilty and alone, lost in a state of irrevocable unhappiness, Nostromo has nothing left but to sit in heavy dignity at the anarchist meetings.

Charles Gould, though scornful of all political theorizing, is the most remarkable political figure in the novel. Perhaps nowhere else in modern fiction does one find so vivid an illustration of the power which ideology can establish over a nonpolitical man. Blindly confident in the rationale of imperialism, hopeful to the end that the San Tomé mine will yield order and peace, he is a good man with an endless capacity for self-delusion in behalf of "material interests." In the political struggle, as Decoud quickly senses, Gould will sacrifice his money, his wife, his skin, everything but the mine. He cannot act, sneers Decoud, "without idealizing every simple feeling, desire, or achievement." Terrible this indictment is, yet not nearly so terrible as Decoud's own assumption that every simple feeling, desire or achievement must, to be measured truly, be stripped of ideal claims.

Nowhere is Conrad's creative tact better employed than in his delicate intimations of a parallel between Gould's political and private fates. The mine has become a token of some "subtle conjugal infidelity," as Mrs. Gould senses when she feels "as if the inspiration of their early years had left her heart to turn into a wall of silver bricks, erected by the silent work of evil spirits between her and her husband." In the innocence of her perplexity Mrs. Gould speaks of evil spirits, but is she not pointing to that mystification of the industrial world which Marx called the "fetichism of commodities," the mystification by which human labor seems to take on an existence independent of the men who perform it? If ever a man has fetichized the production of commodities, if ever a man has surrendered his self to his social role, it is Charles Gould. The sterility of the mine is the sterility of his marriage, the public failure both cause and magnified reflection of his private failure.

Greatly as Mrs. Gould enlists our affections, enchanting as she constantly seems, she too becomes, though not nearly in so gross a measure as her husband, a victim of the

imperialist rationale. Mrs. Gould is all kindness, all goodness, all charity; entirely alert to the most "delicate shades
of self-forgetfulness"; but she does not live in Costaguana,
she has sealed herself off in an enclave of disciplined suffering. The court she holds for the Europeans and a few chosen
"natives" is merely a mirror to her loneliness; the life of the
country on which her comfort depends remains a secret forever closed to her. All Costaguanans, she admits, look alike
to her—she means no malice, not even unfriendliness yet
how fatal an admission it nonetheless is. The rhythms of
Costaguana are alien to her racial conventions, and because
she cannot transcend those conventions—because she lacks
the boldness of Mrs. Moore in *Passage to India*—her life
narrows into a ritual of controlled deprivation. Lovely and
luminous as she seems in her devotion to personal values,
Mrs. Gould signifies the incompleteness of trying to live
merely by those values.

The men who move in her orbit illustrate, through various
patterns of futility, the failure of Europe to cope with
Costaguana. As for the Costaguanans themselves, most of
them are not characters at all but items of drama to which
the Europeans must react. Montero they can all mock; his
manners are coarse, his tone is deplorable, his demagogy
appalling; but what he means and why he springs up they
will never understand.

Captain Mitchell, Don Avellanos, Giorgio Viola, Decoud
—each represents the withering of some European mode of
thought or feeling when it is transplanted to Latin America.
Like Captain MacWhirr of *Typhoon*, Captain Mitchell is
the epitome of endurance and faithfulness, yet in the climate
of Costaguana these qualities are not enough, so that Mitchell appears ridiculous where MacWhirr was not. In his good-
humored imperceptiveness, Mitchell represents Conrad's realization that there are times and places when the solid
English virtues, the always reliable "job sense," will not get
the job done.

Somewhat similarly, though in far more complex terms,
Don Avellanos and Giorgio Viola would impose upon Costa-

guana alien modes of behavior. Avellanos is the agent of classical liberalism, Viola the living emblem of its lost glory. Avellanos is the most admirable political figure of Costaguana; also portentous, somewhat empty, rather a bore. His goodness cannot be admired without qualification if only because it so frequently seems a function of his impotence. And in Viola political impotence is openly manifested; in fact, his grandeur is possible only because, as Avellanos' inspirited double, he stands apart from Costaguana politics, a relic of Garibaldian liberalism unable to survive in a milieu far more complex than Garibaldi could conceive. In Avellanos, Conrad suggests that the classical liberalism of restraint is irrelevant to a country like Costaguana; in Viola he suggests that the classical liberalism of heroic action, the mid-19th century form which is purely national and non-social, is obsolete in a country like Costaguana. In so deprived a land there can be no social margin for the intellectual, and Avellanos, though he fancies himself a defender of the national interest, becomes a helpless aid of the aristocratic Blancos. The principled liberal does the work—he can hardly help it—of Holroyd, apostle of the American Century. Only Viola remains pure; he stands outside the action, a mournful spectator, for he can no longer give his liberalism a vital content, it has declined to a dream of lost fraternity.

Decoud also would like to import European modes of behavior, and he too fails. In Paris he would be a boulevardier, here he is a liberal for lack of anything else; and this is surely characteristic of the modern age, that people who believe in nothing should call themselves liberals. He claims to credit only the truth of his sensations and insists that he enters the civil war merely to win Avellanos' daughter, a furious patriot. But he deceives himself, this man who fears self-deception most of all: the mantle of skepticism cannot protect him from the storm of national feeling, he finds himself swept away by his own glorious phrases. Swept away, but only for a moment. When alone in the Placid Gulf, he finds no resources within himself, his skepticism quickly

crumbles into animal fear. The sentimental idealizing of
Gould is a tragic self-deception, but Decoud's contempt for
all ideas is a tragic self-destruction. He declares the narrowness of all beliefs to be odious, and perishes for lack of such
narrowness. If in Captain Mitchell Conrad gently scratched
at one of his occasional masks, in Decoud he violently tore
at one of his major attitudes.

All of these Europeans and half-Europeans are aliens, but
the Jewish trader Hirsch is an alien among aliens. Socially
he is placed with an exact touch: one soon realizes why
Gould should refuse him financial support. Hirsch is hardly
his kind of European, and while he would not be discourteous
neither would he be helpful. That Hirsch the Jew should
figure as an archetypal outcast is entirely appropriate; that
he should so melodramatically personify cowardice serves
only to obscure this archetypal role . . . unless, of course,
one believes that the sheer quantity of Jewish suffering is
itself evidence of Jewish cowardice. Hirsch's fear is repellent
yet not without reason: he knows what awaits him, he has a
sense of history. One cannot help wondering whether Conrad's scorn is due entirely to Hirsch's being a coward or
perhaps, a trifle, to his not being a gentleman. And one
cannot help wondering, as well, whether Conrad does not
occasionally indulge in the Elizabethan game of having his
Jew sweat.

There remains one major "character," the voice of Conrad
himself, rising to heavy periodic stress and falling to an
austere pathos, but always qualified by an insistent, sombre
irony. In his admirable criticism of *Nostromo* F. R. Leavis
writes that "for all the rich variety of the interest and the
tightness of the pattern, the reverberation of *Nostromo* has
something hollow about it." The remark is acute, though I
cannot feel Mr. Leavis quite accounts for this "hollowness"
by ascribing it to the absence of "the day-to-day continuities
of social living." Something more fundamental, something
lodged in Conrad's creative motives, must be the cause of
this "hollowness," as also of the disconcerting way in which
he drops a good many of the political threads about two-

thirds through the book. I would again suggest that these difficulties may be traced to Conrad's inability to commit himself fully to his own materials. It is the profound distaste of his English side for the wildness of Costaguana—and here Costaguana may be a symbolic extension of the "Russia" of *Under Western Eyes*—which accounts for one's sense of seeing an action through many layers of gauze, and one's discomfort before the narrative skirmishing and ironic over-emphasis.

But it would be false to end on a carping note. For *Nostromo*, like *Middlemarch*, is one of the few novels in our language which commands a whole society, steeping itself in representative modes of behavior, and taking into precise account those delicate interplays of social interest that are so seldom noticed in the English novel. It is the one novel in which Conrad handles the political theme with something very close to mastery, with a balance and poise, a sense of dispassionate justice that can hardly be too much admired. And nowhere more so than in the ending of the book, where society appears resurgent and confident, but of community, of that which makes men human, nothing remains.

CHAPTER FIVE

TURGENEV: THE POLITICS OF HESITATION

"What a torment," writes the Russian playwright Griboyedov, "to be an ardent dreamer in a land of eternal snows." In this complaint, we can be sure, the Russian weather is to be taken as a metaphor of Russian society. Himself implicated in the liberal (Decembrist) revolt of 1825, Griboyedov was thinking of the impossible position —it was never to be anything but impossible—of the enlightened young Russian who desires to serve his country. In Griboyedov's famous comedy *The Mischief of Being Clever* the theme of estrangement from society is pursued with a fullness, and accented with a bitterness, that is hardly to be surpassed in 19th century European literature. The envelope of this play is conventional drawing-room comedy, the content a fierce social criticism, for its "cleverness" refers less to personal endowment than to political value. Chatsky, the hero of the comedy, is perhaps the first in the distinguished line of "superfluous men" that will wind its way through Russian literature; superfluous, not in the sense that he suffers, as do most of Turgenev's heroes, from a psychological malaise but rather that he brings to the homeland, from his several years in the West, an intellectual

vigor and appetite for novelty which to the Russian bureaucrats seems not so much subversive as merely foolish. Eager
for love, eager for friendship, ideas and experience, Chatsky
soon races through the gamut of disillusion; he is exposed to
officials of vast complacence, old soldiers who believe all
books should be burned, courtiers who have perfected the
art of crawling. Having seen all he could bear and discovered
that his wit bounces harmlessly off Moscow's thick skin,
Chatsky flees, apparently to quit Russia once again.

For the Russian writers who follow Griboyedov, *The
Mischief of Being Clever* is both model and inspiration. In
Russia the Byronic hero becomes a type more prevalent,
and with deeper justification, than in any other country of
Europe: here, indeed, the man of sensibility has cause for
despair. Later in the century the novelist Goncharov said of
Chatsky: "His role is to suffer: it cannot be otherwise."
The famous critic Herzen saw "in the figure of Chatsky,
melancholy, retiring into his irony, trembling with indignation and visionary feeling . . . a Decembrist, a man who
completes the epoch of Peter I, and strives to discern, at
least on the horizon, the promised land he will never see."
Griboyedov himself defined his hero with still greater precision: "A man in contradiction to the society that surrounds
him . . . nobody understands him, nobody is willing to
forgive him for being a little above the rest."

That so many Russian literary heroes should be "superfluous men" seems almost inevitable: in 19th century Russia
no other kind of hero is possible. The problem faced by the
Russian writers—I do not mean that they formulated it in
these terms—was whether to conceive of the superfluous hero
as energetic or passive, a man who discards society or a man
whom society breaks. If we glance at a few of the major
heros of 19th century Russian literature—Pushkin's
Onegin, Lermontov's Petchorin, Goncharov's Oblomov—we
see that while radically different in temper they suffer from
a similar disability in relation to the life of their time.
Onegin lacks Chatsky's commanding spirit, his gift for
transcending an immediate problem by seeing it as a public

issue. Onegin is a dandy where Chatsky is a robust young man; Onegin cannot rise to his situation while Chatsky refuses to sink to his. Yet they are complementary figures, both doomed to the role of outsider, the one through an excess of wit and the other through an excess of sensibility.

So too are Petchorin and Oblomov. Petchorin, the most Byronic of the Russian literary heroes, cannot achieve spontaneity in either behavior or feeling: he must watch every move he makes. In Oblomov the will to action has been entirely dissipated: he is the hero run to seed, superfluous even to himself. Petchorin is constantly on the move and Oblomov forever on his back, yet in their distance from society, if not the point from which that distance is to be measured, they are very much alike.

Heroes of estrangement, all of these figures suffer the frustration of being unable to act heroically. As Griboyedov once cried out: "By what black magic have we become aliens among our own! . . . A people of the same blood, our people is estranged from us; and for ever." *

II

Turgenev is invariably described as the most balanced of Russian writers, the cultivated gentleman and spokesman for moderation in a literature of wildness. He is a writer—so the story goes—of soft nostalgia and mellow restraint, of pastel colors and atmospheric shadings; he is notable for a pervasive melancholia rather than psychological intensity.

All of which is true, but not true enough, not the whole truth. If Turgenev is to engage the serious reader of our day, he must be rescued from his reputation, not by twisting him into a miniature Dostoevsky—though this might not be quite so impossible as it may seem—but by restoring to him some of the balancing tensions that were actually present in his life and work.

* For some of the historical material in the above section I am indebted to an excellent book published in England several years ago: *The Hero of His Time* by Henry Gifford.

Deep into his adult life Turgenev struggled against the tyrannical power of his mother, unable to surrender completely to her will or to break fully from her grasp. It is surely not too speculative to suggest that a large amount of his personal and literary indecisiveness can be traced back to this exhausting struggle. Like many men in whom the maternal tie is very strong, he was painfully split in his feelings toward women, most of them absorbing him solely on the level of appetite, while for but one, the singer Pauline Viardot, could he retain a deep romantic attachment. In his ambiguous relations with Madame Viardot, Turgenev seems finally to have accepted the role of an adopted family uncle. Exactly what he meant to her it is hard to say, but for him she seems to have been friend, confidante and surrogate mother.

In Turgenev's novels the sexual relation is almost always frustrated. Except for the conventional ending of *Smoke,* which is also his sourest novel, all of his books end in separation, the loss of the beloved. Remarkable as the lyric-nostalgic tone of his writing often is, Turgenev labored under some deep compulsion—obviously more than a bias of temperament or a preference for realism—to tear his characters away from each other and prevent them from reaching fulfillment. Turgenev's pure and beautiful heroines—those steely maidens who might almost have been raised in 19th century New England—are always wooed but seldom won; and while the heroes admire and appreciate them, it is only to the cold graceful and sophisticated women, the dark lady or bitch enchantress personified by Irina in *Smoke,* that they respond sexually. To rouse the heroes of Turgenev's novels, women must be inaccessible, unpredictable, perverse; they must display feminine attractions but possess unfeminine qualities; the sexual relationship tempts Turgenev's heroes only when stained with guilt. In his novels—so he found it in life—women are strong and men weak; and those few of his heroes, like Bazarov in *Fathers and Sons,* who prove themselves to be men of strength are projections of the traits he knew to be absent in himself.

Turgenev seems to have been a man and, in some senses, a writer of disarranged sexuality; only some such speculation makes intelligible his persistent refusal—in some of his novels it almost comes to sabotage—of the possibilities of love. Yet if the sexual impulse in Turgenev's novels seldom reaches any of the usual resolutions, there is a genuine, if limited, recompense. In his best work, and particularly in the *Sportsman's Sketches*, he achieves a tone of pansexual empathy which can soar to a marvellously tender identification with every living creature.

Behind Turgenev's mildness and sweetness of manner there was an extremely anxious man. He was a notorious hypochondriac; he suffered all his life from a death phobia; his addiction to quarrels bordered on the feline. Subject to violent attacks of spleen, he would try to recover his composure by retreating to a corner and staring at the blank wall: again, the naughty boy punishing himself as once his mother had punished him.

Intellectually, too, Turgenev was far less tranquil, far less resolved than is usually supposed. It is hardly true that he, almost alone among the great Russian writers, was a defender of moderate Western liberalism—or rather, such a statement takes into account the formal conclusion but not the turbulent motions of Turgenev's political thought.

Turgenev wrote in the post-1848 epoch, after the failure of the last purely democratic revolutions on the continent. The "twilight aura" that hangs like a softly pencilled cloud over his work is a reflection, to be sure, of a private condition; but it also has its source in the feeling of hopelessness which overwhelmed many Russian intellectuals during the 1850's. The defeat of the revolution in Germany and its disintegration in France affected them even more deeply than it did the Western intellectuals, for they had looked to the West for help and not only was help now unavailable but the West itself seemed in chronic crisis. The long historical romance between bourgeoisie and proletariat, a romance bred in necessity and uncomplicated by affection, was now at an end; and to the "Westernizing" Russian liberals this brought both dismay and bewilderment, for how could Russia be persuaded to emulate the models they had set before it if those models were themselves beginning to turn rotten? Throughout their careers both Herzen, the most gifted Russian publicist of the time, and Turgenev reflect a sense of having been let down, of being adrift.

Had he died on the barricades in 1848, wrote Herzen, "I would have taken with me to the grave two or three beliefs." At about the same time Turgenev wrote, "An honorable man will end by not knowing where to live"—which was exactly where Turgenev did end. And in another letter he burst out: "I prefer Prometheus, I prefer Satan, the embodiment of revolt and individuality."

Between the politically active Herzen and the passive Turgenev there is a certain loose correspondence of thought and mood. Both are given to wild fluctuations from political enthusiasm to political despair, both are homeless wanderers, both cut off from their native soil, increasingly unhappy in the West, yearning for and dreaming of distant Russia. And both, above all, are men of literary temperament who have been forced by their time and their conscience to turn, Herzen far more than Turgenev, to the life of politics. The journalist Herzen, unable to achieve unity of thought because unable to act decisively in life, fluttered from classical liberalism to peasant socialism and then to radical slavophilism. Herzen's indecisiveness, wrote Lenin with more accuracy than sympathy, was the reflection of a time when "the revolutionary spirit of the bourgeois democracy was already dying, but the revolutionary spirit of the socialist proletariat was not yet ripe . . . This explains the lack of solid ground under Herzen's feet, his pessimism and his many returns to liberalism, which he himself had so often denied and cursed."

These vacillations Turgenev recorded with the sensitiveness of a seismograph. The politics of his novels, running through all of them like a chord of disturbance though dominant only in the final one, may be described as a politics of hesitation, reflecting the dilemmas of a cultivated man whose training and instincts lead him to despise politics ("To a man of letters," he wrote, "politics is poison") but whose intelligence and almost feminine receptiveness to the moods of his day lead him to circle about the world of politics, neither plunging in nor cutting himself off. Burdened with an admirable sense of proportion at a time when all of Russian and almost all of Western politics cries out for something more than proportion, Turgenev himself comes to feel that his finest qualities are paltry, even grotesque. His desire for detachment is constantly undermined by a sarcastic, even nasty bitterness, the extent of which has seldom been measured by his critics, who, like the critics of Chekhov, have a tendency to roll onto their backs and purr. Turgenev's whole experience has taught him the uses of revolt ("I prefer Prometheus, I prefer Satan") but has not endowed him with that monolithic intellectual passion which is necessary for revolt.

In another time, another place, Turgenev would certainly have written nothing at all about politics or political people; but as a Russian, and moreover a Russian liberal, he could not help hovering moth-like around the young radicals, attracted by the brightness and fearful of the heat. Turgenev's relations with the radicals of his day—as with the radicals of his books—are woven out of a series of misunderstandings, a kind of petulant tragi-comedy. He does not really like them, perhaps because he cannot help admiring them. He cannot tolerate their half-baked knowledge and cocksure manner, and in this he is right, of course, except that they are the first to accept this criticism and then to declare it irrelevant. He is disturbed by their rudeness, yet he really understands it very well, understands it better than he wants to, for in *Fathers and Sons* he creates a hero cut from the burlap of rudeness, thereby displaying the most subtle insight into the political meaning and, at times, the political necessity of rudeness. He courts and cultivates the radicals, he draws their portraits with an exactness, though hardly a gentleness, that astonishes them and wins their praise, since they are people who care more about exactness than gentleness. And then—but here we tumble into comedy—he is hurt by their desire to draw *conclusions* from his novels and they, being as scornful of estheticism as almost all 19th century Russians must be, are astonished at his "frivolity" in not desiring conclusions. Yet neither in life nor art can he fully tear himself away from the uncouth Russian radicals; even in his last years, when he was considered passé by the advanced critics, Turgenev kept contributing funds to the émigré journals. That was the dilemma of the Russian liberals: they could express their sense of outrage only in the company of people who must often have struck them as outrageous.

The first important split between Turgenev and the radicals occurred after the publication of his minor novel *On the Eve*. In his first novel *Rudin* he had presented a character too weak to live up to his political claims and in his second novel *A House of Gentlefolk* a character whose strength is large yet not large enough to overcome his circumstances. Now, as his "consciously heroic" hero, Turgenev chose a Bulgarian nationalist, Insarov, who is dedicated to liberating his nation from the tyranny of the Turks and who, alone among Turgenev's heroes, is capable of decisive political action. Insarov wins Elena, one of Turgenev's iron-willed heroines, from her other suitors, who are, not accidentally, a frivolous Russian artist and a meek Russian scholar.

This novel was reviewed by a leading radical critic, Dobrolyubov, who saw in Elena the strength and wholeness of the untried Russian people and in her choice of Insarov a necessary political course. In his review Dobrolyubov went on to wonder how long it would take before Russia could produce *her own Insarovs* to liberate her "from the Turks at home." When Turgenev saw the proofs of this review he tried to have parts of it suppressed; happily, the editor did not yield.

Dobrolyubov, one feels, was essentially correct. He was not reading into Turgenev's novel but was, so to speak, reading out from it. Why Turgenev had chosen a foreigner for his hero was a legitimate topic for critical analysis, and that analysis could be undertaken only after one had considered what it would have meant to make Insarov a Russian. For this kind of hero Turgenev, whether consciously or not, *had* to choose a foreigner; the Insarovs were not yet possible in Russia or if they were, could be found only in the icy corners of Siberia. If, however, Insarov had been a Russian dealing with the problems of Russian life, Turgenev could have preserved him as an insurgent hero only by transforming his relatively safe nationalism—in Russia no one would have objected to *that*—into some kind of radical politics undermining the class structure. Simply by raising this problem, by transferring Insarov from the Bulgarian air to the Russian earth, Dobrolyubov made clear the meaning of Turgenev's hero. *On the Eve* contained revolutionary implications from which Turgenev shied away, and with good reason: he was not a revolutionary; but it was in the nature of 19th century Russian culture that even the faintest touch of liberalism had revolutionary implications. Turgenev's objection to Dobrolyubov's review was not that it failed to tell the truth but that the truth distressed him—a complaint he might better have directed at his own imagination.

Yet it is very much to Turgenev's credit that he realized the difficulties of his own position as a nonpolitical man who had been forced to take account of political life and had displayed a remarkable insight, if not into political ideas, then into political personality. Like so many of his own heroes, he knew his diagnosis and perhaps even the remedy—he simply lacked the power or the possibility for applying it. His novel *Smoke* is a protest, both a groan and a howl, against this dilemma: against Russia, against its radicals and reactionaries, against . . . himself. The book has little intrinsic value yet is of great interest as the revelation of an artist, in the way all uncontrolled books by controlled writers are. *Smoke* is a reflex of frustration, an impotent lashing out against the life Turgenev, and many others more obscure than Turgenev, had to lead.

In his essay *Hamlet and Don Quixote* Turgenev projected this problem ideologically, and in his story *The Diary of a Superfluous Man* he reduced it to psychological outline. The essay is an example of the way a writer's obsession with a problem local in space and specific in time can tempt him into constructing an "eternal" theory of human behavior. Don Quixote becomes the name of his desire, Hamlet the recognition of his reality; and while Turgenev's division of humanity into actors and observers is neither original nor very persuasive, it gains its immediate point, as its immediate pathos, from the political dilemma that has prompted it.

In *The Diary of a Superfluous Man* a young man, clearly intelligent yet without hopes or prospects, is rejected by a provincial beauty in favor of a dandified nobleman and then, after the nobleman has made off, is again rejected, this time in favor of an elderly bystander. Unable to find a place for himself, the superfluous man feels himself overwhelmed by a condition for which it would be pointless to seek the cause, since it is not so much a social disability or a private failure as the sheer catastrophe of being what he is. He thinks of himself not as neurotic or maladjusted or a victim of society; he is simply . . . a mistake. During an absurd duel with the nobleman, he is made the victim of his antagonist's generosity, and it is at this moment of extreme humiliation —a humiliation, to be sure, of relief—that he declares himself to have been "completely unmanned." This phrase, essential to an understanding of Turgenev's work, prefigures both the psychological and political themes of the novels, where the two will become almost indistinguishable. In *The Diary of a Superfluous Man* the sense of being unwanted is a psychological enigma, a fact of existence that cannot be reduced to other terms. In the novels it acquires a social dimension: Turgenev's heroes define their humiliation as a function of their hope.

Not until the appearance of Kafka does any writer explore so thoroughly the sense of being unwanted, of being utterly without significance or value to any other living creature; and in Kafka it becomes again what it was in *The Diary of a Superfluous Man*, the very condition of existence. But because Turgenev complicated, or contaminated, the sense of being unwanted by seeing it partly in social terms, his novels became a miniature history of 19th century Russian liberalism, as of liberalism whenever it enters a state of lassitude and impotence.

If, against Turgenev, we set George Eliot as a representative figure of the best in both English liberalism and English literature, the comparison is nothing less than startling. Eliot seems more aggressive and self-confident, more *manly*—and not because these qualities are impossible to the Russian soul but because they are inaccessible to the Russian liberal of the 19th century. In George Eliot's novels people of the various social levels can still communicate with each other and even find areas of moral solidarity; one seldom senses in or near her books those social wastes that lie, desolate, just off the margins of Turgenev's novels. Eliot assumes that a degree of harmony between public activity and private feeling is still possible, while Turgenev's heroes recoil in weakness or shatter themselves in strength when they try to establish contact with public life.

George Eliot's liberalism was sustained by the religious sense she had inherited from her family, as indeed from the whole tradition of the English-middle-class, and later by the "religion of humanity" which permitted her to transfer her moral energies from the traditional objects of worship to an ethic of duty and sympathy. In *Felix Holt* she instinctively rooted her hero's political radicalism in the tradition of religious dissent—she saw the deep connection between chapel and chartism—so that even her most stringent criticism of English life is also a kind of tribute to its vitality. Turgenev, however, could find no support in the Russian church: he lacked Dostoevsky's appetite for messianism. In him the religious impulse, if it ever existed, had long been dissipated—and the "religion of humanity" could hardly have satisfied a Russian liberal tormented by his distance from humanity. Eliot was a writer of considerable moral security; Turgenev was one of the first esthetes, turning to that worship of art which flourishes whenever more universal forms of belief crumble. Turgenev's liberalism was far less vital than Eliot's, far less imbedded in national realities; yet by a curious spin of history, it now seems closer to us, closer to our indecisions and hesitations.

The most interesting problem in reading Turgenev is to reconcile his two sides, the romantic-idyllic and the political. This can easily lead to trouble, for by imposing an ideological weight upon a lyrical narrative one may destroy its organic quality, particularly if it is a narrative as fragile and delicate as Turgenev's usually are. Yet Turgenev himself prompts us to take the chance, he continually and systematically provides us with the necessary clues. At the risk of being schematic I would suggest that the romantic-idyllic side of his work may profitably be seen as an analogue—not an allegory—of his political side.

Turgenev's least ideological as also his loveliest novel, *A House of Gentlefolk*, is concerned with a hero of strength and integrity, Lavretsky, a democratic slavophile who returns to Russia after a disastrous marriage abroad. Repelled by the West, he has come back to the homeland in order, as he significantly puts it, "to till the land." Here he meets Lisa, the most madonna-like of Turgenev's heroines. Still tied to the peasants yet possessed of a modest cultivation, she is a figure of true moral repose, an embodiment of the idea of Russian purity to which all the Russian writers, whatever their other differences, return again and again. To gain our credence, Turgenev must isolate her from the coarse realities of Russian life; he therefore places his story in one of those shaded country gardens, charming in their slight decay, that appeal so deeply to his sense of nostalgia, one of those gardens that signify traditional Russia minus vodka and the knout. For a moment Lavretsky and Lisa draw toward each other. He hears that his wife has died abroad, he hopes . . . but the wife has not died, she returns, simpering in French, which for Russian novelists is the language of affectation.

Are we to read this story simply as a personal tragedy, another of Turgenev's bitter-sweet tales of disappointment? That element is certainly there and not to be slighted, but I think we must see something more. I think Turgenev is saying, by the most exquisite indirection, that when the Russian intellectual comes home, trying to break away from the West that has become contaminated and turning to the remaining purities of Russia, he will again be frustrated: his cosmopolitan experience, which he cannot undo, makes him unfit for the task of reaching the heart of Russia. The private tragedy of Lavretsky is, on one plane of meaning, the tragedy of Russian liberalism, the tragedy of a politics of homelessness and homesickness. What else are we to make of the following passage—a central passage in the book—where Lavretsky muses to himself about the Russian soil:

"Here I am at the very bottom of the river," thought Lavretsky again. "And always, at all times life here is quiet, unhasting," he thought; "whoever comes within its circle must submit; here there is nothing to agitate, nothing to harass; one can only get on here by making one's way slowly, as the ploughman cuts the furrow with his plough. And what vigor, what health abound in this inactive place! . . ." "In the love of a woman my best years have gone by," Lavretsky went on thinking; "let me be sobered by the sameness of life here, let me be soothed and *made ready, so that I may learn to do my duty without haste.*" (Emphasis added.)

In his best work Turgenev's two sides achieve an organic fusion; in his life, of course, this could seldom happen. "We have hard times to go through," wrote Turgenev to Flaubert, "we who are born onlookers." This is the voice of the Turgenev who wrote *Hamlet and Don Quixote, The Diary of a Superfluous Man, A House of Gentlefolk;* it defines the angle of his vision and the distance he must take from his material. But what he actually sees at that distance, what he *must* see, is perhaps best revealed by a little anecdote he is reported to have once told a friend:

One day we shall be seated behind the house drinking tea. Suddenly there will arrive by the garden a crowd of peasants. They will take off their hats and bow profoundly. "Well, brothers," I shall say to them, "what is it that you want?" "Excuse us, master," they will reply, "don't get angry. You are a good master, and we love you well . . . But all the same we must hang you . . ." "What's that? Hang me?" "Oh yes! There is a Ukase that orders it . . . We have brought a rope. Say your prayers . . . We can easily wait a little while."

III

In all but one of his novels, Turgenev's major characters are students. And most of these students are not young men preparing to enter society, but older men who have failed to enter society. Rudin, the protagonist of Turgenev's first novel and in many ways his greatest character, bursts into one of those manor-houses so frequent in Russian literature, where the mother is silly and modern, the daughter high-minded and serious, and a circle of friends has been tactfully draped around the action in order to set off the hero's mind from a number of perspectives. Burning with enthusiasm, yet already stoop-shouldered and middle-aged, this perpetual student charms everyone by his flow of rhetoric and ideas; a nightingale among provincial sparrows, Rudin brings to stagnant Russia what Turgenev calls "the music of eloquence." His themes are those of a vague bodiless liberalism: man's duty to society, "the special value of education and science," and—speaking as one totally incapable of action —the immediate need for action. We have met these ideas before, on the lips of Chatsky, the Decembrist liberal, who fled from Moscow howling his dismay at the indifference he had suffered. Rudin is a Chatsky grown older, gone to seed, repeating the phrases of his youth. Yet he has a genuine gift for dialectic, a true glow of idealistic fervor: his intelligence is not merely asserted by Turgenev, it is convincingly shown.

Rudin becomes the darling of the household, playing the confidant and fool to its mistress. He knows that he plays the fool yet he cannot stop, so great is his need for solace and flattery; he yearns, like all frustrated politicals, for *the illusion of an audience,* for in his heart he knows what we gradually discover while reading the book: that his ideas have no consequence beyond the moment they bubble from his lips, that they survive only in the kinetic flash he arouses in his listeners. Rudin is a Don Juan of the intellect, a spiritual imperialist whose profit comes from the temporary domination he achieves through rhetoric. He is a man who does not know what an experience is, though he knows every conceivable theory about what experience should be. There is a masterful scene in which Rudin offers the girl of the household advice on her relations with another man as a way of tempting her to confess the love she feels for him, Rudin; he does not want the responsibility this confession entails yet he cannot refrain from the thrill of hearing it.

Rudin is a masterpiece of composition. After a brief play upon our sense of expectation, the major figure is thrust full-face before us; his mind seems as impressive to us as to the people in the book; and then slowly, pitilessly he is stripped, one fault after another being revealed through their impression on the secondary characters. The novel depends on Rudin's initial impact, as if a full rich chord had been struck and all that followed were the lingering diminution of its overtone. This structure reflects, or embodies, Turgenev's meaning, his view of Rudin's liberalism. The second note is never struck—that is the meaning of the book. Yet even as Rudin is so mercilessly deflated, our respect and fondness for him grow; in this paradox lies the greatness of the book. Rudin's weakness is seldom mean, he is not fashionably delusional, his will fails him but his mind never. And this too is marvellously representative of the meaning of liberalism as it registers on 19th century Russia and indeed 19th century Europe: the faults of liberalism multiply yet it lights up a whole epoch of history.

It is characteristic of Rudin that he understands himself completely, both as an individual and a representative figure. In the climax of the novel he proves unequal to the crises he must confront: his emasculated liberalism finds its equivalent in a failure in personal relations. Unmanned politically, he cannot assert his manhood personally. "Nature," he reflects, "has given me much; but I shall die

without accomplishing anything worthy of my powers . . .
My fortune has been strange, ironic; I am always giving myself wholeheartedly, every bit of me—yet in the end can
give nothing. I shall end by sacrificing myself to some piece
of nonsense in which I do not even believe. Heavens! At
thirty-five, still to be preparing to do something!"

Five years after writing the novel Turgenev added the
page that now completes it: Rudin, at the end of July 1848,
is in Paris, the revolution has collapsed, and on a side-street
he appears in "an old frock-coat, belted with a red scarf . . .
in one hand a red banner, in the other a blunt sabre," charg-
ing vainly over an abandoned barricade and being shot down
in casual obscurity. Lord David Cecil thinks that in adding
this page Turgenev's hand faltered, but I would suggest
quite the contrary, that the addition is nothing less than the
stamp of genius. The final page bears the same specific
weight as all that precede it, for in this page the others are
justified, in this page the novel rises from a mere mild pathos
to a high ennobling pathos. Paris is the place where Rudin
dies, and it is no accident: Paris is the one place he could
have lived. It is all delicately right to both Rudin the person
and Rudin the liberal: that he, like Russian liberalism itself,
should come to Paris, to the revolutionary West, only when
it is too late.

If Rudin has partly been created in Turgenev's own
image, Bazarov, the hero of *Fathers and Sons,* is a figure in
opposition to that image. The one rambles idealistic poetry,
the other grumbles his faith in the dissection of frogs; the
one is all too obviously weak, the other seems spectacularly
strong. Yet between the two there is a parallel of social position. Both stand outside the manor-house that is Russia,
peering in through a window; Rudin makes speeches and
Bazarov would like to throw stones but no one pays attention, no one is disturbed. The two together might, like
Dostoevsky's Shatov and Kirillov, come to a whole man; but
they are not together, they alternate in Russian life, as in
Russian literature, each testifying to the social impotence
that has made the other possible.

Like all of Turgenev's superfluous men, Bazarov is essentially good. Among our more cultivated critics, those who insist that the heroes of novels be as high-minded as themselves, it has been fashionable to look with contempt upon Bazarov's nihilism, to see him as a specimen of Russian boorishness. Such a reading is not merely imperceptive, it is humorless. Would it really be better if Bazarov, instead of devoting himself to frogs and viscera, were to proclaim about Poetry and the Soul? Would it be better if he were a metaphysician juggling the shells of Matter and Mind instead of a coarse materialist talking nonsense about the irrelevance of Pushkin?

For all that Bazarov's nihilism accurately reflects a phase of Russian and European history, it must be taken more as a symptom of political desperation than as a formal intellectual system. Bazarov is a man ready for life, and cannot find it. Bazarov is a man of the most intense emotions, but without confidence in his capacity to realize them. Bazarov is a revolutionary personality, but without revolutionary ideas or commitments. He is all potentiality and no possibility. The more his ideas seem outmoded, the more does he himself seem our contemporary.

No wonder Bazarov feels so desperate a need to be rude. There are times when society is so impervious to the kicks of criticism, when intellectual life softens so completely into the blur of gentility, that the rebellious man, who can tolerate everything but not being taken seriously, has no alternative to rudeness. How else is Bazarov to pierce the elegant composure of Pavel Petrovich, a typically "enlightened" member of the previous generation who combines the manners of a Parisian litterateur with an income derived from the labor of serfs. Bazarov does not really succeed, for Pavel Petrovich forces him to a duel, a romantic ceremony that is the very opposite of everything in which Bazarov believes. During the course of the duel, it is true, Pavel Petrovich must yield to Bazarov, but the mere fact that it takes place is a triumph for the old, not the new. Bazarov may regard Pavel Petrovich as an "archaic phenomenon," but the "archaic phenomenon" retains social power.

The formal components of Bazarov's nihilism are neither unfamiliar nor remarkable: 19th century scientism, utilitarianism, a crude materialism, a rejection of the esthetic, a belief in the powers of the free individual, a straining for tough-mindedness and a deliberate provocative rudeness. These ideas and attitudes can gain point only if Bazarov brings them to political coherence, and the book charts Bazarov's journey, as an uprooted plebeian, in search of a means of expression, a task, an obligation. On the face of it, Bazarov's ideas have little to do with politics, yet he is acute enough to think of them in political terms; he recognizes that they are functions of his frustrated political passion. "Your sort," he says to his mild young friend Arkady, "can never get beyond refined submission or refined indignation, and that's no good. You won't fight—and yet you fancy yourselves gallant chaps—but we mean to fight . . . We want to smash other people! You're a capital fellow; but you're a sugary liberal snob for all that . . ." This is the language of politics; it might almost be Lenin talking to a liberal parliamentarian. But even as Bazarov wants to "smash other people" he senses his own helplessness: he has no weapons for smashing anything. "A harmless person," he calls himself, and a little later, "A tame cat."

In the society of his day, as Turgenev fills it in with a few quick strokes, Bazarov is as superfluous as Rudin. His young disciple Arkady cannot keep pace with him; Arkady will marry, have a houseful of children and remember to be decent to his peasants. The older generation does not understand Bazarov and for that very reason fears him: Arkady's father, a soft slothful landowner, is acute enough, however, to remark that Bazarov is different: he has "fewer traces of the slaveowner." Bazarov's brief meeting with the radicals is a fine bit of horseplay, their emptyheaded chatter being matched only by his declaration, as preposterous as it is pathetic: "I don't adopt anyone's ideas; I have my own."

At which one of them, in a transport of defiance, shouts: "Down with all authorities!" and Bazarov realizes that among a pack of fools it is hard not to play the fool. He is tempted, finally, by Madame Odnitzov, the country-house Delilah; suddenly he finds his awkward callow tongue, admitting to her his inability to speak freely of everything in his heart. But again he is rejected, and humiliated too, almost like a servant who has been used by his mistress and then sent packing. Nothing remains but to go home, to his good sweet uncomprehending mother and father, those remnants of old Russia; and to die.

Turgenev himself saw Bazarov in his political aspect:

If he [Bazarov] calls himself a nihilist, one ought to read— a revolutionary . . . I dreamed of a figure that should be gloomy, wild, great, growing one half of him out of the soil, strong, angry, honorable, and yet doomed to destruction—because as yet he still stands on the threshold of the future. I dreamed of a strange parallel to Pugatchev. And my young contemporaries shake their heads and tell me, "You have insulted us . . . It's a pity you haven't worked him out a little more." There is nothing left for me but, in the words of the gipsy song, "to take off my hat with a very low bow."

Seldom has a writer given a better cue to the meaning of his work, and most of all in the comparison between Bazarov and Pugatchev, the leader of an 18th century peasant rebellion who was hanged by a Tzar. Pugatchev, however, had his peasant followers, while Bazarov . . . what is Bazarov but a Pugatchev without the peasants?

It is at the end of *Fathers and Sons* that Turgenev reaches his highest point as an artist. The last twenty-five pages are of an incomparable elevation and intensity, worthy of Tolstoy and Dostoevsky, and in some respects, particularly in their blend of tragic power and a mute underlying sweetness, superior to them. When Bazarov, writhing in delirium, cries out, "Take ten from eight, what's left over?" we are close to the lucidity of Lear in the night. It is the lucidity of final self-confrontation, Bazarov's lament over his lost, his unused powers: "I was needed by Russia . . . No, it's

clear, I wasn't needed . . ." And: "I said I should rebel
. . . I rebel, I rebel!"

This ending too has failed to satisfy many critics,
even one so perceptive as Prince Mirsky, who complains
that there is something arbitrary in Bazarov's death. But
given Russia, given Bazarov, how else *could* the novel end?
Too strong to survive in Russia, what else is possible to
Bazarov but death? The accident of fate that kills him
comes only after he has been defeated in every possible social
and personal encounter: it is the summation of those encounters. "I rebel, I rebel," he croaks on his death-bed,
lying lonely and ignored in a corner of Russia, this man who
was to change and destroy everything; and is not the whole
meaning of the book, political and not political, that for his
final cry of defiance he cannot find an object to go with the
subject and the verb?

The theme of frustrated rebellion reappears in Turgenev's
last and most explicitly political novel, *Virgin Soil*, but this
time in a muted tone. The novel has been mishandled by
Turgenev's critics, most of whom, like Prince Mirsky, have
dismissed it on the (tedious) ground that it failed to give
an accurate picture of the Russian Populists of the 1860's.
If historical accuracy exhausted the interest of the book,
their complaint would count most heavily; but as it happens,
precisely Turgenev's inaccuracies, if such they were, make
for the novel's interest at the present time. Of all Turgenev's
novels, *Virgin Soil* is closest to us in mood and material.

Reading the novel is like being in an erratically lighted
theatre: there are moments of intense brilliance, moments
of annoying dimness, moments when everything blacks out.
The book is a tired, willed book; not that Turgenev doesn't
know what to do, for that he always knew, but that he now
lacks the energy to do it.

As in all of Turgenev's novels, the minor characters—in
this case, the radicals—are beautifully sketched. Mashurin,
the flinty girl immersed in politics yet not quite able to
suppress her vague desires, is a type but a finely conceived

type; a younger version and perhaps the model of Conrad's Sophia Antonovna in *Under Western Eyes*. Paklin and Markelov are as well-drawn as the minor radicals of *The Princess Casamassima* but more acutely and intimately imagined. Paklin is the eternal "sympathizer" whose mixture of admiration and contempt for the radicals he can neither join nor abandon makes him a pathetic gad-fly. Querulous, spiteful, tender, cowardly, he unwittingly betrays them yet utters their final vindication, connecting them with that "Anonymous Russia" to which he can never be joined. Markelov is the radical from personal distemper, an anticipation of that "petty-bourgeois desperation" which is to blow the twentieth century wide open. He too is rooted in the Russian tradition, being one of those inept and helpless small landowners who are trapped between the malice of those above them and the stupor of those below. He tries to institute principles of cooperation among his peasants, and the only result—since you cannot build socialism in one village—is confusion; as one of the peasants says, "There was a pit deep enough before, but now there's no seeing the bottom of it."

The theme of alienation dominates *Virgin Soil*, as it does all of Turgenev's novels; its hero Nezhdanov is a bastard of noble birth and, correspondingly, a spiritual orphan. A lover of poetry, he wishes, in the Russian phrase of the time, to "go to the people." Abstractly, his problem is similar to that of Hyacinth Robinson in *The Princess Casamassima*, though he is never the sticky little *arriviste* that Hyacinth sometimes becomes. He sees his problem not merely in terms of fate but also of character: his eternal wavering, his incapacity for that passionate single-mindedness which is necessary for revolutionary activity. Nezhdanov is finally not very interesting, though he has moments of great interest; the trouble is simply in execution, Turgenev's inability to throw himself into the book which is potentially his best, both as to conception and implication.

The tiredness I have mentioned breaks out in a rough impatience with all the social classes and types of Russia—

an impatience that is the result of Turgenev's increasing and increasingly uneasy distance from his country and his subject. He is persistently satirical, in a not at all gentle way, about the sleek official liberals. He has a fine ear for liberal rhetoric, having himself been guilty of it on occasion. When Nezhdanov quarrels with Kallomyetsev, the reactionary who hails the Russian language as "the language of imperial decrees," their host, a comfortable liberal, declares: "Under my roof, under the roof of the Sipyagins, there are neither Jacobins nor reactionaries, there are only well-meaning people, who, when once they understand each other, are bound to end by shaking hands." This is the real thing: it rings with the true note of golden hollowness. And after he has quieted the argument, the pompous liberal "did not consciously compare himself with Neptune quelling the tempest; but he thought of him with a sort of sympathy."

The book has its dead stretches, but there are at least two chapters as good as anything Turgenev has done, and happily illustrating his two dominant modes. One of these turns back to old Russia, settling upon an old couple, Fomushka and Fimishka, who live like love-birds in their little house, eating old-fashioned dishes, venturing an occasional obsolete phrase in French, leafing through musty old albums, entirely untouched by ideas, tendencies, problems, unrest. The whole meaning of this chapter, in which the very words seem to shrink into miniatures, is revealed in a lovely passage. Fomushka brings out an old carved snuff-box on which it had once been possible to distinguish thirty-six figures in various postures: long ago effaced, they are still seen there by the two old folk. "The spot to which he pointed with his chubby finger . . . was just as smooth as all the rest of the snuff-box lid."

The other chapter I would single out, one of the most brilliant things ever written about the political life, captures once and for all the enlightened intellectual's effort to make his way among the masses whom he hopes to liberate and in whose name he sacrifices himself. Finally gathering his courage, the poet-revolutionary Nezhdanov goes off among the peasants, only to be met with stares of bewilderment when he urges them to "rise." Enticed into a tavern where the peasants pour vodka down his throat, "Nezhdanov began talking, talking, endlessly, shouting wrathfully, malignantly, shaking broad, horny hands, kissing slobbery beards . . ." Turgenev understood it all completely, the effort to be what one is not but feels conscience-bound to emulate: "It appears," says Nezhdanov, "when I am with the people that I am always only stooping to them, and listening . . ." What does it matter that the Populists of the 1860's were not, as the critics insisted, nearly so ineffectual as Nezhdanov, when his experience would be repeated again and again and again?

Set off against Nezhdanov is Solomin, the practical man who sympathizes with the cause yet believes that, for the moment, it is futile. Turgenev did not quite fill in the portrait of Solomin, for he had come upon a type that hardly existed in his time and was only to flourish some decades later. Solomin is seen entirely from the outside, and while this strategy frustrates our curiosity as to his motives and intentions, it must finally be judged correct; for Solomin is not a character being portrayed, he is a character being anticipated. He has usually been seen as the prototype of the political gradualist, the reformer who strikes roots among the masses he would arouse. He is partly that, at least in his capacity as foreman of a factory, but he is also something else. In embryo Solomin is a Lenin type, anticipating Lenin's cool patience, his unromantic belief that revolution, being neither a gorgeous display nor a stroke of fate, must be planned and worked for in a scientific way. Solomin does not dissociate himself from the aims of the Populists, he merely feels them to be hopelessly incompetent. The people, he says, are "asleep" and until they can be awakened all talk of revolution is nonsense—which sounds very much like Lenin arguing with the Populists a few decades later. Solomin is quiet but his insight is very sharp, and even his irony has a tinge of Lenin. Are you ready "to go forward?" he asks Nezhdanov, and when Nezhdanov bridles at this question, he remarks, "I have no doubts of you, Nezhdanov. I only asked because I imagine there is no one ready besides you." But "what of Markelov?" "Yes," answers Solomin, "to be sure, there is Markelov; but he, I expect, was born ready."

Later Nezhdanov has his little revenge. Solomin, he says, "does not believe . . . but he does not need to; he moves calmly forward." What Nezhdanov says is not quite true, but coming as it does from a man who can neither act nor believe, move forward nor remain still, it is a forgivable touch of bitterness. After Nezhdanov's suicide, the psychological and political themes are knitted together in a tragedy of failure. Solomin and the girl who had accompanied Nezhdanov on his mission "to the people" now come together, but in guilt: they have dispossessed Nezhdanov; before his death he had already felt, both in his political fiasco and personal futility, that his manhood was being taken from him. "Why was it she did not dare now to look at Solomin, as though he were her accomplice . . . as though he too were feeling a sting of conscience? . . . Could it be, it had rested with her to save him? Why was it they had neither dared utter a word?" A little later, they come upon Nezhdanov's letter: "What could I do?" he pleads with them, "I could find no other way out of it. I could not simplify myself; the only thing left was to blot myself out altogether."

I could not simplify myself!—for this sentence alone the novel deserves to live.

Turgenev, it has been said, is the one Russian writer who does not attempt to preach, who has no moral or political ideology to advance. In some obvious way this is perhaps true, yet he has very much to say to us, and very much— if a critical heresy may be permitted—to teach us. He speaks to us for those whom history pushes aside, for those who can neither surrender to its passions nor withdraw from its temptations. He speaks to us for the right to indecision, which is almost as great a right as the right to negation. He speaks to us for a politics of hesitation, a politics that will never save the world but without which the world will never be worth saving. He speaks to us with the authority of failure.

IV

Julian Martov was born in 1873. A restless untidy man, stoop-shouldered, hoarse-voiced and tubercular, quick and witty in speech, Bohemian by impulse and experience, Martov was one of the founders of Russian socialism. When the Social Democratic party split into Menshevik and Bolshevik wings, Martov aligned himself with the Mensheviks, though, characteristically, as leader of a left faction among them. When the 1917 revolution came, he found himself caught between the two groups, criticizing both and unable to accept the policies of either. "The moment when the balance is still oscillating," wrote Trotsky about Martov, "is his moment—this inventive statesman of eternal wavering." And with a mixture of admiration and contempt he continued: "As always at times of great historical action Martov floundered hopelessly . . . In 1917, as in 1905, the revolution hardly noticed this unusually able man." At the Congress of Soviets immediately after the Bolsheviks took power, Martov stated his usual cautions and doubts, to which Trotsky, flushed with victory, replied by consigning him to "the rubbish-can of history." Perhaps aware that he was echoing Turgenev's description of the Russian intellectual, Trotsky called Martov "the Hamlet of democratic socialism"; despite which, Martov remained the one opposition leader whom the Bolsheviks respected. He stayed in Russia, as leader of a loyal opposition to Lenin, until the end of 1920, and then he chose voluntary exile in Berlin. In 1924, as Martov lay dying in Berlin, Lenin, who was dying in Moscow, muttered sadly, with an almost prophetic sense of historical drama: "So he too is going." The last encounter between the two extremes of Russian character, and Russian heroism, had taken place. With Martov there went the last of Turgenev's heroes, the last of the superfluous men.

CHAPTER SIX

HENRY JAMES: THE POLITICAL VOCATION

Henry James is a novelist of temptations, temptations resisted, succumbed to, regretted; but the temptation of politics, which has haunted so many modern writers, seems never to have troubled him at all. Politics could rarely excite him to intense emotion or problematic thoughts; he never seems to have regarded it as a human activity with a value, or at least a necessity, of its own. To the degree that it did figure in his world, James was a conservative, though less in formal opinion than as a tangle of what might be called cultural emotions:—a hushed reverence before the great things of the past which had been wrenched from the endless blood and failure of history; a feeling that history being what it was these great things were probably inseparable from the blood and the failure; a distaste for the vulgarity of public life, which had been one reason for quitting America, where life was strenuously public; and a deep distrust, indeed a professional refusal, of abstract ideas. As a writer with a marvellous gift for making the most of his disabilities, James never had to face the question—except, perhaps, toward the very end of his life—whether such attitudes were an artist's privilege or the mark of that American innocence which would remain with him to the end of his life in Europe. He did not have to face such questions because he lived at a time when it was still possible for a writer like himself to make of conservatism a personal esthetic value rather than a mere ideology.

Unlike Dostoevsky, James had never been singed by radicalism, though he had seen it flickering in his father's Fourierist circle and burning in his sister Alice's mind; unlike Conrad he felt no need to discipline or suppress memories of a family tradition of political revolt. James' conservatism was peculiarly the conservatism of an artist who has measured all the effort and agony that has gone into the achievements of the past and is not ready to skimp their value in the name of an unborn and untested future. And it was the conservatism of a man with a profound sense of human disability, an awareness of catastrophe and failure so great as at times to be crippling in its power. So that when he came to write about nineteenth century revolutionary politics in *The Princess Casamassima,* his own opinions were neither risked nor challenged; the book presented itself to him as an experiment in craft and imagination: how well could he survey an area of life he had never explored? In the preface he would later write for the novel he acknowledged this problem bravely, in the novel itself somewhat less so.

The Princess Casamassima fascinated him as a virtuoso flight—or descent—to the world of anarchist London in the 1880's, a world that had recently been brought to anxious public attention by the Trafalgar Square riots. Whatever was unknown, shadowy and fearful in the idea of a radicalism churning beneath the surface of London stimulated his curiosity; he wished to seize upon the potential of destruction while it remained a mere potential ("the sick, eternal misery crying out of the darkness in vain") and to dramatize it against the grimy backdrop of the London slums. It was an exercise in the sheer power, the grasping power, of intelligence to divine that which it did not really know.

"I have never yet become engaged in a novel," he confided to his notebook, "in which, after I had begun to write . . . the details remained so vague." Nor was this vagueness quite the pondered choice he would later claim in his preface when he spoke of "Our not knowing, of society's not knowing, but only guessing and suspecting and trying to ignore, what 'goes on' irreconcilably, subversively, beneath the vast smug surface." Still, there is something admirable in James' creative bravado, his boldness in summoning the unknown and his economy in exploiting his ignorance; there is something even more admirable in his readiness to face the possibility—he seems to have thought it a likelihood—that the society to which he was committed by taste and habit was on the edge of disaster. For if it was James' conscious intention in writing *The Princess Casamassima* to discover how far he could extend the powers of his art into an unfamiliar subject, he was also moved by more intimate needs. The book registered his fear that everything he valued was crumbling, and it would be gratuitous to question the depth or sincerity of this fear; but it also betrayed his doubt whether, in some ultimate moral reckoning that was beyond his grasp, everything did not deserve to crumble. This could hardly affect his conservative temper, which by now had become thoroughly ingrained, but it did permit him an openness and breadth of feeling greater than is usually available to those in whom conservatism is merely an opinion.

The Princess Casamassima is a bewildering mixture of excellence and badness. It sets up at least three main lines of action: the personal faith of Hyacinth Robinson, the career of the Princess, and the activities of the revolutionists, particularly Paul Muniment. Strictly in "technical" terms, the novel suffers from James' failure sufficiently to work these three strands into one another, so that they often seem to be parallel when they should be interwoven. But as one might expect, this "technical" failure is a sign of some deeper failure in conception, indicating that while James was able to imagine, brilliantly for the Princess and indulgently for Hyacinth, the tone and quality of each part, he was weak at connection, at relating one to the other—that is, at precisely the point where general ideas become indispensable *for this kind of novel.*

It is the Princess herself who is the great triumph of the book, the one figure whom James has filled in with avid completeness and with regard to whom it is impossible, except at the very end, to cavil. She is one of a type that was first beginning to appear in James' day and has since become entirely familiar: the woman of superior energies to whom society can offer neither secure place nor proper work, the woman who finds it not enough to be feminine or even female yet cannot establish herself in independence from her sex. She has pushed herself—or rather, if we remember *Rodrick Hudson*, the novel in which she first appeared, she has been pushed—to the summits of society, and finds the conquest not worth the candle: it offers no outlet for her large vague talents; if the lower world is drab the upper is tedious. James knew her type intimately, she was peculiarly the product of the Anglo-American set; he understood her in every respect, including the degree to which sheer sexual boredom can drive such a woman to both fantasy and frenzy.

In his preface he applied three descriptives to her and they are exactly right: she is "the fruit of restless vanity," a woman who would be more than a woman yet knows not what; she displays a conspicuous "aversion to the banal," so that her expedition through society is first a quest for the picturesque and then for the thrilling; and she is "world-weary," her triumphs have come too cheaply. The Princess Casamassima is James' "heroine of all the ages" in her aspect of ugliness, as Isabel Archer from *The Portrait of a Lady* is that heroine in her aspect of loveliness. At times—I suspect the critics miss the snicker that comes from the future Lion of Lamb House— at times she is a creature of high comedy; James is more than a little malicious when he has her say to Hyacinth upon his arrival in her country home: "I wish you had come in the clothes you wear at work." The buzz of pitying solemnity which James affixes to poor little Hyacinth should not be allowed to obscure the fine comedy of the Princess picking Hyacinth's intellectual pocket, quavering before Muniment's delicious because proletarian coarseness, and saturating herself in Bloomsbury dinginess in order to prove she is a serious revolutionary.

There is another, more personal note: the Princess knows that her status, even as far as purchased nobility goes, is false, merely the result of an evil marriage engineered by an adventurous mother. She is in the intolerable position of suspecting that all social currencies may be counterfeit and of wondering whether anyone—be it Hyacinth or Muniment or even the shadowy Hoffendahl—can provide her with a genuine piece of newly-minted revolutionary silver. At a time when the characteristic social climber in the English novel was still laboriously making her way up, following the calculated footsteps of Becky Sharp, James realized that the really interesting and troublesome climbers had begun to hurry down.

When the Princess invites the dispossessed little book-binder to be her houseguest—it is a fine point, incidentally, which she considers the more piquant, his radicalism or his gentlemanliness—she intends it as a deliberate gesture of defiance:

How little the Princess minded—how much indeed she enjoyed the consciousness that in having him about her in that manner she was playing a trick on society, the false and conventional society she had sounded and despised—was manifest from the way she had introduced him to the group they found awaiting them in the hall on the return from their drive. . . .

But the Princess' rather flashy contempt for her own class is not justified or balanced by warmth of feeling toward any other class. She is interested in revolution or at least the idea of revolution, but not in the wretched human beings in whose name the revolution is presumably to be made. There is a neatly arranged incident in the novel where Hyacinth takes her on a mild slumming expedition to a public bar and the Princess reveals her fundamental hardness:

The softer sex . . . was embodied in a big hard red woman, the publican's wife, who looked as if she were in the habit of dealing with all sorts and mainly interested in seeing whether even the finest put down their money before they were served.

The Princess pretended to "have something" and to admire the ornamentation of the bar; and when Hyacinth asked her in a low tone what disposal they should make, when the great changes came, of such an embarrassing type as that, replied off-hand, "Oh, drown her in a barrel of beer."

And even when the Princess indulges in charity—for James is relentless in tracking down her motives—Hyacinth must admit to himself that "her behavior, after all, was more addressed to relieving herself than to relieving others."

As she breathlessly wonders whether the revolution is "real" or not, whether it is a "gathering force" or a "sterile heroism," the Princess becomes a prototype of the upper-class fellow-traveller, a wicked anticipation of the kind of woman who comes to politics searching for experience she can find nowhere else. She is a cousin of Dostoevsky's Varvara Petrovna, but only a distant cousin. For where Varvara Petrovna would peer into the "gathering force," she would plunge into it; and where Varvara Petrovna would yesterday have given cocktail parties, she would today be stealing atom secrets.

It would be a great mistake, and a slighting of James' originality, to think of the Princess as simply an idle woman amusing herself with the idea of radicalism. To suppose that would be to underestimate the explosive power of boredom in modern society, as well as the distance to which the hunger for "the real thing" can take such people. The Princess is a woman of desperate possibilities; one believes entirely in her willingness and capacity to assume Hyacinth's terrorist mission. But if one does credit the Princess' affinity for desperation, it follows that James made a bad mistake in intimating at the end of the novel, through the person of Muniment, that she would return to her mouldy prince for lack of money. On the contrary. Everything James has himself shown us of the Princess, and shown us so superbly, indicates that she would not hesitate to go deeper, to take poverty as still another *experience*, and give herself completely to revolutionary or what she supposed to be revolutionary activities. The only damper upon her enthusiasm would perhaps be her discovery that revolutionary politics, instead of bursting into a gorgeous

total insurrection, required patient and undramatic preparation. But while she might abandon the anarchists—in time
even they might not seem vigorous enough for her—the Princess would not return to her past, she would blunder ahead
into the unknown: desperate, searching, grasping. Above all,
grasping.

II

How well James guessed, for he did not know, some of the
surface qualities of nineteenth century anarchism, Lionel Trilling has noted in his essay on *The Princess*. With instinctive tact James placed his action on Sundays, the one day of
the week workers were then likely to have free for politics—
and he must surely have appreciated the irony in this exchange
of ritual pieties. The anarchists are cast, correctly enough, as
skilled artisans rather than factory proletarians. And the
bursts of discontent that fill the air of the primitive radical
gatherings at the Sun and Moon Cafe ("What the plague am I
to do with seventeen bob—seventeen bloody bob?", "Well,
are we in earnest or ain't we in earnest—that's the thing *I*
want to know") are credible enough in their uncouthness and
aimlessness.

All this rings true, one is ready to call upon one's little
fund of knowledge to attest to its truth; but James was
offering little more than fragments of insight, splinters of
observation, shrewd guesses. Inevitably, some of the guesses
proved to be wrong. George Woodcock, an English critic
thoroughly familiar with the history of anarchism, has written
a sympathetic account of the novel in which he remarks that
"James shows merely a knowledge of the kind of distorted
rumours and journalistic stories by which [the anarchists] were
represented in the newspapers of the late nineteenth century."
Mr. Woodcock points out that the anarchist movement actually consisted of "a loose collection of individuals and groups
devoted to spontaneous direct action and personal propaganda
rather than conspiracy," and that "an authoritarian circle of
conspiratorial leaders, such as James imagines in *The Princess*

Casamassima, was wholly inconsistent with . . . the doctrines and the very name of Anarchism."

This correction is important not because it proves that James drew an inaccurate picture of anarchism, for surely no one would today be troubled on that score, but because it supports the opinion that James, despite many fine touches, was relying far too comfortably on his celebrated lack of knowledge and justifying far too easily his acceptance of second-hand impressions. The result was a novel in which the most brilliant insights into political character jostle a view of politics that reminds one, a little uncomfortably, of the catch-words of melodramatic journalism.

There are times when *The Princess Casamassima* seems almost designed to evade its own theme. Everything is prepared for but little is revealed, doors open upon doors, curtains onto curtains. The elaborate skirmishing around the central brute fact of the novel—I mean, of course, the nature and power of social radicalism—is probably due to James' hesitation at taking it firmly in hand as he had taken other subjects in hand. He is skittish in his treatment because he is uncertain of his material; and he is uncertain of his material not merely because he does not know it intimately, but more important, because he vaguely senses that for a subject so explosive and untried something more is needed than the neatly symmetrical laying-out of his plot or the meticulous balancing of his characters. But what that might be, he does not know.

James tries very earnestly to accumulate sensuous impressions of the London slums; and there are passages in which he bears down hard, turning to an elaborate rhetoric not very common at this stage of his career, in order to convey through eloquence what he does not quite manage through dramatization.

They came oftener this second winter, for the season was terribly hard; and as in that lower world one walked with one's ear nearer the ground the deep perpetual groan of London misery seemed to swell and swell and form the whole undertone of life. The filthy air reached the place in the damp coats of silent men and hung there till it was brewed to a nauseous warmth, and ugly serious faces squared themselves through, and strong-smelling pipes contributed their element in a fierce dogged manner which appeared to say that it now had to stand for everything—for bread and meat and beer, for shoes and blankets and the poor things at the pawnbroker's and the smokeless chimney at home.

If only because such passages indicate how superbly conscious James was of his handicap and how genuine was his sympathy toward the speechless suffering poor who hover in the background of the novel, they are often admirable; yet one cannot suppress the feeling that, for all their local persuasiveness, these bursts of high generalization are there to deflect attention from James' trouble in working out his theme. Precisely in those sections—the sections dealing with the political world—where the novel should be most dense, it is most porous. And again, this failure is not merely the "technical" one of being unable to populate an alien world; it points to another, more serious failure which can be understood only by examining James' treatment of his radical characters.

Taken one by one, they seem entirely successful. Eustache Poupin, veteran of the Paris Commune and the revolution of 1848, "a Republican of the old-fashioned sort . . . infinitely addicted to fraternity and equality," is a perfect specimen of the pre-Marxist but post-Jacobin revolutionary, shown in all his idealism, mental softness and *Schwärmerei*. An amiable blusterer who cannot shed his native respectability—his creed is that of Louis Blanc, his manners those of a French burgher —Poupin is a man of good will but moral sloth, a revolutionist of enthusiasm who is blind to the possibility that enthusiasm can also lead to murder. Poupin is not a very deeply imagined figure, his major function in the novel being to fail Hyacinth, and long before the need arises we know that he *will* fail Hyacinth; but within these limits he serves efficiently. Schinkel, the schematic German comrade, moves in the shadows of the book rather than its forefront, but he is a far more subtly conceived and realized figure than Poupin. He too, I cannot help noticing, seems to spring

from the immediacy of radical experience: the lonely phleg-
matic bachelor who fumbles through a routine of shabby
order, with a perpetual bandage round his neck, a pipe for
companion and the movement as breath and blood of life.
Schinkel's feelings for Hyacinth go deeper than Poupin's, and
so does his betrayal. He does not burble over the bewildered little artisan in the manner of the Frenchman but
watches him from a distance, with longing and affection; and
when it is he who is assigned to inform Hyacinth of the
terrorist mission—for the Schinkels of this world are always
trustworthy—he feels far more poignantly than Poupin the
dilemma of their young friend. He protests to Hyacinth
that he "lofes" him, and it is true, he "lofes" him; yet he
fulfills his part of the mission with precise loyalty. Schinkel
is one of those Jamesian "reverberators" who takes everything
in, who feels it all intensely, so that only at the very end do
we grasp the full extent of his responsibility and his betrayal.
The final sentence of the book is given to Schinkel's reflection
that the revolver with which Hyacinth has killed himself
"would certainly have served much better for the Duke." The
weight assigned these words by their place in the novel, like
the powerful grinding irony they enforce, falls back upon
Schinkel in his role as representative figure of the anarchist
world.

At no point in his invasion of that world is James bolder
than in his handling of Paul Muniment, the minor anarchist
leader; yet one might well complain that finally he is not
bold enough. Muniment is a precise outline—there is more
contour than substance—of the bureaucratic personality, in
one variation the Labor Party parliamentarian and in another
variation the Stalinist functionary. Since Muniment seldom
troubles to develop his ideas, it is not possible to specify the
precise shade of his bureaucratic ambition; but given the
rudimentary state of the radicalism to which he has attached
himself, this can hardly be seen as a serious fault in the
novel. More troublesome is the fact that the interest created
in him is disproportionate to the picture given of him. He is
too prominent for a minor character and too shadowy for a

major one. Though in some ways the most interesting and original figure in the book, we are kept at too great a distance from him and do not experience the full force of his political career. We see it only in its impact on a few of his friends, in his kindly manipulation of Hyacinth and his comic but ruthless struggle with the Princess for personal domination.

Up to a point James' vagueness with regard to Muniment's political life can be justified as part of a strategy for stressing fearful possibilities by refusing to choose among them—a strategy he inherited, of course, from Hawthorne. But once the political thread begins to color the novel, which is to say, about half way through, Muniment should be filled in, if only to make more vivid and substantial one of the forces acting upon Hyacinth. This inadequacy, as I take it to be, is very likely due to James' lack of that deep and intimate knowledge of English working class life which appears to such advantage in D. H. Lawrence's early novels.

Nonetheless, Muniment represents one of James' great strokes of intuition. James caught, almost on the fly, the characteristic traits of the labor bureaucrat: his self-assurance, which seems to rest upon something more than power of intellect; his sense of destiny, reflected in and partly the result of his air of portentous secrecy; his middle-class philistinism in matters of morals and taste; his cool hunger for power; and all the while, his genuine devotion to the cause. These are traits of leadership anxiously familiar to our time; Muniment's very name, taken from the Latin verb meaning to fortify, suggests both the strength and aloofness of his type.

A socialist leader once said he wished to rise not above his class but with it: Muniment foresaw another possibility, he would rise *on* it.

III

Remarkable as was James' insight into political personality, I think it reasonable to say that it does not quite come to a commanding vision of the political life. James showed himself to be brilliantly gifted at entering the behavior of political people, but he had no larger view of politics as a collective mode of action. He had a sense of the revolutionaries but not of the revolutionary movement—which might not have mattered had not the movement been at least as important a character in the novel as the individuals who composed it. He made the mistake of supposing that the whole was equal to a sum of its parts; that if you exhausted the radicals you had gotten at radicalism. He discovered, or thought he discovered, that envy is a major motive among radicals; but even if true, this would not be very illuminating if only because envy works in a great variety of human situations; it does not distinguish one politics from another. To understand a social movement, one must seek to approach it in objective terms, in terms that put aside, at least for the moment, the motives of individual participants and assign a weight and meaning to the group itself. And this James, with his trained inexperience in abstract thought, could not do.

I am not complaining, it had better be stressed, that James the person lacked an ideology, for this fact, if it is one, does not here concern us. My point is that some motivating idea about the revolutionary movement, be it valid or not, was indispensable for bringing into full play the energies that lay waiting in the novel; and James the writer not only lacked such an idea, he did not really grasp the need for it. The idea of which I speak need not be made explicit by the writer, and generally it is preferable that it not be; but it needs to be present as an assumption of what the revolutionary impulse means, what it will do for and to society. It needs to be felt as an unseen force behind the characters, behind the events, behind the very words. That it is not felt means that the politics of the novel remains partly unused. The ensuing loss, like the criticism I am making, is literary, not ideological; it is a loss *within* the book.

But a qualification is needed. For one can see in James' novel a central idea of a sort, an idea once extremely popular in England and France. Nineteenth century publicists liked to depict the political struggle between radicalism and conservatism as a clash between cultural barbarism and cultural refinement. Depending on the bias of a given observer, the barbarism might be seen as vigorously healthy or loutishly destructive, the refinement as the heritage of past greatness or an effete decadence.

In a study of Courbet, the art historian Meyer Schapiro has described a large allegorical painting *L'Atelier* in which this cultural dualism is given physical representation. "The painter presents around him in the studio his two worlds, at the right, the world of art . . . on the other side, the people in their homeliness, poverty and simple interests." • For Courbet this representation did not imply an inherent or terrifying opposition, since he believed that the world of art and the world of the people could be reconciled through the ethos of radical democracy. But for many writers and artists of the nineteenth century no such *rapprochement* seemed plausible, and the rising popular movements were often seen by them as a rude threat to the values of culture.

James absorbed this notion in *The Princess Casamassima*, perhaps a little too uncritically. For the cultural judgment of politics, if pushed too far, can be as trivial as the political judgment of culture, if pushed any distance at all, can be inhumane. An aristocracy of culture, threatened by the indifference of society and the ignorance of rising plebeian movements, is always tempted to mistake its immediate needs for the larger needs of humanity—though sometimes, of course, this is no mistake at all. And in James there is a tendency to judge the movement Hyacinth Robinson joins not as it is morally good or bad, socially creative or destructive, but as it impinges on a cultured sensibility; he is trying, that is, to judge a very complex human enterprise by standards that are both essential and insufficient, and the result is a kind of cultural insularity.

• "Courbet and Popular Imagery," Meyer Schapiro. *Journal of the Warburg Institute*, IV, 3-4.

IV

These weaknesses might have been overcome—or glossed over—if James had chosen as his hero a figure of strength who would impose himself on the political environment and transform it through the force of his will and intelligence. Hyacinth Robinson, however, is one of the most passive of James' heroes. He is a youth, writes James, "on whom nothing is lost," and that is true: one fully credits his talent for registering every nuance of moral chivalry or coarseness. But he is also a youth on whom nothing rubs off; a bastard by birth, he behaves as if he were immaculate in conception. It is his languorous passivity, far more than anything he actually says or does, that constitutes his snobbism. Hyacinth's is the snobbism of the young man who expects things, who waits not rapaciously but wistfully. His desires are pathetically modest, his sensibility is exquisite: how can one help feeling for and with him? That he yearns for the graces of the rich, that he loves the beauties of the evil world, that he is irked by the foulness of the slums and disgusted by the brutalities of the workers he had meant to inspire—only a prig would censure him too harshly for these deviations from his political faith. What is difficult to accept, however, and what finally renders Hyacinth a not very interesting hero, is the curiously feminine insularity of his character, his remarkable gift for being utterly uncontaminated by the world through which he glides.

Had it been James' intention so to cast Hyacinth, one could only regret the choice and applaud the achievement. But clearly his intention is something more; Hyacinth is one of the few characters with whom he seems to have a strong and, I would suggest, a disastrous identification. Hyacinth, says James in his preface, is supremely capable of profiting from all the glories of civilization yet "condemned to see these things from the outside." He is "the trapped spectator," the "poor sensitive gentleman" in a younger version, the fine intelligence which quails before the betrayals and vulgarity of the world. And one side of James is all too susceptible to this figure of pathos, the side of James which takes upon itself the fullest burden of handicap. James does not see what a solemn stick his young man can often be, and he compounds the trouble by identifying not with Hyacinth's temptations but with his refusals. He makes Hyacinth too innocent, not in terms of knowledge, for Hyacinth sees everything, but in terms of motive. Long on chivalry and short on impulse, Hyacinth thrives on renunciation the way heroes thrive on experience; he is too noble to be genuinely interesting and too pathetic to be tragic. In the end, Hyacinth becomes a projection of James' vulnerability.

Not, of course, that Hyacinth is without appetites. He keeps buzzing around the Princess and Millicent Henning, who is a kind of proletarian princess, and in a moment of enthusiasm even pledges his life to the cause. But from some fatal flaw of acquired gentility, he seems unable to act upon his desires: it is a case, I suppose, of a good man ruined by his better instincts.

As his experience widens and he learns to enjoy the Princess' country estate, Hyacinth is torn between a vision of elegance, in which the alloy of snobbism is not always distinct from the gold of culture, and an identification with the suffering millions, in which the indulgence of self-pity softens his wrath against injustice.

When he himself was not letting his imagination wander among the haunts of the aristocracy and stretching it in the shadow of an ancestral beech to read the last number of the *Revue des Deux Mondes*, he was occupied with contemplations of a very different kind; he was absorbed in the struggles and sufferings of the millions whose life flowed in the same current as his and who, though they constantly excited his disgust and made him shrink and turn away, had the power to chain his sympathy, to raise it to passion, to convince him for the time at least that real success in the world would be to do something with them and for them.

As long as this tension continues, this "eternal habit of swinging from one view to another," the book preserves a certain vibrancy and life. In its second half, however, Hyacinth's yearning for beauty and his assumption that it is inseparable from a life of privilege leads him to a moral smugness which James does not really "see through" and, in fact, seems almost to approve. He can now say

that want and toil and suffering are the constant lot of the immense majority of the human race. I've found them everywhere but haven't minded them. Forgive the cynical confession. What has struck me is the great achievements of which man has been capable in spite of them—the splendid accumulations of the happier few, to which doubtless the miserable many have also in their degree contributed.

In defense of Hyacinth, Lionel Trilling has argued that his later phase represents a positive access of knowledge, perhaps even wisdom: "he has learned something of what may lie behind abstract [political] ideals, the envy, the impulse to revenge and dominance." No doubt; but it does not seem to occur to Mr. Trilling, as it did not occur to James, that something equally bad may exist behind the abstract ideals of art to which Hyacinth is now so uncritically pledged. Culture, no less than politics, can harden into ideology.

Yet James is so marvellous an artist that he succeeds in salvaging something from the character of Hyacinth. Intermittently we see another Hyacinth, a Hyacinth who does not readily give himself to the abstract ideals of either politics or art, who knows there is a price to be paid for each advantage in life and is ready to pay it, who realizes both the fatal ambiguities of action and the equally fatal consequences of inaction. In Chapter XXXV, probably the best in the book, this Hyacinth moves into full view and is presented with a directness and firmness that stirs one to reflect on how marvellous a novel *The Princess Casamassima* might have been.

As the chapter opens, the moment of choice is approaching for Hyacinth, and never has he been less prepared to face it. Together with Muniment, he goes off on a radiant Sunday afternoon to a London park, and in the midst of the brimming promiscuous life of the city the two men achieve a sudden closeness. Hyacinth faces both ways, toward his political conscience and his esthetic desire, toward the masses in whose suffering he has been drenched and the art whose radiance has suddenly overwhelmed him. This is the Hyacinth of whom James had given us an earlier glimpse when he wrote, "It might very well be his fate to be divided to the point of torture, to be split open by sympathies that had pulled him in different ways . . ." And now, ruminating on this lonely, lovely Sunday afternoon, "he saw the immeasurable misery of the people, and yet he saw all that had been, as it were, rescued and redeemed from it: the treasures, the felicities, the splendours, the successes of the world."

In the dialogue that runs between them, Hyacinth begins with a provocation: he indulges in the usual jibe against doctrines of equality, that they foster "the selfsame shade of asininity." Muniment's parry is neat: "When those who have no start to speak of have a good one it's but fair to infer they'll go further. I want to try them, you know." Hyacinth cannot stand up to his logical friend, his aggressiveness evaporates, and he pleadingly answers: "I don't want you to think I've ceased to care for the people. What am I but one of the poorest and meanest of them?" And it is here that Hyacinth becomes an almost archetypal figure. Torn between the claims of the future and the claims of the past, between a vision of human fraternity in a world not yet made and the tangible glories of the cultural edifice, he is now, for the first time and at a fearful cost, fully sensitive to the possibilities of life.

His conflict seems insoluble to him, as in a way it is: Paris or the Sun and Moon Cafe, the whole unmeasured gift of past greatness or the grim demands of the political vocation. Here James has come upon—I shall not even try to guess how, except to note that he knew only too well what it meant to live between two worlds—he has come upon a problem that lies at the very center of political life. Hyacinth is trapped in the heart-struggle between beauty and necessity: he wants only to live, only to respond, but it is his very awareness of the unmediated clash between beauty and necessity that destroys him. The world, pressing upon him with its crushing weight, will not let him live; the conflict between taste and belief that has ripped apart his life now proves to be an illusory one. Whatever James has missed in Hyacinth's world, he has understood one thing with a grim finality: that for Hyacinth, as for many in the world like him, the very yearning for choice reveals the power of destiny.

PART TWO

CHAPTER SEVEN

SOME AMERICAN NOVELISTS: THE POLITICS OF ISOLATION

One of the more remarkable chapters in de Tocqueville's *Democracy in America* is entitled, "Why the Americans Have Never Been so Eager as the French for General Ideas in Political Affairs." Writing some forty years later, Anthony Trollope noted in his *Autobiography* the attitude he found common among Americans: that public life is a thing of ugliness, a source of corruption which every honest man does his best to avoid. Other observers of 19th century America, even while reporting the national craze for politics as a "game" or a means of plunder, also testify to the feeling among educated Americans that neither as public activity nor intellectual pursuit is politics to be regarded as quite legitimate.

Political ideas in America have never been as crystallized as in Europe. They have not had to be. The pressures of political choice have seldom closed in upon sensitive minds in America as inexorably as they have in Europe. And it has been part of our good-tempered egotism to suppose that these advantages, made possible by a unique though perhaps temporary joining of historical circumstances, were actually elements of communal wisdom, *choices* testifying to our moderation and maturity. De Tocqueville knew better, of course. In his tantalizing little chapter he points to those "social conditions" which have prompted the French to a passion for ideology, and the absence of which has allowed the Americans to make the suspicion of ideology into something approaching a national creed.

The growth of ideology, I would suggest, is closely related to the accumulation of social pressures. It is when men no longer feel that they have adequate choices in their styles of life, when they conclude that there are no longer possibilities for honorable maneuver and compromise, when they decide that the time has come for "ultimate" social loyalties and political decisions—it is then that ideology begins to flourish. Ideology reflects a hardening of commitment, the freezing of opinion into system. It speaks of a society in which men feel themselves becoming functions of large impersonal forces over which they can claim little control. It represents an effort to employ abstract ideas as a means of overcoming the abstractness of social life. It is the passion of men with their backs against the wall.

Very little in 19th century American experience answers to this description. Except during the Civil War, the one occasion when this country tasted the blood and terror that appear in the kinds of historical moments that give rise to ideology, there has always seemed a way out for Americans. The uniqueness of our history, the freshness of our land, the plentitude of our resources—all these have made possible, and rendered plausible, a style of political improvisation and intellectual free-wheeling. Not, of course, that America has lacked political ideologues. Particularly in the 19th century there have been leaders and theorists—Calhoun, Webster, Stevens, Phillips—who found themselves developing bodies of political ideas that, with some tolerance, can be described as ideologies. But except for Calhoun, none advanced systems of political belief that led to the kind of irrevocable struggles, the repeated "final conflicts" we associate with the life of ideology in Europe.

Nor is it quite true that we have lacked serious political

appetites and impulses. But where such appetites and impulses in Europe would be manifested through coherent theories and massive parties, in America they have generally remained diffuse, eccentric and fluid. One of the most striking facts about American life and literature is the frequency with which political issues seem to arise in non-political forms. Instead of confronting us as formidable systems of thought, or as parties locked in bitter combat, politics in America has often appeared in the guise of religious, cultural and sexual issues, apparently far removed from the contentions of Europe yet difficult to understand except in regard to those contentions.

Most American novels that have dealt with politics have been unable to sustain the theme. It is a characteristic rhythm of such novels that they begin promisingly, even brilliantly, in the portrayal of some area of American political life and then, about mid-way, withdraw from or collapse under the burden of their subject. The idea of politics can seldom seem so "natural" a subject to American novelists as to European; our writers tend to think of it as a special "problem," with all the awkwardness and self-consciousness that entails, while the Europeans take politics for granted as they take sex or social manners or national feeling for granted. If a 19th century American novelist chose a political theme, he generally did so to expose the evils of corruption in government (America's substitute, as someone has said, for ideology) or to bemoan the vulgarities of public life that were driving sensitive men into retreat. The first made for a journalistic novel of the sort that was popular in the last few decades of the 19th and the first few of the 20th century, but with a handful of exceptions, such as DeForest's *Playing the Mischief,* these books are too parochial in their outlook, too caught up in the particularities of local problems, to absorb the modern reader.

It is the second kind of novel, the novel colored by the emotions of political loss, that seems closer to our interests today. In such novels—Henry Adams' *Democracy* is the prime example—one comes up against the despairing cry: *It is too late, there is no place for the sensitive and thoughtful man, perhaps there never was.* This cry is also to be heard in Henry James' *The Bostonians,* though without the bitterness of Adams, and one may even detect muffled anticipations in Hawthorne's *The Blithedale Romance.*

For Adams and, to a lesser extent, James, the sense of despair and disgust with American politics is aggravated by a longing for the tradition of political intelligence and disinterestedness—Adams looks back to it in his own family, James in his social world—which they associate with the political leaders of revolutionary America. The humane imagination of a Jefferson, the rectitude of a John Adams are powerful and attractive elements in a political tradition that is patrician in quality yet not aristocratic in bias. Seen from the post-Civil War years, this political patriciate of early America can easily take on almost legendary qualities, and one can understand the temptation to idealize it a little by supposing it to have been above class interest or political sectarianism. By contrast, the politics of America after the Civil War can only seem vulgar and amoral, something to be approached with explicit antipathy—if also, at times, a fascinated antipathy.

Very few American writers have tried to see politics as a distinctive mode of social existence, with values and manners of its own. Even those who understood that a fruitful subject for the novel might be the *idea* of politics, could not find enough supporting material in their experience or their environment with which to give this theme a full embodiment. Adams' novel is the most obvious example of this difficulty, but neither James nor, somewhat earlier, Hawthorne is exempt from it. The result was that in those 19th century American novels that do deal with politics, ideology or what passes for it in this country is seen in a far more intimate relation to personal experience than in the European political novel; in fact, ideology is sometimes treated by the American novelists as if it were merely a form of private experience. Those massive political institutions, parties and movements which in the European novel occupy the space between the abstractions of ideology and the intimacies of personal life are barely present in America.

The Americans failed, they could not help but fail, to see political life as an autonomous field of action; they could not focus upon politics long and steadily enough to allow it to develop according to its inner rhythms, for it bored or repelled them even as it tempted them. Personalizing everything, they could not quite do justice to the life of politics in its own right, certainly not the kind of justice done by the European novelists. Personalizing everything, they could brilliantly observe how social and individual experience melt into one another so that the deformations of the one soon become the deformations of the other. This theme is first touched upon in *The Blithedale Romance,* is given a special turn in *Democracy,* and reaches its fulfillment in the *The Bostonians.* Though we cannot find in these novels a treatment of politics nearly so full or rich as in the work of the 19th century Europeans, it is to them that we must look for a tradition of American writing in which the idea of politics, and sometimes the life of politics, is seriously treated.

Hawthorne: Pastoral and Politics

No portrait of Hawthorne, wrote Henry James, "is at all exact which fails to insist upon the constant struggle which must have gone on between his shyness and his desire to know something of life; between what may be called his evasive and inquisitive tendencies." This remark provides a clue not merely to Hawthorne but to a good many other American writers, including James himself, for it focuses on the dualities of moral attitude and literary approach that cut through so much of our literature. In the work of Hawthorne, and especially in *The Blithedale Romance,* they are particularly severe: his outer moral conventionality (the "blue-eyed Nathaniel") as against his suppressed recalcitrance, which sometimes breaks out as an extreme boldness of moral speech; the frequent Augustan deadness of his prose as against its occasional release into pure and passionate lucidity; the mild and almost somnolent surface of his mind, so utterly unimpressive in its own right, as against the vital emotional strength beneath.

Throughout his life Hawthorne was caught up in what we would now call a crisis of religious belief. His acute moral sense had been largely detached from the traditional context of orthodox faith, but it had found little else in which to thrive, certainly no buoying social vision—which may explain why he turned so often to allegory, the one literary mode in which it might be possible to represent the moral sense as an independent force. Estranged from the dominant progressivist thought of his time, Hawthorne could summon no large enthusiasms nor pledge himself to any social movement; his prevalent temper was skeptical, though a powerful impulse within him worked to assault and deride his skepticism. But what is so curiously "modern" about Hawthorne's crisis of belief is that he seems to have been drawn less to belief itself—he was quite free from the mania for certainty—than to the enlargements of feeling that might come with belief, the passions it might release and regulate. In its assumptions this attitude toward religious belief might almost be called "pragmatic," odd as that word seems in relation to Hawthorne.

As a 19th century American he could not acquiesce in Puritan dogma, but as a man who had neither the enthusiasm nor the fatuousness of Transcendental optimism he could not break free from the Puritan mode of vision. He did not see *what* the Puritans had seen, he saw *as* they had seen. He felt that no matter how questionable the notion of "original sin" might be as doctrine or how distasteful if allowed to become the substance of a practical morality, it nonetheless touched upon a fundamental truth concerning human beings. This truth he reduced from a dogma to an insight, defending it on empirical grounds rather than as revelation.

Similar problems of belief troubled him, though far less acutely, in politics. A democrat by hesitation rather than conviction, he disliked reformers, distrusted the Abolitionists, and sympathized with that wing of the Democratic Party, a mediocre small-souled wing, which hoped to patch up a truce of expediency with the slave-owning South. In an age blazing with certainty, he had to make his way on doubt. The breakdown of faith in God, human capacity and social progress that would later shake the world, was foreshadowed in his life, and though he seldom made these opinions explicit, they form the buried foundations of his visible work.

Yet one cannot read his novels without seeing that in addition to the skeptic there is a man so eager for experiment in personal life that at times the "inquisitive tendency" becomes sheer hunger. This Hawthorne finds himself drawn, against his will and sometimes without his conscious knowledge, to moral outlaws who dare what he himself never even desired to dare. This Hawthorne yearns for some great liberating transformation which will bring him, for the first time, into full vibrant life. His mind was sluggish, mild, rationalistic; his creative self was passionate, warmly receptive, sometimes even sensual. It would be oversimplifying to see these two strands as always in opposition, for that would have made his life unendurable; but the two strands are there.

The quiet of Hawthorne's life was interrupted by a few adventures, a few raids on experience, of which the most interesting was perhaps his brief participation in Brook Farm, the utopian community of the 1840's. Most of Hawthorne's biographers, refusing to reach beneath the surface of his reminiscence, have assumed that since he did not agree with the ideas of the reformers he entered the Brook Farm community simply to find a way of supporting his future wife. But that hardly seems a sufficient reason, for it is unlikely that so hard-headed a man as Hawthorne would have thought Brook Farm a good financial investment, or would have thought of it primarily as a good investment. More plausible, though admittedly speculative, is the assumption that Hawthorne, apart from motives of convenience and perhaps without fully realizing it himself, was seeking in Brook Farm another kind of investment, an investment in shared life. What may have tempted him was not the ideas of the reformers, but their large enthusiasm, their animating idealism, their implicit faith in the possibility of human communication.

And despite its antipathy to the reformers, despite the tone of aggressive mockery it generally takes toward them, *The Blithedale Romance* makes it abundantly clear that Brook Farm had struck deeply and forever into Hawthorne's consciousness. In his own secretive way he had come up against many of the problems that would dominate the 20th century novel: the relation between ideology and utopia, the meeting between politics and sex.

The dualism that controls almost everything in *The Blithedale Romance* is that between subject and object, narrator and event. At the several points where the novel breaks down, the trouble is not merely one of literary structure, it also involves a radical uncertainty as to the possibilities of knowledge. Everything is seen through the eyes of Coverdale, a timid "minor poet" recalling his stay at Blithedale, the utopian community modelled after Brook Farm; and so methodical is the evasiveness and mystification with which he presents the action that one begins to suspect the book is hampered less by literary clumsiness than by some psychological block of which he is merely the symptom.

Coverdale is a self-portrait of Hawthorne, but a highly distorted and mocking self-portrait, as if Hawthorne were trying to isolate and thereby exorcise everything within him that impedes full participation in life. The tendency to withdrawal that is so noticeable in Coverdale represents not merely a New Englander's fear of involvement in the dangers of society; it is also a moony narcissism by means of which an habitual observer, unable to validate his sense of the external world, tries magically to deny its reality. This symbolic annihilation of whatever resists control of the will reaches its climax when Hawthorne destroys, physically and psychologically, the two main characters who threaten Coverdale, though nothing in the logic of the plot requires so violent or extreme a conclusion.

As against the ineffectual Coverdale—who, by the way,

lacks neither intelligence nor shrewdness—Hawthorne sets up several centers of anxiety. Blithedale itself, a place of idealism and effort; Zenobia, a sexually magnificent and intellectually daring woman who is shown as the central figure of the community; Hollingsworth, a reformer who has come to Blithedale to "bore from within" in behalf of a monomaniacal scheme for salvaging convicts; and finally Priscilla, a sweet priss of a girl who represents the feminine principle in its most conservative aspect (that which makes the family go round)—all these challenge Coverdale, for all tempt him to break out of the circle of selfhood. His problem then becomes, how can he drain off some of their energy and power without himself taking the risks of commitment? Emotional parasitism is an obvious course, but with obvious limitations; in the end Hawthorne simply "rescues" Coverdale by suppressing the conflicts that threaten to liberate him—and thereby, it might be added, destroying the novel.

Coverdale's relation to the utopian community is one of the first but still among the best treatments in American writing of what happens when a hesitant intellectual attaches himself to a political enterprise. Looking back from his withered bachelorhood Coverdale is proud that at least once in his life he dared to plunge: "Whatever else I repent of, let it be reckoned neither among my sins nor my follies that I once had force and faith enough to form generous hopes of the world's destiny. . . ." And throughout the book Hawthorne retains a qualified affection for that side of New England utopianism which would later prompt Parrington to speak of Brook Farm as "a social poem fashioned out of Yankee homespun."

When Coverdale finally leaves Blithedale, he does so from a feeling—it will reappear in many American novels—that he is inadequate to public life, incapable of the monolithic enthusiasms a utopian politics demands. ("The greatest obstacle to being heroic," he shrewdly notes, "is the doubt whether one may not be going to prove one's self a fool.") Partly, too, he "sees through" the utopian impulse, discovering what would hardly surprise or shock a more realistic and experienced man: that behind its ideal claims it often shelters personal inadequacy and ideological fanaticism. And finally he grows weary of that constant depreciation of the present in the name of an ideal future which seems so necessary to utopian radicalism: "I was beginning to lose the sense of what kind of world it was, among innumerable schemes of what it might or ought to be."

Yet all of this, though pointed enough, is not very far from the usual criticism of utopian politics or, for that matter, from the usual attack upon 19th century ideas of progress; and what really distinguishes *The Blithedale Romance* is another kind of criticism, double-edged, subtle and generally unnoticed. Hawthorne saw that, motives apart, the formation of isolated utopian communities is seldom a threat to society; he understood that no matter how pure its inner moral aspirations might be, the utopian community could not avoid functioning as part of the materialistic world it detested.

I very soon became sensible [says Coverdale] that, as regarded society at large, we stood in a position of new hostility, rather than new brotherhood . . . Constituting so pitiful a minority as now, we were inevitably estranged from the rest of mankind in pretty fair proportion with the strictness of our mutual bond among ourselves.

And at another point:

The peril of our new way of life was not lest we should fail to become practical agriculturists, but that we should probably cease to be anything else.

It is interesting, and a little amusing, to note how closely these caustic observations approach the Marxist criticism of utopian communities. For if Hawthorne's sentences are transposed into economic terms, what he is saying is that by virtue of being subject to the demands and pressures of the market, the utopian community becomes a competitive unit in a competitive society ("we stood in a position of new hostility") and must therefore be infected with its mores. The utopian who would cut himself off from the ugly world must, to preserve his utopia, become a "practical agriculturist"—which means to model his utopia upon the society he rejects.

This criticism,* which strikes so hard a blow at the political fancies of many 19th century American intellectuals, is advanced by Hawthorne with a cruel and almost joyous insistence, but that does not make it any the less true. Hawthorne, of course, was as far from the Marxist imagination as anyone could be, but almost any criticism of utopian politics from a point of view committed to struggle within the world would have to render a similar judgment.

If Hawthorne criticizes the utopian impulse on the ground that it does not really succeed in avoiding the evil of the great world, he also implies that another trouble with utopianism is that it does not bring its followers into a sufficiently close relation with the evil of the great world. And in the context of the novel these two ideas are not as incompatible as they might seem.

For the whole utopian venture at Blithedale, with its effort to transform the impulse of political idealism into a pastoral retreat, bears a thoroughly innocent air. It is an innocence peculiar to many 19th century American intellectuals, who believed that politics, when it was not simply a vulgarity to be avoided, could be engaged in by proclaiming a series of moral precepts. (Though Emerson shied away from the utopian communities, they were actually founded on his principle that individual regeneration must precede social politics—the only difference being that in the utopian communities a number of individuals came together to seek their regeneration in common.) This innocence—or perhaps one should speak of a willed search for innocence—was of course related to the hopelessly crude and corrupt nature of our

* Nor was Hawthorne alone in making it. His sister-in-law Elizabeth Peabody wrote in the 1840's that Brook Farm proved little beyond the fact that "gentlemen, if they will work as many hours as boors, will succeed even better in cultivating a farm." And Emerson, who understood very well the precarious relation between intellectuals and society, wrote in his journal that he refused to join Brook Farm because to do so would be "to hide my impotency in the thick of a crowd."

"ordinary" national politics, and it showed itself in no more endearing form than its assumption that "ordinary" politics could be gotten away from, or supplanted, by the politics of pastoral retreat. America itself having in some sense gone astray, utopianism would remake it in the small.

The characters in *The Blithedale Romance*, even those who are meant as figures of worldliness, also partake of this New England innocence. For while Zenobia and Hollingsworth, the one a radical in behavior and the other a radical in ideology, are treated as figures of enviable passion and experience, there is a tacit recognition throughout the book that it is only by Coverdale's standards that they can seem so rich in passion and experience. Hollingsworth, writes Hawthorne, "ought to have commenced his investigation of [the reform of criminals] by perpetrating some huge sin in his proper person, and examining the conditions of his conscience afterwards." To be sure, this trenchant observation is put into the mouth of Coverdale, who is frequently envious of Hollingsworth's political passion; but there is surely nothing unfamiliar, or at odds with our sense of psychological realism, in Coverdale's need to depreciate that which he most admires. It is as if Hawthorne, soon to punish Zenobia and Hollingsworth for their putative boldness, can accept his desire to punish them only through a half-suppressed feeling that, in reality, they are not bold enough.

The uneasy mixture of skepticism and yearning that complicates Hawthorne's treatment of the utopian community can also be seen in his approach to Zenobia and Hollingsworth as individuals. Zenobia rules the book. "Passionate, luxurious, lacking simplicity, not deeply refined," she is the frankest embodiment of sensuality in Hawthorne's work. Except for Hollingsworth, whose appetite runs to political notions rather than human flesh, everyone in the book is drawn to her. For she alone is really alive, she alone is open in her sexuality. As if to cover up the freedom of his characterization, Hawthorne also endows her with a somewhat operatic manner, but this does not seriously detract from Zenobia's power and when one remembers how difficult and damaging the role of feminine reformer must have been in 19th century New England it even has a certain appropriateness. Throughout the book Zenobia is celebrated in rhapsodic outbursts:

> Zenobia had a rich, though varying color. It was, most of the while, a flame, and anon a sudden paleness. Her eyes glowed. . . . Her gestures were free, and strikingly impressive. The whole woman was alive with a passionate intensity, which I now perceived to be the phase in which her beauty culminated. Any passion would have become her well; and passionate love, perhaps, the best of all.

In her opulent, inaccessible sexuality Zenobia becomes a kind of New England earth goddess—though, given Hawthorne's estimate of New England women, a very intellectual goddess too. Both ways, she is the name of his desire.

Hawthorne quickly penetrates to the source and nature of Zenobia's sexuality; he relates it, both in its power and its limitations, to her political boldness. He understands that in her person is realized the threat to traditional modes of life which the others merely talk about. And he sees how, in turn, her political boldness contributes to and sanctions her personal freedom:

> She made no scruple of over-setting all human institutions, and scattering them as with a breeze from her fan. A female reformer, in her attacks upon society, has an instinctive sense of where the life lies, and is inclined to aim directly at that spot. Especially the relation between the sexes is naturally among the earliest to attract her attention.

This powerful insight Hawthorne puts to two uses, making Zenobia into a vibrant woman who challenges established social norms but also showing how this very challenge twists and depletes her life. For as Zenobia ruefully admits, "the whole universe, her own sex and yours, and Providence, and Destiny, to boot, make common cause against the woman who swerves one hair's-breadth out of the beaten track."

But if Zenobia's intellectual and political audacity makes possible a new kind of personal freedom, it also involves the danger of a confusion of sexual roles. Zenobia's unconventionality as a woman allows her a certain masculine energy and arrogance, and while this brings her public satisfactions it also prevents her from winning Hollingsworth's love; for he is one of those reformers who prefers that his own wife be tame and submissive. In a brilliant little passage Hawthorne hints at the tragi-comic difficulties of Zenobia's position. Asked at the beginning of the book whether she knows Hollingsworth, Zenobia replies, "No, only as an auditor—auditress, I mean—of some of his lectures."

Can Zenobia, however, be both the personification of forbidden sexuality and a woman capable of so revealing a slip as the one I have just quoted? Is Hawthorne "cheating" when he portrays Zenobia as a richly feminine figure yet particularly open to the dangers of subverting the feminine role?

Whatever the difficulty may be with Zenobia, it is not in Hawthorne's initial conception of her, which is marvellously deep and subtle; in fact, it is one of his major intuitive strokes that he notices how the political atmosphere which encourages a freer sexuality also threatens the feminine role. The trouble lies in Hawthorne's presentation, his unwillingness or incapacity to live up to the promise of his opening pages. For, like everything else in the book, Zenobia comes through only in flickers; we do not see her in a developed action that would call upon the intelligence she undoubtedly has; the speculative insights into the relation between her public and private selves appear mainly as occasional remarks that do not affect the bulk of the novel. Either because he draws back from his subject, fearful of his own boldness, or because he could not work up an action by which to sustain his subject, Hawthorne does not show us Zenobia in the motions and gestures of life. And that, of course, is one reason he can imply that she is not so thoroughly a figure of passion and experience as Coverdale supposes. The more she is to be shown as a temptress, the more must her temptations be called into question.

What is true for Zenobia as a projection of desire is truer still for Hollingsworth as a warning against the dangers of ideology. A number of recent critics have praised Hawthorne's presentation of Hollingsworth as a prophetic anticipation of the reformer who is cold to everything but his own scheme. Were Hollingsworth "there," were he endowed with a certain contingency and thickness and color of presentation, this point might well be true. For it is clearly Hawthorne's intention to show in Hollingsworth the utopian impulse as it has hardened into an inhumane ideology. But in the novel as Hawthorne wrote it, Hollingsworth is a dismal failure. He never *does* anything, he seldom displays any emotional fluidity or complexity, he is rarely given one of those saving human touches which, by their very presence, would make more credible his essential inhumanity.

There are, of course, a few passages in which Hawthorne breathes a little life into him—as when Hollingsworth, with that single-minded sincerity which is a form of blindness, asks Coverdale, "How can you be my life-long friend, except you strive with me toward the great object of my life?" or when Zenobia bursts out that Hollingsworth's political dedication "is all self! . . . Nothing else; nothing but self, self, self!"

Such passages, however, do little but suggest how great was Hawthorne's opportunity and how seldom he seized it, for Hollingsworth conforms so neatly to Hawthorne's skepticism concerning reformers that he cannot have much reality of his own. Nothing is granted any scope in the book that would allow Hollingsworth to resist or complicate the point he is meant to illustrate. Presumably a warning against the terrible consequences of a fanatic ideology, he is seldom allowed any vitality as a character because Hawthorne's sense of him is itself so thoroughly ideological. What Hawthorne had wished to warn against in his portrait of Hollingsworth becomes a crucial deficiency of the portrait itself.

Any critic who cares enough to write about *The Blithedale Romance* runs the risk of suggesting that it is a better book than it actually is, for its themes would appear so close to our current preoccupations that they need merely be stated in order to arouse interest. And with a novel so abundant in potentiality and so limited in realization there is the further danger of writing about the book it might have been—a very great book, indeed!—rather than the one it is. Yet by any serious reckoning *The Blithedale Romance* must be called a remarkable failure of a very remarkable writer.

One way of testing this judgment is to consider how difficult it is to specify the novel's controlling significance. It is possible to trace the assumptions behind Hawthorne's treatment of utopian radicalism; to observe the partial success with which he has drawn figures appropriate to the utopian community and has noticed the relationship between politics and sex, ideology and utopia as they take shape in such an environment. But none of this is yet to see the book as a coherent work of art, a disciplined whole that is informed by a serious moral interest—and that, I think, is precisely what cannot be done.

One can, to be sure, offer a number of generalized thematic statements. But it is not possible closely to relate Hawthorne's serious thematic intentions with most of the happenings in the book, which consist of mistaken identities belatedly discovered, secret marriages long repented of, spiritual exercises and hypnotic experiments, melodramatic suicides and Gothic flim-flam. Between the serious matter, confined mostly to the first fifty pages, and a tedious gim-crack plot there is seldom any vital relation.

How then are we to account for this radical incoherence?

In a recent essay on Hawthorne, Philip Rahv has written that "the emotional economy" of *The Blithedale Romance* "is throughout one of displacement . . . the only genuine relationship is that of Coverdale to Zenobia: the rest is mystification. But the whole point of Coverdale's behavior is to avoid involvement." The remark is keen, though I would qualify it by adding that there does seem to be one other relationship which for Coverdale has elements of risk and involvement: his aborted discipleship to Hollingsworth. He draws back from Zenobia's personal freedom, he draws back from Hollingsworth's political commitment, and in both cases he finds reasons, often good enough in their own right, with which to rationalize his timidity. Zenobia and Hollingsworth together stand for "the world," the dangerous beckoning world of experience and liberation. To cheat Coverdale of these temptations, Hawthorne must end the novel by drowning Zenobia and breaking Hollingsworth's spirit.

And yet . . . one feels drawn to the book, to its sudden sparks of perception, its underground passions. Henry James saw enough possibilities in its subject to base one of his major novels upon it: *The Bostonians*, in many ways, is the masterpiece that Hawthorne's book might have been. But even James did not exhaust its possibilities, and if ever a novel is written that dives beneath the surface of political life in 20th century America its author may find a storehouse of hidden reserves in Hawthorne's great failure *The Blithedale Romance*.

Henry Adams: Politics and Nausea

Henry Adams knew American politics through birthright, but by the time he came to compose *Democracy*, in 1879, he also knew it from close and painful observation. He had spent several years in Washington, at the rim of the political trough, and if he had not plunged his arm in, he had dipped a few fingers. For the remainder of his life he seemed to feel that he could never wipe them clean, and he suffered, sardonically and a little self-pityingly, from a nausea he could neither release nor suppress. The play of social manners which lights *Democracy* and the current of intellectual contempt which darkens it were both the result of his application to the *task*, for so he now conceived it, of seeing things from the outside. In the America that had honored the name of Adams as few others, he chose to live and write as an alien; but it was neither a light-hearted nor a whimsical choice. He assumed the posture of estrangement because it seemed to him the only way of preserving the integrity of the tradition that had brought his grandfather and great-grandfather to the centers of American power. *Democracy*, a novel as congenial to its time as a prophet to a barbecue, is filled with the reverberations of the clash between Adams' moral expectations and the grotesque realities of American machine politics, though the book testifies not so much to the trauma of this meeting as to Adams' effort to compose himself after the trauma. At times one feels that if Adams had been somewhat less successful in simulating the tone of composure, if he had allowed a little more of the original pain and anger to break through, it would have been a better book.

For if read simply as a novel it suffers from the thinness of texture that, inevitably, is the price of composing fiction as an illustration rather than a representation; it is the point, far more than the people, that Adams really cares about. And his concern with corruption in government—though merely, as it turns out, a surface concern—may strike one as too much ado about a problem that, by our standards, seems quite innocent. Yet it would be a pity to read the novel in this way: *Democracy* can take only a rather light application of the historical sense, it is a book that must be salvaged from its context.

It is not, of course, a political novel in the way *The Possessed* or *Virgin Soil* or *Felix Holt* may be said to be a political novel. Classes in combat, voices threatening from the social depths, intellectuals yearning to reach "the people" —not these are the ghosts that haunt Henry Adams. The best thinking of the young republic had concerned itself with procedures of and, often, against government rather than with strategies for insurgent or imperilled classes; and the corruption that troubled Adams was far less the corruption of the till than of the mind. It was the pall of good-natured mediocrity, sanctioned by the popular will and awesome in its indifference to the idea of self-doubt, that outraged him; it was the uniquely American complacence—the aptitude of the democratic mind for self-congratulation—which de Tocqueville had noticed a few decades earlier and which, by the time of Grant and Hayes, had visibly thickened. The question the book implicitly raised was relevant not merely to

American politics but to the whole of American experience: how, in this atmosphere, can an intelligent man survive?

In writing *Democracy* Adams refused—I think it was at least as much a refusal as a failure—to commit himself to the needs of the novel as a form; he was not prepared for and, except perhaps in *The Education*, would never permit that surrender to the imagination which is implicit in the literary act. He needed always to be in tight control, and always to manifest this control through the polished composure of his style. And because he could not take the novelist's risk—that the imagination will bring to awareness more than he means it to—Adams often showed a distinct impatience with the demands of the novel. At times, his amateur's impatience reminds one, rather oddly, of the professional's weariness in Turgenev's last novels: both know where the imagination should be called into play yet neither is able to do so.

Adams' style is hard, clear, witty, pungent; it almost covers the gaps in his novel; but his cool elegance often suggests a withdrawal from his subject rather than an immersion in it. His elegance comes to seem a token of embarrassment and contempt; very rarely, of pathos. The style turns into an enemy of the novel, shaping its meaning and constricting its emotion more than Adams intended; it reveals his fear of the psychic hazards that would arise from a genuine struggle with his materials; and it makes his response to politics that of an esthete rather than a moralist, giving him too high-perched and nose-pinched an air.

Adams speaks through three voices in the novel: first, as the cultivated but unoccupied heroine, Mrs. Lee ("there was a very general impression in Washington that Mrs. Lee would like nothing better than to be in the White House"); second as Nathan Gore, a disabused historian retiring from politics half in sorrow and more in petulance (he has frequently been taken as a portrait of James Russell Lowell, but in the structure of the novel he serves as a chorus of intellectual disapproval, expressing the formal ideas about democratic government that Adams would like to set up against his drama of democratic corruption); and third, in his own right, the narrator and skilled observer given to such slightly sour jokes as "democracy . . . is the government of the people, by the people, for the benefit of Senators." The problem that is sounded through all of these is the problem of participation: what place is there for a sensitive person in a government devoted to swilling? But this problem is never sufficiently explored, for Mrs. Lee is too naive, Gore too stiff and weak, and Adams himself given to fastidious *longueurs*.

Mrs. Lee begins bravely enough, wanting, as Adams puts it,

to see with her own eyes the action of primary forces; to touch with her own hand the massive machinery of society; to measure with her own mind the capacity of the motive power. She was bent upon getting to the heart of the great American mystery of democracy and government . . . What she wished to see, she thought, was the clash of interests, the interests of forty millions of people and a whole continent, centering at Washington; guided, restrained, controlled or unrestrained and uncontrollable, by men of ordinary mould . . . What she wanted, was POWER.

With an appetite apparently so imposing, she descends upon Washington, open to enlightenment and experience. There she establishes a salon for the wits of the capital, who include European diplomats politely cynical about "the American experiment," and, in a more dour tone, her distant cousin Carrington, a ruined Southern lawyer who serves Adams as a counterweight of chivalrous integrity against the gross and grabbing Northerners. Senator Silas Ratcliffe, a leading mid-Western politician, is also drawn to this salon. He hopes to win Mrs. Lee and thereby acquire both a distinguished partner for a possible residence at the White House and a mentor in taste who will nurture and guide his dim yearnings toward cultivation.

There are fine scenes in which Ratcliffe is baited by a European diplomat for making the *unforgivable* error of confusing Voltaire with Molière, and others in which he is seen in his squalid, lonely "rooms" lined with oilcloth and crammed with job-seekers stationed near spittoons. Later, when he listens to Mrs. Lee's friends chatter about art, Ratcliffe wishes he "understood precisely what tones and half-tones, colors and harmonies, were." His effort to subjugate Mrs. Lee, conducted with the elaborate strategy of a political campaign, forms the central action of the novel. It is an effort that almost succeeds, for Mrs. Lee, with more time and intelligence on her hands than experience, is impressed by his looming masculine power and sometimes even by his sonorous rhetoric. In the end Ratcliffe is thwarted only because Carrington, by breaching the code of his profession, proves to Mrs. Lee that the Senator had once accepted bribes. Shocked by this discovery, Mrs. Lee abandons Washington and returns to the amenities of private life.

The situation has been set up for tension, but does not build into tension. Adams does not sufficiently let go, nor does he quite see through the characters who think and speak for him. It is hard to extend Mrs. Lee the sympathy she solicits—for having put her pretty fingers near the fire, what could she expect but to be singed? (Nor is the case improved by her thinking she has been charred.) Carrington is a stick, a clump of Southern furniture. Henry James, in *The Bostonians,* was also to use a Southerner as a counterweight to the busy scheming North, but one need only read the caustic sentences James heaped upon him to see that, unlike Adams, he was not taken in by his own devices. And as for Gore, he does little but stand on the side-lines, where he is allowed one or two impressive declarations but is neither vibrant in his own right nor significantly related to the main action of the book.

Ratcliffe, however, is very powerful, and more so, I suspect, than Adams meant him to be. Whenever his gross and massive figure lumbers into sight, the book comes triumphantly alive, for Adams, himself a little abashed before this wicked old man, senses that no measure of contempt, no clever or cutting phrase, can call into question his enormous vitality—which may suggest that when a writer lacks the energies of love he would do well to turn immediately to hate. What Ratcliffe possesses so abundantly, and far more so than any of his opponents, is experience—the experience of a man for whom nothing has been prepared or easy, a man who has had

to make his own life. And while experience does not constitute a moral quantity, it has a way of confounding moral
assumptions. Not that Adams intends Ratcliffe to defeat his
opponents, nor that he actually does so—that is not my claim.
But surely as we watch him maneuvering, ponderously and
shrewdly, between his political interests ("The beauty of his
work consisted in the skill with which he evaded questions of
principle") and his budding private desires ("He felt that
Mrs. Lee was more necessary to him than the Presidency itself; he could not go on without her; he needed human com-
panionship; some Christian comfort for his old age . . ."),
we cannot help feeling that here at least is a man who, in his
own dubious way, has lived, has plunged, has taken risks.

The arguments allowed Ratcliffe are too good for the figure
he is supposed to cut. That morality must be complicated by
political necessity or expediency ("Only fools and theorists
imagine that our society can be handled with gloves or long
poles"), seems to me true; but surely this difficult and dangerous point of view deserves a better defender than Ratcliffe
and is not, in any case, necessarily dependent on his kind of
political behavior. And against Ratcliffe, Adams has surpris-
ingly little to offer. Because Adams had seen the social basis
of his family's politics washed away by industrialism, he re-
treated to a pose of aggrieved moralism which, despite the
obvious intelligence and integrity behind it, could not help
turning sour from lack of any possibility for realizing it in action. Mrs. Lee, in the shrewd phrase of R. P. Blackmur, represents "the intelligence which is willing to tamper with the
actual without being willing to seize it." She is shocked to discover that the source of Ratcliffe's power is, in part, corruption
—though she lacks the acuteness to see that it is also far more
than that. She does not trouble to recognize that Carrington
too has employed deceit in order to expose Ratcliffe, or for
that matter, that the source of her comfortable income may be
as tainted as the source of Ratcliffe's vulgar power. In the
end, this charming but dilettantish woman "had got to the
bottom of this business of democratic government, and found

out that it was nothing more than government of any other kind"—a conclusion neither weighty nor accurate.

At other times Adams was to realize the futility of the simple moralistic pose he struck in *Democracy*, and to recognize that against the Ratcliffes of this world more supple weapons are needed. For though in the end Ratcliffe is caned by a European diplomat who despises his vulgarity (which strikes one as rather petulant evidence of Adams' inability to deal with him dramatically or intellectually), it is he, the shamed politician, who retains the field and his opponents who flee. This, of course, does not give him a moral victory, but to anyone concerned with more than easy gestures it raises the most grievous moral problems. Adams himself would seem to realize as much, since in the undisposed figure of Nathan Gore he has tried to create a force of resistance to the whole despairing drift of his book. With "the energy of despair" Gore declares his faith in democracy:

I accept it. I will faithfully serve and defend it. I believe in it because it appears to me the inevitable consequence of what has gone before it. Democracy asserts that the masses are now raised to higher intelligence than formerly . . . I grant it is an experiment, but it is the only direction society can take that is worth taking; the only conception of its duty large enough to satisfy its instincts; the only result that is worth an effort or a risk.

Eloquent as this speech is, and reflecting as it does a deep bias of Adams' mind, it remains a mere speech. Nowhere in the book is it dramatically embodied in a figure who might struggle in behalf of its assumptions and thereby bring a significant quantity of opposition to Ratcliffe's ideas and activity. The "experiment" Mrs. Lee had undertaken proves insufficiently an experiment, there is not enough intellectual uncertainty or dramatic risk. The book lacks moral tension. Perhaps, however, Adams was capable only of seeing everything in society that made a mockery of Gore's speech—and as for the speech itself, only of repeating it. In any case, *Democracy* makes its claim upon us less as a dramatization of political life than as a gesture of political withdrawal and helplessness.

Since Adams wrote, politics in America has become heavier with ideology, though far less so than in Europe. The peculiar position of this country still permits the luxury of a party system unrelated to alignments of principle; as one character in *Democracy* brilliantly remarks, "You Americans believe yourselves to be excepted from the operation of general laws." Indeed, our unique form of egotism is to take transient advantages for transcendental virtues. But the direction of American politics may yet turn toward Europe, and if it does Adams' famous "mood," partly evident in *Democracy* and fully in *The Education*, will seem justified as an anticipation of the age of ideology. That he may have been wrong about the second law of thermodynamics or the role of the Virgin in medieval life, hardly matters; he was right about something far more important, the feelings that led him to speculate about the second law and the Virgin.

Henry James: Politics and Character

The theme of estrangement, which receives treatments so varying in *The Blithedale Romance* and *Democracy*, appears again in James' great novel, *The Bostonians*. The debt to Hawthorne's earlier work is obvious, and at least similarities can be noted between *The Bostonians* and Adams' novel. James, who had fewer hopes or illusions than most American writers, shared in the feeling of distance and separation that Hawthorne and Adams had expressed, yet he found a way of avoiding its literary price; he found a way of avoiding that surrender to the "evasive tendency," that withdrawal from the urgencies of the subject matter, which occurs about midway through so many American novels dealing with the life of politics.

James generally started a novel with a clear sketch in mind of his essential themes and structure. In a notebook entry for 1883 he wrote concerning the relationship of Olive Chancellor and Verena Tarrant that it "should be a study of one of those friendships between women which are so common in New England." After remarking that the idea for the book had been suggested to him by Daudet's *Évangéliste*, he goes on to say:

If I could only do something with that *pictorial* quality. At any rate, the subject is very national, very typical. I wished to write a very *American* tale, a tale very characteristic of our social conditions, and I asked myself what was the most salient and peculiar point in our social life. The answer was: the situation of women, the decline of the sentiment of sex, the agitation on their behalf.

What is more, the device through which James generally works out a disciplined relation to his material—the strict confinement of a novel's "point of view" to one or two observing characters—does not seem to interest him very much in *The Bostonians.* Judged by narrowly "Jamesian" standards, *The Bostonians* might even be said to suffer from an undisciplined pictorial looseness. If so, we have every reason to be grateful. Much of its charm, even some of its wit, comes from James' affectionate rendering of places and scenes. The elegance of Olive Chancellor's drawing room, the dinginess of the Cambridge street in which the Tarrants live, the glimmering mildness of Cape Cod in the summer—these are among the permanent values of the book. The musty mumbling circle of reformers meeting, and sagging, in Miss Birdseye's rooms, the wonderful and gently satirized Miss Birdseye as she summons the heroic past of Abolitionism, the moment when Ransom and Verena stand gravely before the scroll of the dead in Memorial Hall, the brutal clash between Ransom and Olive at Verena's New York debut—these scenes, etched with a dry clarity, stay fresh and alive in one's mind.

But even in terms of strict loyaly to his theme, James was entirely right in turning to the pictorial method. The dramatic concentration that is gained from seeing an action through the eyes of one or two observers is sometimes possible in *The Bostonians,* and then the camera narrows down to the blighted vision of Olive Chancellor or Basil Ransom. But such a narrowing is not always desirable. For *The Bosto-*

nians as conceived, and its first 150 pages as written, it is essential that we gain a sense of the larger workings and rhythms of society, which in most of James' novels, confined as they are to private dramas, he can afford to skimp. One of the ways, for example, in which James suggests that the glories of Abolitionism and the Boston reform movements are a thing of the past is by showing us the slowly accumulating seediness of the city itself as it stumbles into the factory age:

> [From Olive Chancellor's window one could see] a few chimneys and steeples, straight, sordid tubes of factories and engine-shops, or spare, heavenward finger of the New England meeting house. There was something inexorable in the poverty of the scene, shameful in the meanness of its details, which gave a collective impression of boards and tins and frozen earth, sheds and rotting piles, railway-lines striding flat across a thoroughfare of puddles . . . loose fences, vacant lots, mounds of refuse, yards bestrewn with iron pipes, telegraph poles and bare wooden backs of places.

Apart from such superb descriptive passages, James' yielding to the pictorial impulse makes possible a treatment of character that sets *The Bostonians* apart from most of his other novels. James' excessive identification with the weakness and deprivations of his more vulnerable characters— which mars such books as *Roderick Hudson, The Portrait of a Lady* and *The Princess Casamassima*—is here no problem at all. There are no "poor shabby gentlemen" in *The Bostonians* over whom James can quiver and softly moan, no brave American girls trapped in the moral pits of Europe. The luxury of renunciation, one of the few to which James was ever susceptible, does not tempt him in *The Bostonians,* for the characters of this novel do try to live by their desires. In *The Bostonians* James keeps his distance, often a quite cool and hostile distance, from almost all of his characters; he is not, in any damaging sense, involved with their destinies.

But James' concern with the pictorial does something even more remarkable for *The Bostonians.* It allows him a free and happy release of aggressive feelings such as he seldom ventures in his other novels: he needn't in *The Bostonians*, "consider" his characters too tenderly, they are fair game, at times mere objects of satire—and it would be sanctimonious to deny that James finds a distinct pleasure, or that we share it, in swooping down on the intellectual frauds and quacks of Boston. When we first meet Olive Chancellor, we are told that a smile playing about her lips "might have been likened to a thin ray of moonlight resting upon the walls of a prison." Selah Tarrant, mesmerist father of Verena, "looked like the priest of a religion that was passing through the stage of miracles"; Matthias Pardon, the poisonous reporter, "regarded the mission of mankind upon earth as a perpetual evolution of telegrams." In such sentences, and in the passages from which they are drawn, the prose races forward with a spontaneous sharpness and thrust, it breathes an assurance that permits James to risk, and control, the broadest touches of burlesque.

The qualities I have related to James' striving for pictorial effects are central to the book, and all of them contribute to its underlying tone or attitude. *The Bostonians* is infused with skepticism, not only in regard to New England reformers but also to the claims and pretensions of American society as a whole. The idea of social reform is treated less with hostility—for it isn't ideas as such that form his main target—than with cool and ironic misgivings. This may be offensive to our liberal or radical pieties, but there, as James might say, it is. Nor is the offense to conservative pieties any the less, for it is precisely the conservative mood of the book that brings it into severe conflict with conservative doctrine.

James' skepticism is that of a man who is living, and knows he is living, in the backwash of a great historical moment. It is the skepticism of a man who in his own life has known something about the reformers of yesterday (many of them friends of his father, Henry James, Sr., himself one of the more attractive figures of the Emersonian Age) and who wants little to do with them, except perhaps to honor their memories. Though entirely nonpolitical in the ordinary sense, James had been a warm partisan of the North during the Civil War, and the fact that the years of sacrifice and consecration had been followed by a time in which mediocrity and downright venality dominated national life, had left a scar upon his consciousness. James, to be sure, felt none of the frustration at having been brushed aside by the politics of his time that ate into the heart of Henry Adams, but he understood—or sensed—the nature of the social and moral changes that were brushing aside people like Adams. The bitterness that rises from every page of Adams' *Democracy* is a far more intense emotion that the skepticism of *The Bostonians*, but given the differences in temperament, character and ambition of the two men, they still share many implicit attitudes toward the America of the 1870's and 1880's. Both stand on the margin of American society, estranged from its dominant powers, helpless before the drift toward a world of industry and finance, money and impersonality. Only, Adams grows heart-sick watching the death of the earlier America to which he is emotionally pledged, while James finds a kind of solace, to say nothing of a remarkable fulfillment, in the practice of his art.

The Bostonians charts the parallel disarrangement, sometimes verging on a derangement, of public and private, political and sexual life. James was bold enough to see that the two spheres of experience could not be kept apart, and that it would be a fatal error for a novelist if he tried to. He was even bolder in supposing that the ideological obsessions which form so constant a peril for public life will leave their mark, not merely on social behavior, but also on the most intimate areas of private experience.

This boldness of observation is beautifully mirrored in James' prose. Because he is so thoroughly in command of the relation between public and private experience, James can allow himself an epigrammatic swiftness and "hardness" of style that is rare in both his earlier and his later work. For he is writing on the secure assumption that the social surface can be made to yield the necessary clues as to what is happening beneath it—and this may help explain why in *The*

Bostonians James is so much less concerned than in his other novels with getting to the "essence" of characters and situations, why he places a higher value on the outer grain and texture of experience. It is for similar reasons that neither Olive Chancellor nor Basil Ransom changes very much in the course of the novel, and that no revelation is made of previously unseen depths in their characters. Both are essentially the same at the end as they were at the beginning, except that one has triumphed and the other has been defeated; and it is precisely to the clash leading to the triumph and the defeat that our main attention is directed. We are concerned here primarily with the terms of their struggle and concerned on the assumption that in the hands of a writer like James, this will tell us all we need to know.

In seeing how ideology can penetrate even the most private areas of experience, James anticipated one of the great insights of psychoanalytic theory: that the price of a complex civilization is often the complex diminution of pleasure. And he understood, as well, that civilization seems to take a malicious delight in exacting this price from those most intent on reforming it. All the major characters in *The Bostonians*—Olive Chancellor, through her need to reject both the masculine and feminine modes of life, Verena Tarrant, through her need to believe in the wisdom of those who make demands on her, Basil Ransom, through his need to proclaim his masculinity as if it were a manifesto—are victims not only of each other but also of themselves. Olive Chancellor is an open enemy of the pleasure principle, because she knows it cannot be reconciled with her peculiar brand of feminism; Verena Tarrant is a befuddled enemy, because she has "bad lecture-blood in her veins"; and even Basil Ransom, the one character ready to invoke the pleasure principle, does not and cannot really live by it.

The Bostonians, said James, was to be concerned with "the decline in the sentiment of sex"—a phrase that can be read in at least two ways. One of them would point to the problematic status of women in modern society, the other to the equally problematic relation between pleasure and civilization. Not one of the people in *The Bostonians* has a secure sense—so secure, that is, as to require neither affirmation nor discussion—of what his culture expects from him in his sexual role. All of them are displaced persons, floating vaguely in the large social spaces of America.

What one notices first is the extent to which a breakdown has occurred in the traditional role of women—a role more exalted in national legend than in actuality. And while Basil Ransom is ready to talk about the proper place of women, who are for him the solacing and decorative sex, James is far too much a realist to suggest that they can or ever will again assume this place: even Ransom's lady relatives in Mississippi, deprived of their darkies, have been reduced to hard work. If Ransom is expressing James' views at all, it is in a style so deliberately inflated as to carry the heaviest ironic stress. In the hidden depths of the novel there may be some notion of what a harmonious relationship between the sexes should be, but it is not the relationship Ransom advocates and, except for vague intimations of a comely conservatism, it is not a relationship James could easily have specified. Nor was there any reason why he should have. It was enough that he so brilliantly observed the dislocations of sentiment and status which create, in almost all the characters of the novel, a nagging, distinctly "modern" anxiety.

Part of the humor in *The Bostonians*—at times, it must be admitted, a rather hard-spirited humor—comes from James' quickness at seizing upon those large glaring elements of the ridiculous that were inherent in the feminist movement and, for that matter, in the whole feminine effort to find new modes of social conduct. Yet James is fair enough to grant that feminism cannot be understood as if it were a mere sport of the New England mind. That such a movement could hardly avoid neurotic and morbid contaminations seems obvious enough: no social movement can. But this fact would hardly be very interesting if James did not also see feminism as inseparable from the conditions of American culture, as emblematic of a social and moral malaise. James understood that, while his immediate task was to focus on whatever might be strange and eccentric in his subject, his final aim could only be to present a critical vision of American life.

Far from indulging any notions about "eternal" wars between the sexes—Olive Chancellor and Basil Ransom can hardly be said to represent the sexes!—James established his drama in the actualities of late 19th century American life. The form, the tone, the quality of feminism in *The Bostonians* is not to be imagined as existing anywhere and at any time but those specified by James—which is to say that it is part of the vast uprooting of American life which begins after the Civil War and has not yet come to an end.*

If, then, *The Bostonians* is concerned with dramatizing a parallel disarrangement of social and sexual life, what are we to make of the underlying view of society or, if you wish, of human behavior from which the book is written?

Part of the answer, I think, has already been suggested. James writes from a conservative skepticism that is more readily understood as a cultural value than as an explicit politics. This conservative skepticism is a remnant of politics, not his own, but that of his family and tradition, which James is perhaps repudiating but more likely shedding. Like many writers who appear after an age in which politics has been important, James registers a certain impatience with the idea or the need for politics. And like the good innocent American that on one side of himself he was to remain throughout his life, James is also registering an uneasy contempt for the very idea of "public life," which for him would always be at odds with private values.

At times this comes rather close to being an esthetic (perhaps even an esthete's) reaction to the life of politics, a judg-

---

* The disposition to speak of society in metaphors drawn from personal life was to remain with James throughout his career. Some twenty years after *The Bostonians*, he wrote of devastated Richmond:

"The femininization is there just to promote for us some eloquent antithesis; just to make us say that whereas the ancient order was masculine, fierce and mustachioed, the present is at most a sort of sick lioness who has so visibly parted with her teeth and claws that we may patronizingly walk all around her."

ment of one area of experience in terms of another, which is almost always a dangerous kind of judgment to make. One of the few times that James relaxes his hostility to Olive Chancellor is the moment she draws back from the feminists because they offend, not her moral sense, but her fastidious sensibility. Throughout the book there are occasions in which James seems to be applying small measures to large matters, judging difficult social and moral issues by esthetic criteria a little too neat for the job.

But both his conservative skepticism and his occasional estheticism are secondary to the perception that lies at the heart of the novel: that somehow, for reasons he cannot quite grasp, the proportions and rhythms of life in America have gone askew. In the mass industrial society that was coming into existence toward the end of the 19th century, the role of the sexes with regard to one another was no longer clear, the centers of authority and affection had become blurred, the continuity of family culture was threatened, but most important of all: the idea of what it meant to be human had come into question. All that we have since associated with industrial society was moving into sight—call it depersonalization or *anomie*, the sapping of individuality or the loss of tradition. James could not quite meet this problem through a frontal attack, but in *The Bostonians* he approached it in his own way. He did not specify the social coordinates, the fundamental causes, of the problem, but he dramatized and elaborated it with a critical sharpness that no American novelist has yet surpassed. Basil Ransom, the recalcitrant Southerner, was a convenient device for marshalling the possibilities of opposition to things as they were: he appealed to James' sense of complaint and his sense of humor; but it went no further, James' irony spared him no less than it spared anyone else in *The Bostonians*.

For a writer who is often said to shy away from physical experience, James, in *The Bostonians*, seems remarkably aware of the female body. It is an awareness that comes into play somewhat negatively, since he is presenting a singularly unattractive group of women; but his acute and witty apprehension of their sexlessness or their sexual distortions would be quite impossible if he did not have in reserve a sense of sexual possibilities.

Mrs. Luna's "hair was in clusters of curls, like bunches of grapes, her tight bodice seemed to crack with vivacity." Verena Tarrant, predictably, has "a flat young chest" and Miss Birdseye "no more outline than a bundle of hay." Dr. Prance is "spare, dry, hard, . . . If she had been a boy she would have borne some relation to a girl, whereas Dr. Prance appeared to bear none whatever." Olive Chancellor's appearance is deliberately left vague, except for the clue given our sense of catastrophe when we learn, upon her first meeting with Ransom, of "the vague compassion which [her] figure excited in his mind."

Not only do these descriptions quiver with a life of their own, they also point to the social relations and complications that James is trying to illuminate. The disarrangements of society, as sometimes the obsessions of politics, are embodied in the often deformed and grotesque sexual lives of the characters, and particularly the women.

Mrs. Luna, that bound and bulging female, claims to command the traditional resources of her sex, but the claim is so preposterous as to become a subject for comic by-play. She seems always to have just emerged from the armory of her boudoir, wielding the weapons of sexual calculation with so absurd a belief in their power that they quite obliterate her personal sex. ("Mrs. Luna was drawing on her gloves; Ransom had never seen any that were so long; they reminded him of stockings, and he wondered how she managed without garters at the elbows.") Yet she is at least as far as any woman in the novel from the norm of womanliness James seems to have intended, for her sexuality has turned rancid, it has been corrupted into a strategy for social acquisition.

For all the moral and psychological differences between them, Mrs. Luna and Olive Chancellor occupy symmetrical points of distance from their society: it is hardly an accident that James imagined them as sisters who despise one another.

Olive Chancellor regards the sexual impulse as an enemy of her purpose, Mrs. Luna employs it as a convenience of her ego. In Olive the sexual impulse has been starved by her radical fanaticism, in Mrs. Luna it has been debased by her conservative parasitism. Olive feels nothing but aggression toward society, Mrs. Luna wishes merely to appropriate its comforts. Nonetheless, Olive's rejection of the feminine role and Mrs. Luna's exploitation of it have many elements in common. Both are self-betrayed in their life as women, the one through the grandeur of ideology and the other through the paltriness of vanity. Neither really "belongs" anywhere, Olive keeping a finicky distance from the reformers with whose cause she identifies, Mrs. Luna being unable to break into the elegant social circles to which she aspires. And in both women the waste of sexual power is paralleled by a social malaise that seeps into their very souls, leaving one of them embittered and the other petulant.

Except for the still impressionable Verena, all the women in the novel seem, by intent, off-center and abnormal, lacking in womanliness or femininity. Dr. Prance, for example, represents an extreme possibility of feminism; she is a comic grotesque, rather likable for her blunt commonsense but also frightening in her disciplined incapacity for emotion. She is a *reductio*, though hardly *ad absurdum*, of feminism, a warning of what it could become if driven to its extreme. For she has done what Olive Chancellor would like to do but cannot quite manage: she has totally denied her life as a woman. This, James seems to be saying, is how you may yet prance, dear ladies—like the good and terrible Mary Prance.

But James was too shrewd an observer, and too skilled a novelist, to set off against this grim spectre of feminism an ideal or idealized figure of feminine loveliness. Verena Tarrant has little but her promise, and her promise consists of little but her malleability. If all the other characters are seen in their activity, she alone is treated in terms of her "essence," so that no matter how much her outer, social being has been tarnished by the quackery of Boston there remains a pure feminine center, available to none but Basil Ransom.

If James meant Verena as the one "positive" moral force, the one figure toward whom our response should be more sympathetic than ironic, he failed; for she is unable—she simply is not interesting enough—to assume so crucial a role. But if she is intended mainly as a charming creature over whose imperilled innocence a violent battle of ideologies is being fought, he brilliantly succeeded. For seen in this way Verena need exert no active power, she need only be more attractive and receptive than the other women—which, in the circumstances, is not very difficult.

Still, James is not given to romantic idealizations in *The Bostonians* and even toward Verena, one of its few attractive figures, he can show a healthy disrespect. In a chilling passage toward the end of the novel, he proves himself quite aware that even at its most apparently innocent the feminine character can have a biting malice of its own and an aggressiveness that is almost as great a threat to male assurance as the open assaults of the feminists. When Verena asks Ransom, "Why don't you write out your ideas?", James remarks with a stress that is unmistakable: "This touched again upon the matter of his failure; it was curious how she couldn't keep off it, hit it every time." And this, we may surmise, will be Verena's role in the future; to "hit it off every time," her all too normal contribution to the felicities of domestic life in America.*

But it is through Olive Chancellor that James registers the full and terrible price that is paid by a first-rate intelligence as it is ravaged by social disorder and psychological obsession. Her condition is analyzed with so fine a touch that for a time it almost seems true, as some critics have argued, that she is merely the sum of her symptoms. Finally, however, it is

---

* The idea that passive femininity can subdue male energy as aggressive feminism cannot is another link between *The Blithedale Romance* and *The Bostonians*. In Hawthorne's novel the saturnine reformer, Hollingsworth, is finally captured and tamed by Priscilla, a pale New England maiden who, like Verena, has been involved in mesmerist exercises. Toward the Priscilla-Verena figure and all that she stands for Hawthorne betrays a deeper, if more cautious, hostility than James: he had more at stake.

not at all true, for precisely the ruthlessness in James' treatment of Olive, his refusal, except perhaps at the very end, to offer her a shred of sympathy, drives him to the most intense dramatization of her predicament. Were he sympathetic to Olive, James could risk a number of literary short cuts, but being hostile he must, for persuasion's sake, depict and penetrate and comment with a particular fullness.

Conceiving of herself as a St. Theresa of Beacon Hill, Olive is afflicted with a yearning for martyrdom that can find no satisfactory release, if only because she cannot bear to acknowledge the private and contaminated sources of this yearning. Her rejection of femininity goes far beyond a distaste for the traditional status of women: it is part of her fundamental impatience with the elementary conditions of human life. ("It was the usual things of life that filled her with silent rage; which was natural enough inasmuch as, to her vision, almost everything that was usual was iniquitous.") She rejects the idea of "the natural," either as fact or category. Olive's sexual ambiguity, like her social rootlessness, is in part due to her fastidious incapacity for accepting any of the available modes of life. It would be a gross error to see her feminist ideas simply as a rationalization for her private condition, since part of what she says—it might be remembered—happens to be true. Partly her rebellion *is* against society, but her mistake is to suppose it entirely against society; she does not see—how can she bear to see?—that it is also against herself, and not merely against that which, by accident or luck, is misshapen in herself but against all that is biologically "given" or conditioned in human life.

Olive's lesbianism becomes both cause and emblem of her social incapacity. Though James hardly presents heterosexual relations in any ideal light, he implies that they at least make possible sustained and regular communication between human beings, thereby becoming one of the tacit means by which society is knit together. Olive's lesbianism, however—partly because it is antipathetic to society, partly because it is suppressed—cuts her off from everyone, except for a time Verena, and renders her incapable of genuine communication in either public or private life. Only in light of this fact can one grasp how overwhelming, indeed almost shocking a humiliation James imposes upon her in the final scene where she is forced to placate an audience roaring with impatience to hear her lost and beloved Verena.

Seen from one point of view, Olive is a descendant of Hawthorne's villains—but with this crucial difference, that James realizes she commits the great sin of manipulating human beings not from some sourceless malignity but from her own clearly specified sickness and vulnerability. Actually, she is the most vulnerable figure in the book and toward the end James allows not merely an awareness of how painful her defeat is (for she is never even granted a confrontation, she is simply run away from) but also a sense that in defeat she achieves a gloomy sort of magnificence.

Her symptoms are presented with a remarkable directness: persistent hysteria, a will to power that is inseparable from a will to prostration, an unqualified aggression toward men. Her activities always demand analysis in terms of something other than their apparent meaning. When she talks about politics, we think of sex; when she talks about love, we think of the urge to power; when she talks about history, we think of humiliation. Yet, as James keeps insisting, she is a woman of attainment and rectitude—were she not at least the intellectual equal of Basil Ransom, her defeat would hardly matter. Her fanaticism is a function of a gnarled and impoverished psyche; her destructive will, the means by which ideology is transformed into hysteria. Both as a person in her own right and as the agent of a mean and narrowing culture, she is lost.

In opposition to this disordered world Basil Ransom stands for—for what? It is a temptation to see him as the representative of masculine strength, traditional order, conservative wit. Thus, one critic:

Of first-rate intelligence, completely "unreconstructed," holding "unprogressive" ideas of manliness, courage and chivalry, Basil Ransom . . . has a set of civilized principles to fall back upon . . .

Another critic:

> By choosing a Southerner for his hero, James gained an immediate and immeasurable advantage . . . When he involved the feminist movement with even a late adumbration of the immense tragic struggle between North and South, he made it plain that his story had to do with a cultural crisis . . .

> James conceived Ransom as if he were the leading, ideal intelligence of the group of gifted men who, a half-century later, were to rise in the South and to muster in its defense whatever force may be available to an intelligent romantic conservatism . . .

> [Ransom] has the courage of the collateral British line of romantic conservatives—he is akin to Yeats, Lawrence and Eliot in that he experiences his cultural fears in the most personal way possible, translating them into sexual fear, the apprehension of the loss of manhood.

These remarks seem to me an instance of how critics can be "taken in" by a character who never deluded his creator. From the very moment we see him, Basil Ransom—an opinionated provincial ("he had read Comte, he had read everything")—is treated by James with a cool and detached irony. Ransom *does* have a considerable attractiveness, if only because he is trying, by the force of his will, to extricate himself from defeat. But he can lay claim to none but personal powers; his cultural tradition is smashed and no one knows this better than he. It is true that he is free from some of the less attractive qualities of the New England mind in its decline, but neither does he command anything resembling its original power; for him, writes James, vice was "purely a species of special cases of explicable accidents." And while he lays claim to a disenchanted realism, he reveals more than a touch, as James meant he should, of the sentimental and callow. He considered that women "were essentially inferior to men and infinitely tiresome when they refused to accept the lot which men had made for them"—an example, no doubt, of the "civilized principles" upon which he can fall back.

James' tone is unmistakable. Ransom's appearance, he writes, "might have indicated that he was to be a great American statesman; or, on the other hand, [it] might simply prove that he came from Carolina or Alabama." A little later James remarks of Ransom that "he had an immense desire for success," thereby noting that side of the Southern conservative which, if given half the chance, will out-Northern the Northerners. Still later, James writes that Ransom's "scruples were doubtless begotten of a false pride, a sentiment in which there was a thread of moral tinsel, as there was in the Southern idea of chivalry . . ."

But most remarkable of all is the incident in which Ransom solemnly declares himself ready for both marriage and the future on the extraordinary ground that one of his essays has finally been accepted by "The Rational Review," a journal of which the title sufficiently suggests both its circulation and influence. If nothing else, this would be enough to convince us that Ransom is as naively and thoroughly, if not as unattractively, the victim of a fanatical obsession as Olive Chancellor—this characteristic delusion of the ideologue (the pathos of which is one of the few things that makes poor Ransom endearing) that if only his precious words once appear in print, the world will embrace his wisdom and all will be well.

Were Ransom an "ideal intelligence," the novel would be hopelessly unbalanced. For what possible drama or significance could there be in a clash between the exalted figure he would then be and so wretched an antagonist as Olive Chancellor? The truth, I would suggest, is that in his way Ransom is as deeply entangled with his ideology as Olive with hers, and that the clash between styles of culture which is supposed to be reflected in their struggle is actually a rather harsh comedy in which both sides, even if to unequal degrees, are scored off by James.

And nowhere is this truer than in Ransom's presumed "apprehension of the loss of manhood." For while it is a common assumption of our culture that the "biological" is the most profound and fundamental variety of experience, before which all else must seem pale and unreal, it is worth remembering that the biological, or the sense of it, can also become imbued with ideology. In the case of Ransom, his "apprehension of the loss of manhood," in addition to being an authentic personal emotion, is frequently part of his rhetoric of moral and intellectual aggrandizement.

This, indeed, is the great stroke of *The Bostonians:* that everything, even aspects of private experience supposedly inviolable, is shown to be infected with ideology. When Ransom, in his Central Park speech, appeals to Verena to break from Olive, he does so not merely in the name of his personal love but also through a catch-word of politics, and curiously enough one that is closer to New England radicalism than to Southern conservatism: he urges her to stand forth in the name of *personal freedom.* When Olive and Verena listen to Beethoven, "symphonies and fugues only stimulated their convictions, excited their revolutionary passion . . ."—the very music becomes a medium of ideology. Everything is touched by it, from politics to sex, from music to love.

That being so, we are in a better position to judge the complaint often made about *The Bostonians,* that there is a loss of certainty and brilliance midway through the book. It is true that *The Bostonians* does falter about half way, but only because James is not quite sure how to manage one of the boldest and most brilliant transitions of his entire work. The first 150 pages of the novel present directly a world of contention and decline; there follows a somewhat hesitant section, set mainly in New York—and then the struggle is resumed, more bitterly, more fiercely, more poisonously, on the face of it a struggle of love but in its depths a struggle of politics.

Ransom wins. Despite all of James' qualifications in regard to Ransom, he grants him certain attractions and powers. Ransom is no poor shabby gentleman watching life glide away; he is a man of energy and will, as hard as Olive and less frenetic. And for James, always a little uneasy before the more direct forms of masculine energy, there is a fascination in seeing this energy exert itself. But the logic of the book itself demands that Ransom win. For if the struggle between Ransom and Olive over Verena is a struggle between competing ideologies over a passive agent of the natural and the human, then it is a struggle between ideologies that are not equally in opposition to the natural and the human. When she is finally driven to her choice, Verena chooses in accordance with those rhythms of life which Olive bluntly violates but Ransom merely exploits. In a dazzling final sentence James writes that "It is to be feared that with the union, so far from brilliant, into which she was about to enter, these [tears] were not the last she was destined to shed." What James thought of Ransom's pretensions, what he made of the whole affair, how thoroughly he maintained the critical and ironic tone throughout the book, is suggested in this hint that Ransom and Verena, married at last, would live unhappily ever after.

From *The Blithedale Romance* to John Dos Passos' *USA*, from *Democracy* to Lionel Trilling's *The Middle of the Journey*, from *The Bostonians* to Robert Penn Warren's *All the King's Men*—is there a significant connection to be noticed here, a connection, I mean, that is more than an academic device, that helps establish a genuine continuity of interest and response in American writing?

It does not seem promising, at first sight. The distance is enormous, a chasm separates two worlds. The turning point, or breakdown, in modern history that, for purposes of dramatic simplification, can be located in 1914, surely marks us off from Americans of a century ago; and the novels that touch upon the political experience of contemporary America surely raise spectres—the spectres of totalitarianism, defeated radicalism, disabled liberalism—that are unique to us and incomprehensible in terms other than our own.

But we should not be too hasty, nor too certain. It is profitable to look upon American experience and American literature as arising from a clash between the heritage of our past and the complicating influences of European thought. True, much that contributes to 20th century American writing *is* unique, there *is* historical novelty, totalitarianism *is* unprecedented. Yet continuities remain, even amid the newness and perplexity of our time.

Consider the images of political man with which Dos Passos, Warren and Trilling end their novels. Ben Compton, a shattered revolutionary, walking the streets of New York, without belief or hope or even self-regard. Jack Burden, asking himself how he could place his trust in a puny dictator like Willie Stark and wondering, in the total isolation that has overcome him, what is to become of his life. John Laskell, waiting alone in a railroad station to begin the middle of his journey, his pieties and passions behind him, and little before him but spiritual exhaustion and a bleak integrity. The image raised by all these critical scenes is one of isolation, an isolation that a wounded intelligence is trying desperately to transform into the composure of solitude. And once every allowance has been made for the differences in the experience of mid-19th and mid-20th century America, are we not here recalled to the dilemmas and anxieties of *The Blithedale Romance, Democracy* and *The Bostonians?*

PART THREE

CHAPTER EIGHT

MALRAUX, SILONE, KOESTLER:
THE TWENTIETH CENTURY

The central event of our century remains the Russian Revolution. For a moment, one of the most fervent in all history, it stirred the hope among millions of people that mankind had at last begun to lift itself, however painfully, from the realm of necessity to the realm of freedom. That hope, like the heroic phase of the revolution from which it sprang, did not long survive, and in the literature of our time there are few direct reflections of its original intensity. A "law" of history would seem to require that a considerable time elapse before a great event can be appropriated by the creative imagination —and in this case the event had been fatally disfigured before the novelist or poet could reach it. In two books, though hardly more than two, we can still see the revolution in its pristine enthusiasm: John Reed's *Ten Days That Shook the World* and Leon Trotsky's *History of the Russian Revolution*. The first is a work of journalism, a remarkably vivid rendering of the revolution as physical experience, while the second is history in the grand style and like all histories in the grand style, also a work of the literary imagination. Apart from its claim to being a faithful record and true interpretation, Trotsky's book is one of the few in our time that is able to sustain the kind of stylistic scrutiny now reserved for Shakespeare's plays, James' novels and minor poets. The book unfolds from a simple but commanding image: the meeting of Russian worker and Russian peasant, their first hesitant gropings toward each other, the pattern of retreat and reconciliation and finally, a clasp of unity. I quote a key passage:

The workers at the Erikson, one of the foremost mills in the Vyborg district, after a morning meeting came out on the Sampsonievsky Prospect, a whole mass, 2,500 of them, and in a narrow place ran into the Cossacks. Cutting their way with the breasts of their horses, the officers first charged through the crowd. Behind them, filling the whole width of the Prospect, galloped the Cossacks. Decisive moment! But the horsemen, cautiously, in a long ribbon, rode through the corridor just made by the officers. "Some of them smiled," Kayurov recalls, "and one of them gave the workers a good wink." This wink was not without meaning. The workers were emboldened with a friendly, not hostile, assurance, and slightly infected the Cossacks with it. The one who winked found imitators. In spite of renewed efforts from the officers, the Cossacks, without openly breaking discipline, failed to force the crowd to disperse, but flowed through it in streams. This was repeated three or four times and brought the two sides even closer. Individual Cossacks began to reply to the workers' questions and even to enter into momentary conversations with them. Of discipline there remained but a thin transparent shell . . . The officers hastened to separate their patrol from the workers and, abandoning the idea of dispersing them, lined the Cossacks out across the street as a barrier to prevent the demonstrators from getting to the center. But even this did not help: standing stock-still in perfect discipline, the Cossacks did not hinder the workers from "diving" under their horses. The revolution does not choose its paths: it made its first steps toward victory under the belly of a Cossack's horse.

There is no novel of comparable stature which attempts to absorb the same experience. To be sure, the Russian Revolution had a lasting effect on the contemporary novel, as on every other phase of our life, but the effect was belated and indirect. The myth that one can see emerging from Trotsky's paragraph—I do not, of course, use myth as a polite synonym for lie—dominated the imagination of most political novelists until a very few years ago, but for the more serious writers it was largely "negative" domination, forcing them to think in terms of separation rather than unity, the split between worker and peasant rather than fraternity. The contrast between early political hope and later disillusion becomes the major theme of the twentieth century political novel: Malraux, Silone, Koestler—all are obsessed by the failure, or betrayal, of the revolution. Their books can be read as footnotes, half tragic half ironic, to Trotsky's paragraph.

I

Where Dostoevsky looked upon radicalism as a marginal conspiracy, a disease that had infected the intelligentsia and the *lumpenproletariat,* Malraux and Silone, in their major novels, recognize it as the occasion for the first independent entry of the masses into history. For Dostoevsky and Conrad the very possibility of revolution meant a catastrophic breakdown of order, a lapse into moral barbarism; for Malraux and Silone the breakdown of society is a long-accomplished and inevitable fact, and what matters now is the energy, the heroism, the pathos of the effort to achieve socialism. The view of "human nature" shared by Dostoevsky (at least the official Dostoevsky) and Conrad is one of radical pessimism: man must be strapped by ordained moral law so that the chaos within him will not break loose. Malraux's view is existentialist: man is whatever he makes himself, either in victory or defeat, and only through a chosen act can he fulfill the unmeasured possibilities of his being. For Malraux it is the appearance of millions of speechless men, climbing up from the silence of centuries, that is the overwhelming fact of our political life. From the feeble conspiracies of *The Princess Casamassima* and the feeble chatter of Peter Ivanovitch's circle in *Under Western Eyes* to the desperate revolt of the Shanghai workers in *Man's Fate*—that is the distance which the political novel, as indeed our world itself, has travelled.

The political novelist of our century feels the pressures

of ideology far more intensely than his predecessors of the nineteenth century. He sees ideology not as a symptom of some alien disease but as both the burden and challenge of history: necessary in times of social crisis, frightening in its rigor, and precisely because it can be put to such terrible uses, a temptation most dangerous to those most in need of it. Yet he recognizes that ideology must be confronted, history allows no alternative; for like some discovery of atomic physics, ideology is in itself neither good nor bad, being a mode of thought that permits the widest spectrum of moral application.

From the nineteenth to the twentieth century there is a radical shift in perspective, in the distance the political novelist establishes between himself and his materials: Conrad and James probe beneath the surface of society to measure the plebeian threat while Malraux and Silone are themselves engaged in the struggles they portray. It is significant that both Malraux and Silone were active political figures shortly before they turned to literature, this very turn itself being a political act of the most desperate kind. In a sense, the true hero of their novels is the author himself: Kyo is not Malraux nor is Pietro Spina quite Silone but the problems of Kyo and Spina are the problems of Malraux and Silone. It is from their creators that Kyo and Spina draw their obsessive need to shift the direction of history, to put, as the hero of *The Royal Way* says, "a scar on the map." The result of this personal involvement is at once a gain in political authority and a loss of subtlety and range in the traditional skills of the novel. In the work of these writers there is far less penetration into individual motives and behavior than in the novels of, say, Conrad and James— and the difference is due not merely to the greater talent of the nineteenth century authors, nor even to the advantages that Conrad and James gained from working within a still vital cultural tradition while Malraux and Silone venture into unexplored regions of mass consciousness and mass revolt; it is due, rather, to the fact that Conrad and James wrote from positions of isolated social comfort while Malraux and Silone expose themselves, they *are* in their tragedies, their blood and hope are ground into the defeated revolutions over which they mourn.

II

In one of André Malraux's earliest books, a European writes to a Chinese friend that Western man is "committed to the test of the *act*, hence pledged to the bloodiest fate." This sentence might stand as an epigraph to Malraux's career, for it leads directly to the paradox at the heart of his work: his effort to assimilate, perhaps even to "capture" history while yet refusing to acknowledge historical categories. This tension is partly a consequence of Malraux's idea that man, doomed to dissolution in a world where God and the hope for immortality have died, must live within the claustrophobic circle of his ego and can achieve certainty neither as to what he knows nor what his life means. But there is another side to Malraux, intellectually less imposing or at least less fashionable, which also tempts him into the desire to force history to its knees—I refer to his impatience with ideas, his tendency to lump them together without caring or trying to discriminate as to their possible truth, his inclination for supposing them mere facades for obscure, irrational compulsions. All of these elements are present— raw, unassimilated, rather callow, but charged with tremendous urgency—in his first political novel, *The Conquerors*.

The claim often asserted but not always demonstrated by modern critics—that the structure of a novel determines, or is a chart of, its meaning—is radically true for *The Conquerors*. A novelist turning to political life in the twentieth century cannot help being attracted by the modes and devices of journalism, for they promise him the power of immediacy. He knows, too, how imperious is the tyranny of public over private experience, how the apparently transient incident can corrode the hidden values by which men try to live. The very perspective from which he has chosen to examine human life requires him to place a valuation on *the event* that implies a sharp break from the absorption in private consciousness which has dominated the novel in the twentieth century. *The Conquerors* begins as a diary that could as well be a document or record noting a sequence of objective occurrences; it is, at the beginning, rigidly sparse and noncommittal, for its author implies that nothing anyone might say or feel could equal in significance the fact he is reporting: that in Canton and Hong-Kong thousands of Chinese workers are engaged in a general strike which has closed the ports and left British imperialism helpless. The power of the event, the necessity for acknowledging the ludicrous disproportion between historical occurrence and subjective response—these shape the nervous bits of action with which the book begins. We are to be overwhelmed by the inexorableness of what is happening, until we come to feel that nothing can be done to deflect, let alone resist, the fatality of the impersonal.

Only then is there a shift in the perspective of the novel. We begin to stumble, and then to speed, toward the subjective consciousness of its hero Garine, the character who in all of Malraux's novels seems most to embody his own attitudes and desires. For it is central to Malraux's vision of heroism in our time that the moment of trial, the gesture which defines and embodies the heroic, should come into being primarily in anticipation of defeat. The effort to mount history having failed, it becomes possible to acknowledge once again the claims of private feeling. Yet the hero, even as we now begin to see him in his vulnerability and pain, must persist in an action he now views as philosophically absured, a mere token of vanity—and not the least of its absurdity is that the enlargement of consciousness which has led to this realization is itself the product of the action to which he remains pledged. By the end of the book we have penetrated not merely to the core of subjectivity, but to a subjectivity that is sick, distraught, intolerably alone. The commitment to the impersonality of history has led, through the painful circle of paradox, to a history of personality.

Insofar as this is the scheme of the novel (I have eliminated other elements without scruple), it achieves a striking success: the sense of history in motion is conveyed with a saturating fullness. We do not doubt for a moment that we have participated in a major experience—but whether in the company of vibrant human beings is another matter.

For Malraux as a novelist, and particularly in *The Conquerors*, is guilty of a curious double standard: he is infinitely ready to accept the "given" in history yet ruthlessly imposes his metaphysical predilections on his characters, even when those predilections violate the psychological needs created in them by their participation in history. The result is that the movement of history, which we have been prepared to see as rigorously objective, takes on the freedom and even the caprice of subjectivity, while the behavior of his characters, which was to suggest the possibilities of the human will, takes on an aura of the impersonal and determined. This is particularly true for Garine, the revolutionary leader who works with the Chinese Communists yet is himself not a Marxist—a character in whom obsession is frequently in danger of declining from a living psychological trait to a metaphysical abstraction. (One might say that Garine behaves as if he had read too many of Malraux's novels.)

"Garine," writes Nicola Chiaramonte in his excellent essay on Malraux, "is a man of action unleashed. To him, 'there is only one reason that is not a parody: it is the most effective use of force,' and there is only 'one thing that counts: not to be defeated.' He says of himself that he has put 'a·complete lack of scruples at the service of something which is not my immediate interest.' An adventurer? Of a sort. But since he does not seek personal profit, since he has chosen a cause and not a career, Garine finds himself bound by laws that he cannot control. He is committed to his action and to the demons evoked by it. He cannot simply kill and send people to be killed. He must account for his acts, to himself as to others. He must follow to the bitter end the course he has chosen. If he had wanted just adventure, then he is indeed trapped: 'Those who want to soar above the earth soon come to realize that the earth sticks to their fingers.'"

Chiaramonte's analysis needs to be extended a step further. Though Garine has made a mystique out of activity and power, he must nonetheless make political choices and decisions, if only because he is a leader of a great historical action and a leader, moreover, who has begun to doubt the wisdom of its guiding strategy. He develops what we would now call Trotskyist deviations, but the rigid structure of his (or Malraux's) metaphysical pressupositions keeps him from working out the meaning of these deviations. Like most of Malraux's heroes, Garine is a highly contemplative man; but he does not think.

Given the assumptions with which Malraux organizes his novel, it is impossible for the act of critical thought to take its rightful place in the process of historical action. That is why *The Conquerors,* for all its atmospheric authenticity, lacks the kind of definition—I am not speaking of an ideological "line"—which a novel dealing with politics must have. The mystique behind Garine's loneliness, the mystique that has brought him into so poignant a conflict with the role it has assigned to him, keeps him from the act of cognition which might lead to the self-awareness that is the traditional privilege of a tragic hero in his moment of defeat.

By the time Malraux came to write *Man's Fate,* five years later, none of his fundamental dispositions had changed yet he had grown profoundly as a writer. His dominating ideas are now embodied in more humane and less compulsive forms: for one thing, they are dispersed among a richer variety of characters instead of being bundled, improbably, into one hero. But the concern with heroism remains, and *Man's Fate,* which is set in the disastrous Chinese revolution of 1927, is one of the very few novels of our time where a deliberate and, I think, successful effort is made to reach the plane of heroic action. Its protagonist, Kyo, is the best kind of pre-Stalinist revolutionary: dedicated, idealistic, intelligent enough to be concerned about the relation between his private self and the movement to which he has gladly consigned it. So far as heroic action is possible to our time, Kyo is a tragic hero: he confronts his fate despite a foreknowledge of doom, he believes that in the twentieth century death can take on heroic dimensions only if it is the necessary consequence of revolt and revolt is an act of *choice*. Not without a certain pathos, he hopes that in revolt men can establish that "virile fraternity" which enables them to live both as individual persons and in community, thereby escaping, at least in moments of crisis, the paired terrors of loneliness and anonymity. His life significantly exists for him only in terms of certain minimal conditions for dignity. Asked by the Shanghai police chief, "You want to live?" Kyo replies, "It depends how." Challenged by the police chief, "What do you call dignity?" he answers, "The opposite of humiliation."

Despite occasional drops into melodrama *Man's Fate* is a remarkably authentic account, written from "the inside," of civil war; by which I mean not that Malraux has personally participated in civil war (though he has) or that he has adhered faithfully to the Chinese events of 1927 (though he has not) but rather that he is a man who has fully reckoned the price of historical action and is prepared to pay it. I doubt that there is another novel of our time that so superbly gathers into itself the fervor and tension which a revolution can bring forth, so fully dramatizes the abrasive interlocking of private wills and their momentary communion in struggle. *Man's Fate* becomes a paean to revolution yet a strangely nonpolitical one, for Malraux is concerned with revolution not as an algebra of ideology but as an arithmetic of emotion, not primarily as a political act but as the incarnation of human desire, the first stirrings to consciousness of dormant millions. That this consciousness must now be acquired at the price of death seems insignificant by comparison with the possibility of giving "to each of these men whom famine, at this very moment, was killing like a slow plague, the sense of his own dignity." What matters most, Malraux has written, is "to tie oneself to a great action of some kind, not to let go of it, to be haunted and intoxicated by it"—and in this view the revolution becomes a deliberate engagement with death as a means for measuring the possibilities of freedom.

Malraux's conception has clear, though limited, affinities with the values one finds in Trotsky's *History of the Russian Revolution*. For Trotsky history is an almost personified force moving through time with the élan of a romantic hero, and the revolutionary party, in its moments of purity and exaltation, becomes the collective agent of historical law. The movement of history and the passion of men come together in an epiphany of struggle; the claim that there is a tragic incommensurability between history and man is for him a sterile notion hindering the immediate need to shape history. To his Marxist imagination, the possibilities of history are limited, but within the limits imposed by a given epoch there are always significant choices to be made. Malraux finds common ground with Trotsky in his emphasis on activity, Trotsky focusing on the initiative of the revolutionary party and Malraux on the initiative of the revolutionary person. By contrast, however, Malraux has a rather poor because uncultivated sense of historical movement. He rejects as "doctrinal rubbish" the Marxist claim that there is an observable order in history which enforces a sequence of limitation, for he is concerned far more with the activist term in the Marxist vocabulary, the thrust of will, than with the resistance of society or tradition.

Sometimes, however, Malraux is able to reach a deeper human vision than Trotsky: he acknowledges the authority of defeat, he offers a kind of pity, even if a rather cold and impersonal kind, while in Trotsky's pages, perhaps because they still burn with the fires of civil war, the absense of pity is a major fault. In other respects Malraux is far inferior to Trotsky: his mystique of action keeps him from making the concrete analysis of any given choice which the political mind, at its best, can make, and in *Man's Hope*, his one meretricious novel, the *literary* consequences are disastrous.

There are at least two Malrauxs: the one who gives himself irrevocably to some historical momentum and, almost always for too long a time, does not stop to wonder whether it has been deflected from its original or proclaimed purpose, and the other who knows that in all historical action blood will be shed without good reason, without recompense or possibility of recompense. Neither of these figures is interesting in himself, only through the unity of their struggle does Malraux become a significant writer. All too often, however, his infatuation with action leads him to exalt the will at the expense of the mind, thereby betraying him into a dubious adventurism. Starting with the valid, or at least defensible, assumption that in modern times inertia is a form of self-betrayal, he proceeds to the dangerous conclusion that one must follow through to the desperate end an action in which one no longer retains faith. In *Man's Hope* this leads to a contrived and shabby rationale for the brutalities of Stalinism in Loyalist Spain, an exaltation of efficiency in a context that makes it both inhuman and, finally, inefficient. But in *Man's Fate,* his one genuinely important novel, there is a delicate, often poignant counterposition of commitment and temptation, morality and politics, the individual and the collective, emotion and ideology. A counterposition but not a cancelling-out—for even as he places his hope in socialism and insists that political problems require political solutions, the author of *Man's Fate* sees life as essentially tragic: Man and Fate are the unbalanced terms in the equation of existence.

In the novel these terms are brought into clash through a hierarchy of characters. Ch'en the revolutionary terrorist cannot content himself with anonymous acts of destruction: he longs for intimate contact with his victims. In the opening scene of the novel, he is presented in a kind of terrible dumb-show: he bends over a sleeping man—unnamed, unknown, merely a person who has a paper desperately needed by the revolutionists—and prepares to kill him. No word is said, no sign exchanged between victim and executioner. All that we see of the sleeping man is his white foot extending beyond the mosquito netting: the white foot that has become a symbol of aliveness. At first Ch'en is appalled by the loneliness of his task, he desires a victim who will respond and resist. But once he strikes, he feels that strange pleasure which killing has begun to give him: "There was a world of murder and he was staying in it as if in a warm place."

The thought that he has private motives unsanctioned by his public discipline, motives that bear no relation to the revolutionary ends in whose behalf he commits his acts of terrorism, is a source of ineradicable anguish to Ch'en: he cannot accept the possibility that men engage in selfless political activity which yet releases obsessions of the self, he yearns (like Kirillov in *The Possessed*) for a purity of engagement, a monolithic correspondence between motive and act, which politics can never give and religion but rarely, if at all. Ch'en finds that the life of terrorism imposes upon him its own psychic economy: he must now stand apart from other men, including the workers in whose name he acts. Death soon seems to him the only release, for he sees no way of reentering the community of men; death becomes an appetitie, a desire; he is one of those unfortunate men who become revolutionaries not merely from conviction— his conviction is not to be doubted—but because they are inherently unable to live in ordinary society. Useful as the destructive agent of the revolution, he cannot even savor the dream of the future which sustains his comrades. He hopes only to "die on the highest possible plane."

Kyo, however, wishes to *live* on the highest possible plane, and for him the choice of death has meaning only as it follows from a passion for life. Though he chooses martydom, he is not driven by a death-wish; he acts from a sense of responsibility to his cause and himself, and not only to these but to the men whom he has helped lift to political awareness. Because he does want to live on the "highest plane" of consciousness available to him, his inner life is beset by uncertainty and anguish. Kyo is not nearly so much the victim of obsessional drives as Ch'en, yet he too faces the same disjunction between private emotion and public commitment, he too finds that the mere fact of having made a political choice, while enough for determining the shape and even the duration of his life, is not enough for determining its quality. The conflict between acting and being, the anguish of discovering that while a political man can choose his ends he cannot always settle upon the most desirable means for reaching them, the distress he feels at the increasing separation between his inner reflections and his outer motions—these are the central problems of the book, faced by all the characters in their various ways but by Kyo with the greatest intensity and intelligence.

When Kyo learns, on the day the worker's revolt is to begin, that his wife has been unfaithful to him, his outward response is an "enlightened" shrug. But within himself he is wounded, not least of all because his wife explains it as a mere act of caprice or stray pity, and he is a man who values too highly the possibilities for human relationships to accept this discounting of the sexual act. It is precisely because he knows that his wife does love him, because he realizes that in terms of his commitment he can make no pertinent objection to what she has done, that Kyo is all the more disturbed. He understands that he is experiencing a clash between his convictions and the tradition in which he has been raised, and he is too sensitive not to be troubled by the thought that his way of solving it may be pat and evasive. What matters most, however, is not the problem itself but the time of its appearance, the fact that this needle of pain should bite into his flesh at exactly the moment he must prepare for an insurrection he knows to be doomed. Even as he goes off to a collective action, he finds himself in "solitude, the inescapable aloneness."

Kyo is also troubled by political doubts: he rejects the line of the party leadership. Subordinating the workers to Chiang Kai-shek in the common struggle against the warlord government, surrendering arms to an ally who tomorrow will turn them against the workers, seems to him a catastrophic blunder—though he has not yet reached the point of asking why such blunders occur. When he travels to Hankow with Ch'en in an effort to persuade the party leadership to change its course, his independent personality is brought into strong contrast with Vologin, the Russian representative in whom one sees the revolutionary movement as it is rapidly becoming corrupted and Stalinized. Obedience, urges Vologin, is "the only logical attitude" for a revolutionist; Kyo's inner reply is voiced by Ch'en: "It's not through obedience that men go out of their way to get killed—not through obedience that they kill . . . Except cowards."

But Kyo suffers at deeper levels than those involving private unhappiness and political doubt. By nature he is a reflective man: part of him responds, because he *is* reflective, to Katov, the completely involved revolutionary, but another part is tied to his father, a man whose knowledge of suffering has driven him to opium. Kyo has the rare gift of being able to surrender himself to an historical action while observing it, in some part of himself, as if he were outside time; he senses the vanity of all action when measured against the certainty of death, yet he is also accessible to those claims for human continuity which lead men to act in behalf of values they cannot hope to see realized in their lifetime. That life may be, in some sense, absurd does not mean one should live absurdly; only through a refusal to surrender to the absurdity of the human situation can life gain a sanction beyond the clamor of appetite. Kyo's humanist disposition and his need for dignity lead him to political struggle, but also to a desparing realization that political struggle is not the true end of man's life and that he, Kyo, will not live to see any other.

Malraux acknowledges that the ideological life exacts severe moral and esthetic deprivations yet insists that without it man, in our time, is nothing. Through the character of Katov, who surrenders his pinch of cyanide to another imprisoned comrade though he knows it means his being burned alive, Malraux justifies this belief. Katov has been the least obviously humane, the most ideological of the revolutionaries; he is a professional while they are amateurs; but in his final act he proves equal to Kyo's conception of necessary heroism: here ideology, being pure and selfless, transcends itself to become something better than itself.

Katov has previously succeeded in submerging his true self into the social task, but it is Malraux's central theme that his humanity can fully emerge only when he succeeds in realizing his self through—and more important, above and beyond—his social task. Nothing in Katov's ideology, nothing in any political doctrine, requires him to make the sacrifice he does. Nothing *can* require that but his sense of being a man. Yet—and here Malraux aims a blow at the liberal humanists—it is Katov's dedication which gives him the possibility and the strength to make his sacrifice. At the very least, then, Kyo's Marxism, as embodied in Katov, helps modern man to find a proper way of dying. Katov represents not a conventional shift from ideology to humane heroism, but their ordering into a proper relationship; he comes finally to embody what the Malraux of *Man's Fate* regards as the most one can hope for in the present age: the humanization of ideology.

III

In Ignazio Silone's first novel, *Fontamara*, the image of worker and peasant, which had achieved a symbolic elevation in Trotsky's *History*, appears again, this time in a state of decomposition, its two parts split into figures of hostility. One of the few modern novels that has the genuine quality of a folk tale, or perhaps better, a comic fable, *Fontamara* tells the story of a peasant village in the Abruzzi resisting in its pathetic way the onthrusts of the Mussolini regime. To the peasants, the political problem first presents itself as one of city against country, town against village—and they are not entirely wrong, for they, the peasants, are at the very bottom, suffering the whole weight of Italian society. Simple but not simple-minded, unable to generalize very well from their suffering yet aware that they must learn to, they show an acute insight, through their complicated jokes and sly stories, into the nature of the social hierarchy. When a minor government flunkey, the Hon. Pelino, comes to gather their signatures for a petition that, as it happens, has not yet been composed, one of the peasants tells him a marvellous little fable:

"At the head of everything is God, Lord of Heaven. After him comes Prince Torlonia, lord of the earth. Then comes Prince Torlonia's armed guards. Then comes Prince Torlonia's armed guards' dogs. Then nothing at all. Then nothing at all. Then nothing at all. Then comes the peasants. And that's all."

"And the authorities, where do they come in?" (asks the Hon. Pelino.)

Ponzio Pilato interrupted to explain that the authorities were divided between the third and fourth categories, according to the pay. The fourth category (that of the dogs) was a very large one.

From their bloody experience the peasants must learn that they need the help of the town, and one way of reading *Fontamara* is as a series of explorations into, or encounters with, the town where the peasants try to discover their true allies—not the priest, who is corrupt and bloated; not the old landowners, who are being squeezed by Mussolini's agents yet remain as much as ever the enemies of the peasants; not the liberal lawyer, Don Circostanza, who betrays them with his windy rhetoric. Only when the most violent of the peasants, Berardo—it is significant that he owns no land and is therefore free from the conservative inclinations of even those peasants who have nothing more than a strip of rock or sand—only when he goes to Rome does he meet, after a series of tragi-comic blunders, the agent of the revolutionary underground. At the end of the novel, a union has been achieved—hesitant, not fully understood and quickly broken—between peasant and worker. The underground revolutionary brings to the peasants a miniature printing-press, a product of urban technology, and the peasants print one issue of a little paper called *What Is To Be Done?* As one of them explains with a truly masterful grasp of political method, the question must be asked again and again, after each statement of their plight: *They have taken away our water. What is to be done? The priests won't bury our dead. What is to be done? They rape our women in the name of the law*. What is to be done? *Don Circostanza is a bastard*. What is to be done?

The question echoes, not accidentally, the title of Lenin's famous pamphlet, in which he first outlined his plan for a disciplined revolutionary party; nor is it an accident that both Lenin's pamphlet and the paper of Silone's peasants are written in times of extreme reaction. For *Fontamara* is the one important work of modern fiction that fully absorbs the Marxist outlook on the level of myth or legend; one of the few works of modern fiction in which the Marxist categories seem organic and "natural," not in the sense that they are part of the peasant heritage or arise spontaneously in the peasant imagination, but in the sense that the whole weight of the peasant experience, at least as it takes form in this book, requires an acceptance of these categories. What makes *Fontamara* so poignant as a political legend—despite the apparent failures, upon occasion, of Silone's language to equal in richness his gift for anecdote—is that he is a *patient* writer, one who has the most acute sense of the difference between what is and what he wishes. The peasants are shown in their nonpolitical actuality and the political actuality is shown as it moves in upon them, threatening to starve and destroy them; Silone does not assume the desired relationship between the two, though he shows the possibilities for a movement into that relationship; the book is both concrete—wonderfully concrete—in its steady view of peasant life and abstract—a brilliant paradigm—in its placing of peasant life in the larger social scheme. The political theories behind the book resemble the lines signifying longitude and latitude on a map; they are not the reality, not the mountains and plains and oceans; but they are indispensable for locating oneself among the mountains and plains and oceans; they are what give the geography of society meaning and perspective.

Fontamara ends in defeat yet it exudes revolutionary hope and élan. Silone's next novel, *Bread and Wine*, is entirely different in tone: defeat is now final, the period of underground struggle at an end, and all that remains is resignation, despair and obeisance before authority. The novel's hero, Pietro Spina, who partly reflects the opinions of his creator, is a revolutionary leader who from exile has returned to the peasant areas of his native Abruzzi in order to reestablish ties with his people and see whether his Marxist theories will hold up in experience. As he wanders about the countryside, the sick and hunted Spina gradually abandons his Marxism, but not his social rebelliousness; the priest's frock that he has adopted as a disguise begins to be more than a disguise; he must fulfill the responsibilities of his public role or what appears to be his public role, and must adjust his private emotions to this necessity; he becomes or aspires to become, a revolutionary Christian saint. He asks—in the words of Albert Camus—"Is it possible to become a saint without believing in God? That is the sole concrete problem worth considering nowadays." But he sees even further than Camus: he dimly envisages, and in *The Seed Beneath the Snow* tries to realize, a fraternity beyond sainthood and then beyond good and evil.

Soon after arriving in the Abruzzi, Spina decides that the usual kinds of political propaganda are irrelevant in a fascist country. People have been misled by slogans too long and too often; they instinctively distrust all phrases. To refute the government propaganda is pointless since no one, least of all its authors, believes it. Why argue against ideas that everyone realizes to be absurd? People understand the truth well enough; it is courage and energy that they lack, not understanding; they are not ready to sacrifice themselves. Spina feels that what is now needed is not programs, even the best Marxist programs, but examples, a pilgrimage of good deeds: men must be healed, they must be stirred to heroism rather than exhorted and converted. Something more drastic, more radical than any kind of political action is needed to cope with the demoralization and corruption Spina finds in Italy.

Before coming to these conclusions Spina had already been uneasy about his political allegiance: "Has not truth, for me, become party truth? . . . Have not party interests ended by deadening all my discrimination between moral values?" The political doubts prompting these questions, together with his feeling that the Marxists in exile have lost touch with the realities of Italian life, lead Spina to the ethical ideal, the love concept, of primitive Christianity, which for him becomes "a Christianity denuded of all religion and all church control." Spina believes not in the resurrection of Jesus, only in his agony; Jesus figures for him entirely in *human* terms; in fact, the significance of Jesus is that he is the first, and perhaps the last, fully human being. To live as a Christian without the church means, for Spina, to shoulder the greatest possible insecurity before man and God. Spina rejects that duality between means and ends which is common to *all* political movements; unwilling to stake anything on the future, he insists that the only way to realize the good life, no matter what the circumstances, is to live it. "No word and no gesture can be more persuasive than the life and, if necessary, the death of a man who strives to be free, loyal, just, sincere, disinterested. A man who shows what a man can be."

Abstracting this political view from its context in the novel, as Silone virtually invites us to, we reach mixed conclusions about its value. Much of what Silone says is undoubtedly true: anyone trying to organize a political underground would have to demonstrate his worthiness not only as a leader but as a man and a friend. But here we reach a difficulty. Once Silone's militant and saintly rebels acquired followers, they would have to be organized into some sort of movement, even if it claimed to be nonideological and were not called a party; and then that movement would be open to bureaucratic perils similar to those of the Marxist party which Spina has rejected—bureaucratic perils that would be particularly great in an atmosphere of saintly, even if not apocalyptic, Messianism. Has not something of the sort happened to Christianity itself, in its transition from primitive rebelliousness to a number of accredited institutions?

Silone has here come up against a central dilemma of all political action: the only certain way of preventing bureaucracy is to refrain from organization, but the refusal to organize with one's fellow men can lead only to acquiescence in detested power or to isolated and futile acts of martyrdom and terrorism. This is not, of course, to deny the validity of specific organizational rejections; it is merely to question Silone's belief, as it appears in *Bread and Wine*, that political goals can be reached without political organization.

It is, however, entirely to Silone's credit that he recognizes this dilemma and embodies it in the action of his book; he does not try to pry his way out of it with some rusty formula. One of his finest strokes in *Bread and Wine* is the scene in which Spina takes off his priestly frock—this occurs, significantly, as soon as some possibility for political action appears. He takes off his priestly frock but we are not to suppose that his experience as Paolo Spada the false priest has not left a profound mark upon him. The duality between Spina and Spada—between the necessity for action and the necessity for contemplation, between the urge to power and the urge to purity—is reflected in Silone's own experience as novelist and political leader. Even after he wrote *The Seed Beneath the Snow*, a novel in which he exemplifies a kind of Christian passivity and mute fraternity, he continued to participate in the quite worldly Italian Socialist movement. In his own practise as an Italian Socialist, he has been forced to recognize that the vexatious problem of means and ends involves a constant tension between morality and expediency which can be resolved, if resolved at all, only in practice.

Yet it is precisely from these scrupulous examinations of conscience and commitment that so much of the impact of *Bread and Wine* derives; no other twentieth century novelist has so fully conveyed the pathos behind the failure of socialism. *Bread and Wine* is a book of misery and doubt; it moves slowly, painfully, in a weary spiral that traces the spiritual and intellectual anguish of its hero. The characteristic turning of the political novelist to some apolitical temptation, is, in Silone's case, a wistful search for the lost conditions of simple life where one may find the moral resources which politics can no longer yield. This pastoral theme, winding quietly through the book and reaching full development only in its sequel, *The Seed Beneath the Snow*, is not an easy one for the modern reader to take at face value: we are quick, and rightly so, to suspect programs for simplicity. But in Silone's work it acquires a unique validity: he knows peasant life intimately and, perhaps because he does not himself pretend to be a peasant, seldom stoops to pseudo-folk romanticizing; he is aware that a return to simplicity by a man like Spina must have its painful and ironic aspects; his turn to pastoral does not imply social resignation but is on the contrary buttressed by a still active sense of social rebelliousness; and most important of all, he employs the pastoral theme not to make a literal recommendation but to suggest, as a tentative metaphor, the still available potentialities of man.

Bread and Wine is a work of humility, unmarred by the adventurism or the occasional obsession with violence and death which disfigures the political novels of Malraux and Koestler. Whatever the ideological hesitations of Silone's novels, they remain faithful to the essential experience of modern Europe; and to the harsh milieu of political struggle they bring a cleansing freshness, a warmth of fraternity.

Perhaps as a sign of the drift of our age, Silone has gradually become one of the most isolated among Italian writers. In the intellectual world of Italy he is seldom honored or admired. The memory of his refusal to accommodate himself to the fascist regime stirs feelings of bad conscience among literary men who were more flexible. His continued rejection of the traditional elegance of "literary" Italian confounds and disturbs the conventional critics. And his politics—for in some vague but indestructible way he remains a socialist, indifferent to party or dogma, yet utterly committed to the poor and the dispossessed—annoys those Italian writers who have tied themselves to one of the party machines or the far greater number who have remained in the shelters of estheticism.

This last factor may also account for the decline of Silone's reputation in the United States. Those American intellectuals who have settled into social conformism or a featureless liberalism find in Silone's politics little more than sentimental nostalgia—or so they would persuade themselves; those who have turned to religion, whether it be the Catholic Church or the crisis theology of Protestantism, cannot help realizing, with a discomfort in proportion to their sensitiveness, that Silone's struggle for the ethic of primitive Christianity has little in common with the religious institutions and doctrines of the twentieth century.

Yet each man, if he is to remain one, must go his own way; and Silone, in his clumsy uncertainty, his humorous irritability, his effort to speak without rhetoric or cant, has become a kind of moral hero for those of us who have been forced by history to put aside many of the dogmas of social radicalism but who remain faithful to the rebellious and fraternal impulse behind the dogmas. Silone's most recent novel, *A Handful of Blackberries*, has been received with some conventional appreciation and more conventional depreciation; neither of these is an adequate response. So deeply opposed is this book to the moods, the assumptions, the values of our time, so thoroughly is it imbued with the forgotten emotions of humaneness, that one can only assert that in years to come it will be looked back upon, if anything is looked back upon, as a cultural and spiritual act helping to redeem a terrible age.

Simply as a novel, *A Handful of Blackberries* has large, obvious faults: it reads more like a scenario than a realized work, it is occasionally flabby in structure and scratchy in style, it betrays a tone of great weariness (but from that weariness also comes a kind of greatness.) One soon suspects that Silone, like many other novelists for whom writing is not merely portrayal but also a form of implicit prophecy, has become a little impatient with the mechanics of literature, the game of creating illusions. He has reached almost, but not quite, the position of the serious artist whose very seriousness causes him to shed the forms in which he has scored his greatest successes.

Yet these matters, though they have an intrinsic interest, are as nothing beside the overwhelming fact to which the novel testifies: that in an age of faithlessness Silone has kept faith. He has remained with the *cafoni*, the landless peasants in whose name he first began to write, and in this novel he tells us that, through the noise and the muddle of shifts in regimes and parties, nothing has changed for the peasants except the names of those who exploit them and the catchwords by which their exploitation is rationalized.

The surface action of the novel traces the disillusion of a young engineer who begins as a local leader of the Communist Party and comes gradually to realize that he must choose between the peasants who trust him and the party machine, which is as inhuman and repressive as the machine of the fascists. The inner action of the novel is a fable enriched with Silone's marvellous anecdotes*—a fable about a trumpet by which the peasants, when their misery becomes unbearable, called one another together and which the Communist Party, in its false claim to be their spokesman, now wishes to appropriate. But while it may be true that the peasants are unable to act positively in their own behalf, they do have a long and rich experience in collective resistance. They do not surrender the trumpet.

Once again, as in *Fontamara* and *Bread and Wine*, the city

* "Silone's characters exchange anecdotes like gifts; it is all they have, but it is everything. If genuine life is communion, according to Silone, its seed is the anecdote; so that his notion of life and his notion of fiction are not to be detached. The role of fiction, like the end of life is (for Silone) to be companionable; and its nature is the account of individuals failing or succeeding in coming together, in being companionable, in putting themselves in touch with reality and with each other by the telling of stories." This fine observation appears in an essay about Silone written by R. W. B. Lewis, in *Kenyon Review* (Winter 1955). The essay has other such insights, but is, to my mind, marred by an unwillingness to take Silone's politics with full seriousness, that is, as an activity needing no "translation" into moral or quasi-religious terms. Thus, Mr. Lewis speaks of Silone's politics as a "fortunate fall, a bruising experience invaluable for both the man and the artist." This seems to me a curious view of the relation between life and literature, as if experience were merely fodder for composition. But more important, it indicates, I think, a refusal to understand that for Silone the failure of socialism, far from being a "bruising" experience—let alone anything so providential as a "fortunate fall"—was the decisive and tragic event of his life.

is counterposed to the country: neither can understand the other, and given the inequity of social arrangements it can hardly be avoided that the one should exploit the other. The life of the peasants remains as miserable, as buried in darkness, as ever before. And so long as this remains true, Silone sees no reason to make his peace with the world as it is. Nor is he at all sentimental about the peasants, for the sardonic humor that twists through the book is often turned against their coarseness and gullibility. But they are his, by adoption of blood, and he remains hopeful, with a hopefulness that has nothing to do with optimism, that from the hidden inarticulate resources of the poor, which consist neither of intelligence nor nobility, but rather of a training in endurance and an education in ruse—that from all this something worthy of the human may yet emerge. When will the trumpet blow again? "How can I know?" answers the peasant Lazzaro. "It doesn't depend on me, you know. Maybe next year, or twenty or five hundred years from now." But the trumpet remains.

Silone's novels contain the most profound vision of what heroism can be in the modern world. Like Malraux, he appreciates the value of action, but he also realizes that in the age of totalitarianism it is possible for an heroic action to consist of nothing but stillness, that for Spina and many others there may never be the possibility of an outward or public gesture. If we compare his view of heroism with that of Hemingway, we see the difference between the feelings of a mature European and, if I may say so, an inexperienced American. For Hemingway heroism is always a visible trial, a test limited in time, symbolized in dramatic confrontations. For Silone heroism is a condition of readiness, a talent for waiting, a gift for stubbornness; his is the heroism of tiredness. Hemingway's heroic virtues are realized in situations increasingly distant from the social world, among bullfighters and hunters and fishermen; Silone's heroic virtues pertain to people who live, as Berthold Brecht has put it, in "the dark ages" of modern Europe, at the heart of our debacle.

IV

The twentieth century political novel moves along a line of descent, an increasingly precipitous fall into despair. To turn from the revolutionary ardor of *Man's Fate* to the rebellious doubt of *Bread and Wine,* and from these to the symbolic triumph of Stalinism in Arthur Koestler's *Darkness at Noon,* is to see in miniature a history of our epoch.

Since it is in the grip of a fixed idea, *Darkness at Noon* has little of the intellectual fluidity, the richness of absorbed life, the complex interplay between emotion and ideology, that distinguishes the political novel at its best. Though the subject of Koestler's book can be seen as the increasingly problematic nature of all modern politics, it seldom yields itself to the problematic as a mode of feeling or observation. Can one say that a certain kind of commitment to the problematic may itself become a form of ideological fanaticism? If so, that is how to describe *Darkness at Noon.* For Koestler is the sort of writer who manipulates his characters with a ruthless insistence that they conform to his will, that they illustrate prefabricated themes rather than fulfill their inner possibilities. Only intermittently does he do the novelist's job and, as one might expect, it is then that he is at his best, relaxing his ideological hold—that grim insistence upon the dazzling formula which is all too often a sign of intellectual panic— and letting his imagination work freely.

Darkness at Noon is an account of the arrest of an Old Bolshevik, Rubashov, by the Stalin government and his gradual capitulation to its inquisitors; but it also carries a superimposed intellectual framework intended as an explanation of why the Old Bolsheviks confessed in the Moscow Trials of 1936-39. In the first regard, the novel is often superb. Confined to one locale, one line of action, one dominating character, it accumulates great dramatic intensity, and in a climactic scene, where the prisoners drum an anguished threnody on their cell walls as an old oppositionist is dragged out to be killed, it reaches a concentrated expression of all the horror of modern politics. There are other remarkable scenes. One remembers the terrible incident of the Communist who had been imprisoned in some wretched Balkan country and upon his release and arrival in Russia, imprisoned once more; he believes, with the literal sincerity of the damned, that he is not in Russia at all, he was put on the wrong train . . . Nor is it possible to forget the flash-back in which Rubashov, sent by the Russians to persuade the Belgian Communists to break their boycott of oil for Mussolini during the Italo-Ethiopian war, tries to cajole the dock workers into doing what he knows is evil and in the process takes another step toward his own degeneration.

But the novel is crucially flawed, and Rubashov thinned into abstractness, by Koestler's simple and often crude theorizing about the moral premises which, he claims, were the basis of the Old Bolshevik capitulation to Stalin. Koestler makes the error of discussing an enormously difficult and complex problem in abstract and ultimatistic moral terms: the Old Bolsheviks like Rubashov believed that "the end justifies the means" and once they decide that because of "the immaturity of the masses" Stalin's terroristic regime is unavoidable, they feel obliged to suppress their "own conviction when there is no prospect of materializing it." Since, argues Rubashov to himself, "the only moral criterion which we recognize is that of social utility, the public disavowal of one's conviction in order to remain in the party's ranks is obviously more honorable than the quixoticism of carrying on a hopeless struggle." And thus Rubashov comes to hope that his confession and death may even form a gesture in behalf of the socialism he knows Stalinism is betraying.

Either in or out of the novel's context, Koestler's explanation of Rubashov's behavior is open to challenge—and since *Darkness at Noon* cleaves to the surface of contemporary politics, we can speak of the event in history and the report in the novel almost as if they were the same. The capitulation of some, though by no means all, of the Old Bolsheviks is hardly to be explained by attributing to them a series of rigid deductions from a moral precept which, in the unmodulated form that Koestler employs it, they would not merely have rejected but would have considered malicious. What appears to be the iron logic in Rubashov's reflections is achieved by a ruthless elimination of complicating alternatives at each point of his argument; Koestler is imitating not any possible version of the Rubashov type but his own self-confirming hypothesis of the "inner necessity" of Rubashov's capitulation. Indeed, it is precisely the apparent rigor of Rubashov's argument which renders Koestler's portrait of him suspect, for it assumes that Rubashov's gradual surrender to Stalinism is a dialectical process within his own thought, a valid deduction from the premises of his political career. But this is manifestly untrue to our sense of human behavior, even the behavior of Bolshevik politicians. Between the assumptions of theory and the conclusions of defeat there must lie a whole middle ground of Rubashov's experience, the gradual destruction of his will and integrity as he takes step after step toward acquiescing to the regime he knows to be vile. By the time of the action described in *Darkness at Noon,* Rubashov has already been destroyed or has already destroyed himself, and the *post hoc* rationalizations in which he might be supposed to indulge, and which for Koestler are the heart of his dilemma, would bear little relation to the actual process of his disintegration.

This point has been made so well by Harold Rosenberg, in an article written shortly after the novel appeared, that I feel obliged to quote a crucial passage from his analysis:

Koestler approaches politics with a fixed philosophical dualism that distorts his understanding of the tragedy of the left intellectuals of the past decade. In *Darkness at Noon* . . . he did not attack the jailors of Rubashov for specific violations of socialist values but placed the responsibility on Rubashov himself as representing with them a metaphysical absolute—"the logic of history"—opposed to the individual by the nature of things. The effect of this mechanical dichotomy (which also appears in Koestler's essays) was to cause Rubashov, introduced as one of the revolutionary founders of the USSR, to conceive his political life as nothing more than a series of crimes against the individual—it was the guilt he incurred in "representing history" that he expiated at the trial.

Such a criticism of the [Moscow] Trials is a metaphysical not a political or historical criticism, and in effect it accepts the political and historical claims of the Communists while rejecting their moral ones.

Fully to understand the Rubashov type, it would be necessary to place him, as Koestler hardly does, against the background of a gradual counterrevolution, in which deeply antagonistic social forces are pitted against each other, *social forces that cannot be reduced to moral categories*, though they are, of course, open to moral criticism.

What finally gives *Darkness at Noon* so "unreal" a quality, and this despite its interludes of brilliant realism, is that Koestler approaches the problem of historical action with a wilful insistence upon an either / or dilemma—either amoral activism or moral passivity. This rigid fascination with absolutes and an equally rigid elimination of any possible choices of action lying between these absolutes, lends his novels the appearance of intellectual clarity, of getting down to "fundamentals"; but the fundamentals prove to be little more than a dazzling phrase and the clarity that of an over-focussed and thereby untrustworthy picture. To insist upon the Yogi-Commissar dichotomy—I use the sloganized personifications Koestler made popular in a later book, though they are already implicit in *Darkness at Noon*—is to ignore the vast preponderance of choices made by men in history, choices that involve a tension between the demands of historical pressure and the demands of moral standards, not to mention a reliance upon the tact of instinctual response. Koestler's method of analysis—which, in his case, is the same as saying, his method of writing a novel—may give a momentary illusion of logical rigour; but it cannot yield a credible portrait of a man thinking or, more important, of a man suffering from the need to rethink ideas that he once had accepted on faith. Rubashov may seem to reason, but he does not breathe. And partly that is because Koestler is so terribly impatient a writer, impatient as only a journalist can be when he finds himself trying to "use" the novel. More concerned with the phrase than the experience it is supposed to illuminate, Koestler is quite incapable of that calm surrender to the rhythms of an imagined situation which is indispensable to the true novelist. As American journalists sometimes say, he always has to be "on top of" his subject.

The criticism I have been developing here, if it has any point at all, applies equally to Koestler the political journalist and Koestler the political novelist. If a simplified moral dialectic which makes no allowances for the nuance of human decision cannot explain history, it must surely prove even less adequate for portraying the fine textures and ambiguities of human experience. But the irony of this failure—it is no small irony, since Koestler is an enormously talented writer—is that Koestler himself writes as a conscious opponent of ideology. A major part of his intention in writing *Darkness at Noon* must surely be to warn against the abstractions of ideology, those abstractions which, if allowed to spawn too freely, tend to dehumanize our lives—yet every line Koestler writes, and one doubts that he can avoid it, is suffused with ideology. He is like a stricken Midas yearning for the bread of life yet, with every touch, turning experience into the useless gold of ideology.

But is this not part of the fascination he holds for contemporary readers? The word that has been most used to praise him—and on the whole, it is a praise he has earned—is "relevant"; one feels that, with all his faults and all his journalistic glibness, he has been one of the few writers in our time to drive immediately toward the problems that most concern intelligent men. Koestler is so skillful a journalist that his very phrases distil the anxiety of Europe, and if it is sometimes hard to credit his claim to being a diagnostician one is ready to grant that his work always constitutes a noteworthy symptom. As a novelist, however, he has never quite managed to achieve the poise and the patience that are required for knowing when to turn to his sense of "relevance" and when to resist it.

The result is that even a book like *Darkness at Noon,* with its many claims to distinction and its obvious interest for our time, comes finally to seem an example of how the modern appetite for ideology can harm a novelist when he turns to public themes. One can reject the political implications of *Bread and Wine* and still be moved by Spina's experience in reaching them; one can be disturbed by the political theories behind *Man's Fate* and still be stirred by the human effort it dramatizes; but reject Koestler's essential thesis and Rubashov has no reality whatever—all that remains, and that of course is considerable, is an excellent but highly limited evocation of the Stalinist milieu. The politics of *Man's Fate*, in view of the subsequent triumphs of Stalinism, does raise a special problem in reading. Yet a moment's reflection should convince one that the book deals primarily with those human indecisions and torments which Stalinism, or even the Stalinist party, makes impossible; that the whole history of Stalinism is a destruction of the Kyos and the Katovs; that so long as the party in Malraux's book still can have in its ranks a Kyo, a Katov, a Ch'en, it is not yet the party of Stalin as we have come to know it. *Darkness at Noon*, however, depends for its impact almost entirely upon its ideology. At the end of the novel Rubashov is convinced of the need to return to what he once considered the "grammatical fiction" of the first person singular, but it is a curious irony, and the mark of Koestler's inferiority as a novelist to, say, Silone, that this claim for the "I" remains entirely impersonal and abstract.

I want, finally, to turn to a second-rank novel, to look at a work that is not quite successful in its effort to absorb modern politics into fiction. *The Case of Comrade Tulayev*, a novel about Stalinist Russia, is the work of Victor Serge, a very gifted journalist with a vast revolutionary background. The faults of the book need not concern us here; I want merely to notice two small passages in which Serge does manage to suggest the possibilities for the political novel.

In one remarkable scene Rublev, a Bolshevik leader who has been slowly broken by the Stalin regime, arranges a meeting with two old comrades, veterans of the revolution and distinguished intellectuals, in the woods near Moscow. In desultory terms they discuss what can be done, quarrel a bit,

and reach no particular conclusion. Suddenly their spontaneous life-force is stirred by the coldness and the purity of the
snow, by the warmth and pathos of this, their final meeting—
and they begin . . . not to talk about purges, programs, or
politics; it is too late for that, they are doomed. *They begin
throwing snowballs at each other,* laughing like boys and for
an unbearably pathetic moment innocent and forgetful. "They
leaped, laughed, sank into snow up to their waists, hid behind trees to make their ammunition and take aim before
they let fly. Something of the nimbleness of their boyhood
came back to them . . . Wladek stood where he was, firmly
planted, methodically making snowballs to catch Rublev from
the flank, laughing until the tears came to his eyes, showering
him with abuse: 'Take that you theoretician, you moralist, to
hell with you' and never once hitting him . . .'"

The second incident concerns another Old Bolshevik,
Ryzhik, who has not capitulated. In distant exile he lives
faithfully by the original passion of the revolution, hardly
caring whether or not he survives. As he is being brought
back to Moscow for a confession he will not make, Ryzhik
encounters in a cell another old oppositionist, Makarenko.
They embrace in a flare of excitement, talk for a while;
Ryzhik begins a political discussion; the other man listens—
yes, he agrees; but he is restless, it is too late for such talk.
"Our meeting," Makarenko bursts out, "is extraordinary . . .
An inconceivable piece of negligence on the part of the serv-
ices . . . We are living through an apocalypse of Socialism
. . . Why are you alive, why am I—I ask you!" Unimagina-
tively, Ryzhik answers this question in routine political terms,
and the other man, full of affectionate impatience, must insist: "I am a Marxist, too. But shut your eyes for a minute,
listen to the earth, listen to your nerves." Here is the direct
counterposition of ideology and emotion—in a dialogue between two men who are surrendering their lives in behalf of
their ideological conviction.

Neither of these two incidents could have been conceived
by anyone but a writer intimately related to modern politics;
the political knowledge never appears on the surface but the

surface would be impossible without the political knowledge. In both of these incidents the tragedy of politics is counterposed to the possibilities of experience, the commitment to an idea shown as it brushes against the commitment to compassion—the capitulators, brilliant but futile dialecticians, throwing snowballs; the oppositionists, secure in their belief, reaching for a moment of closeness before death.

This seems to me as good a prescription for the political novel, if there must be a prescription, as we are likely to get: amidst the clamor of ideology—the indispensable, inescapable clamor—listen to your nerves.

CHAPTER NINE

ORWELL: HISTORY AS NIGHTMARE

About some books we feel that our reluctance to return to them is the true measure of our admiration. It is hard to suppose that many people go back, from a spontaneous desire, to reread *1984:* there is neither reason nor need to, no one forgets it. The usual distinctions between forgotten details and a vivid general impression mean nothing here, for the book is written out of one passionate breath, each word is bent to a severe discipline of meaning, everything is stripped to the bareness of terror.

Kafka's *The Trial* is also a book of terror, but it is a paradigm and to some extent a puzzle, so that one may lose oneself in the rhythm of the paradigm and play with the parts of the puzzle. Kafka's novel persuades us that life is inescapably hazardous and problematic, but the very "universality" of this idea helps soften its impact: to apprehend the terrible on the plane of metaphysics is to lend it an almost soothing aura. And besides, *The Trial* absorbs one endlessly in its aspect of enigma.

Though not nearly so great a book, *1984* is in some ways more terrible. For it is not a paradigm and hardly a puzzle; whatever enigmas it raises concern not the imagination of the author but the life of our time. It does not take us away from, or beyond, our obsession with immediate social reality, and in reading the book we tend to say—the linguistic clumsiness conceals a deep truth—that the world of 1984 is "more real" than our own. The book appals us because its terror, far from being inherent in the "human condition," is particular to our century; what haunts us is the sickening awareness that in 1984 Orwell has seized upon those elements of our public life that, given courage and intelligence, were avoidable.

How remarkable a book 1984 really is, can be discovered only after a second reading. It offers true testimony, it speaks for our time. And because it derives from a perception of how our time may end, the book trembles with an eschatological fury that is certain to create among its readers, even those who sincerely believe they admire it, the most powerful kinds of resistance. It already has. Openly in England, more cautiously in America, there has arisen a desire among intellectuals to belittle Orwell's achievement, often in the guise of celebrating his humanity and his "goodness." They feel embarrassed before the apocalyptic desperation of the book, they begin to wonder whether it may not be just a little overdrawn and humorless, they even suspect it is tinged with the hysteria of the death-bed. Nor can it be denied that all of us would feel more comfortable if the book could be cast out. It is a remarkable book.

Whether it is a remarkable novel or a novel at all, seems unimportant. It is not, I suppose, really a novel, or at least it does not satisfy those expectations we have come to have with regard to the novel—expectations that are mainly the heritage of nineteenth century romanticism with its stress upon individual consciousness, psychological analysis and the study of intimate relations. One American critic, a serious critic, reviewed the book under the heading, "Truth Maybe, Not Fiction," as if thereby to demonstrate the strictness with which he held to distinctions of literary genre. Actually, he was demonstrating a certain narrowness of modern taste, for such a response to 1984 is possible only when discriminations are no longer made between fiction and the novel, which is but one kind of fiction though the kind modern readers care for most.

A cultivated eighteenth century reader would never have said of *1984* that it may be true but isn't fiction, for it was then understood that fiction, like poetry, can have many modes and be open to many mixtures; the novel had not yet established its popular tyranny. What is more, the style of *1984*, which many readers take to be drab or uninspired or "sweaty," would have been appreciated by someone like Defoe, since Defoe would have immediately understood how the pressures of Orwell's subject, like the pressures of his own, demand a gritty and hammering factuality. The style of *1984* is the style of a man whose commitment to a dreadful vision is at war with the nausea to which that vision reduces him. So acute is this conflict that delicacies of phrasing or displays of rhetoric come to seem frivolous—*he has no time, he must get it all down.* Those who fail to see this, I am convinced, have succumbed to the pleasant tyrannies of estheticism; they have allowed their fondness for a cultivated style to blind them to the urgencies of prophetic expression. The last thing Orwell cared about when he wrote *1984*, the last thing he should have cared about, was literature.

Another complaint one often hears is that there are no credible or "three-dimensional" characters in the book. Apart from its rather facile identification of credibility with a particular treatment of character, the complaint involves a failure to see that in some books an extended amount of psychological specification or even dramatic incident can be disastrous. In *1984* Orwell is trying to present the kind of world in which individuality has become obsolete and personality a crime. The whole idea of the self as something precious and inviolable is a *cultural* idea, and as we understand it, a product of the liberal era; but Orwell has imagined a world in which the self, whatever subterranean existence it manages to eke out, is no longer a significant value, not even a value to be violated.

Winston Smith and Julia come through as rudimentary figures because they are slowly learning, and at great peril to themselves, what it means to be human. Their experiment in the rediscovery of the human, which is primarily an experiment in the possibilities of solitude, leads them to cherish two things that are fundamentally hostile to the totalitarian outlook: a life of contemplativeness and the joy of "purposeless"—that is, free—sexual passion. But this experiment cannot go very far, as they themselves know; it is inevitable that they be caught and destroyed.

Partly, that is the meaning and the pathos of the book. Were it possible, in the world of 1984, to show human character in anything resembling genuine freedom, in its play of spontaneous desire and caprice—it would not be the world of 1984. So that in a slightly obtuse way the complaint that Orwell's characters seem thin testifies to the strength of the book, for it is a complaint directed not against his technique but against his primary assumptions.

The book cannot be understood, nor can it be properly valued, simply by resorting to the usual literary categories, for it posits a situation in which these categories are no longer significant. Everything has hardened into politics, the leviathan has swallowed man. About such a world it is, strictly speaking, impossible to write a novel, if only because the human relationships taken for granted in the novel are here suppressed.* The book must first be approached through politics, yet not as a political study or treatise. It is something else, at once a model and a vision—a model of the totalitar-

---

* Some people have suggested that *1984* is primarily a symptom of Orwell's psychological condition, the nightmare of a disturbed man who suffered from paranoid fantasies, was greatly troubled by dirt and feared that sexual contact would bring down punishment from those in authority. Apart from its intolerable glibness, such an "explanation" explains either too much or too little. Almost everyone has nightmares and a great many people have ambiguous feelings about sex, but few manage to write books with the power of *1984*. Nightmare the book may be, and no doubt it is grounded, as are all books, in the psychological troubles of its author. But it is also grounded in his psychological health, otherwise it could not penetrate so deeply the social reality of our time. The private nightmare, if it is there, is profoundly related to, and helps us understand, public events.

ian state in its "pure" or "essential" form and a vision of what this state can do to human life. Yet the theme of the conflict between ideology and emotion, as at times their fusion and mutual reinforcement—a theme that has been noticed repeatedly in the previous chapters of this book—is still to be found in *1984*, as a dim underground motif. Without this theme, there could be no dramatic conflict in a work of fiction dominated by politics. Winston Smith's effort to reconstruct the old tune about the bells of St. Clement is a token of his desire to regain the condition of humanness, which is here nothing more than a capacity for so "useless" a feeling as nostalgia. Between the tune and Oceania there can be no peace.

1984 projects a nightmare in which politics has displaced humanity and the state has stifled society. In a sense, it is a profoundly antipolitical book, full of hatred for the kind of world in which public claims destroy the possibilities for private life; and this conservative side of Orwell's outlook he suggests, perhaps unconsciously, through the first name of his hero. But if the image of Churchill is thus raised in order to celebrate, a little wryly, the memory of the bad (or as Winston Smith comes to feel, the good) old days, the opposing image of Trotsky is raised, a little skeptically, in order to discover the inner meanings of totalitarian society. When Winston Smith learns to think of Oceania as a *problem*—which is itself to commit a "crimethink"—he turns to the forbidden work of Emmanuel Goldstein, *The Theory and Practise of Oligarchical Collectivism*, clearly a replica of Trotsky's *The Revolution Betrayed*. The power and intelligence of *1984* partly derives from a tension between these images; even as Orwell understood the need for politics in the modern world, he felt a profound distaste for the ways of political life, and he was honest enough not to try to suppress one or another side of this struggle within himself.

II

No other book has succeeded so completely in rendering the essential quality of totalitarianism. *1984* is limited in scope; it does not pretend to investigate the genesis of the totalitarian state, nor the laws of its economy, nor the prospect for its survival; it simply evokes the "tone" of life in a totalitarian society. And since it is not a realistic novel, it can treat Oceania as an *extreme instance,* one that might never actually exist but which illuminates the nature of societies that do exist.*

Orwell's profoundest insight is that in a totalitarian world man's life is shorn of dynamic possibilities. The end of life is completely predictable in its beginning, the beginning merely a manipulated preparation for the end. There is no opening for surprise, for that spontaneous animation which is the token of and justification for freedom. Oceanic society may evolve through certain stages of economic development, but the life of its members is static, a given and measured quantity that can neither rise to tragedy nor tumble to comedy. Human personality, as we have come to grasp for it in a class society and hope for it in a classless society, is obliterated; man becomes a function of a process he is never allowed to understand or control. The fetichism of the state replaces the fetichism of commodities.

There have, of course, been unfree societies in the past, yet in most of them it was possible to find an oasis of freedom, if only because none had the resources to enforce total consent. But totalitarianism, which represents a decisive break from the Western tradition, aims to permit no such luxuries; it offers a total "solution" to the problems of the twentieth century, that is, a total distortion of what might be a solution. To be sure,

---

* "My novel *1984*," wrote Orwell shortly before his death, "is *not* intended as an attack on socialism, or on the British Labor Party, but as a show-up of the perversions to which a centralized economy is liable. . . . I do not believe that the kind of society I describe necessarily *will* arrive, but I believe . . . that something resembling it *could* arrive."

no totalitarian state has been able to reach this degree of "perfection," which Orwell, like a physicist who in his experiment assumes the absence of friction, has assumed for Oceania. But the knowledge that friction can never actually be absent does not make the experiment any the less valuable. To the degree that the totalitarian state approaches its "ideal" condition, it destroys the margin for unforeseen behavior; as a character in Dostoevsky's *The Possessed* remarks, "only the necessary is necessary." Nor is there a social crevice in which the recalcitrant or independent mind can seek shelter. The totalitarian state assumes that—given modern technology, complete political control, the means of terror and a rationalized contempt for moral tradition—anything is possible. Anything can be done with men, anything with their minds, with history and with words. Reality is no longer something to be acknowledged or experienced or even transformed; it is fabricated according to the need and will of the state, sometimes in anticipation of the future, sometimes as a retrospective improvement upon the past.

But even as Orwell, overcoming the resistance of his own nausea, evoked the ethos of the totalitarian world, he used very little of what is ordinarily called "imagination" in order to show how this ethos stains every aspect of human life. Like most good writers, he understood that imagination is primarily the capacity for apprehending reality, for seeing both clearly and deeply whatever it is that exists. That is why his vision of social horror, if taken as a model rather than a portrait, strikes one as essentially credible, while the efforts of most writers to create utopias or anti-utopias founder precisely on their desire to be scientific or inventive. Orwell understood that social horror consists not in the prevalence of diabolical machines or in the invasion of Martian automatons flashing death rays from mechanical eyes, but in the persistence of inhuman relations among men.

And he understood, as well, the significance of what I can only call the psychology and politics of "one more step." From a bearable neurosis to a crippling psychosis, from a decayed society in which survival is still possible to a totalitar-

ian state in which it is hardly desirable, there may be only
"one step." To lay bare the logic of that social regression
which leads to totalitarianism Orwell had merely to allow his
imagination to take . . . one step.

Consider such typical aspects of Oceanic society as telescreens and the use of children as informers against their
parents. There are no telescreens in Russia, but there could
well be: nothing in Russian society contradicts the "principle" of telescreens. Informing against parents who are political heretics is not a common practise in the United States,
but some people have been deprived of their jobs on the
charge of having maintained "prolonged associations" with
their parents. To capture the totalitarian spirit, Orwell had
merely to allow certain tendencies in modern society to spin
forward without the brake of sentiment or humaneness. He
could thus make clear the relationship between his model of
totalitarianism and the societies we know in our experience,
and he could do this without resorting to the clap-trap of science fiction or the crude assumption that we already live in
1984. In imagining the world of 1984 he took only one step,
and because he knew how long and terrible a step it was, he
had no need to take another.

III

Through a struggle of the mind and an effort of the will
that clearly left him exhausted, Orwell came to see—which is
far more than simply to understand—what the inner spirit or
ethos of totalitarianism is. But it was characteristic of Orwell
as a writer that he felt uneasy with a general idea or a total
vision; things took on reality for him only as they were particular and concrete. The world of 1984 seems to have had
for him the hallucinatory immediacy that Yoknapatawpha
County has for Faulkner or London had for Dickens, and
even as he ruthlessly subordinated his descriptions to the
dominating theme of the book, Orwell succeeded in noting
the details of Oceanic society with a painstaking and sometimes uncanny accuracy.

There are first the incidental accuracies of mimicry. Take, as an example, Orwell's grasp of the role played by the scapegoat-enemy of the totalitarian world, the rituals of hate for which he is indispensable, and more appalling, the uncertainty as to whether he even exists or is a useful fabrication of the state. Among the best passages in the book are those in which Orwell imitates Trotsky's style in *The Theory and Practise of Oligarchical Collectivism*. Orwell caught the rhetorical sweep and grandeur of Trotsky's writing, particularly his fondness for using scientific references in non-scientific contexts: "Even after enormous upheavals and seemingly irrevocable changes, the same pattern has always reasserted itself, just as a gyroscope will always return to equilibrium, however far it is pushed one way or another." And in another sentence Orwell beautifully captured Trotsky's way of using a compressed paradox to sum up the absurdity of a whole society: "The fields are cultivated with horse plows while books are written by machinery."

Equally skillful was Orwell's evocation of the physical atmosphere of Oceania, the overwhelming gloomy shabbiness of its streets and houses, the tasteless sameness of the clothes its people wear, the unappetizing gray-pink stew they eat, that eternal bureaucratic stew which seems to go with all modern oppressive institutions. Orwell had not been taken in by the legend that totalitarianism is at least efficient; instead of the usual chromium-and-skyscraper vision of the future, he painted London in 1984 as a composite of the city in its dismal grayness during the last (Second) world war and of the modern Russian cities with their Victorian ostentation and rotting slums. In all of his books Orwell had shown himself only mildly gifted at visual description but remarkably keen at detecting loathsome and sickening odors. He had the best nose of his generation—his mind sometimes betrayed him, his nose never. In the world of 1984, he seems to be suggesting, all of the rubbish of the past, together with some that no one had quite been able to foresee, is brought together.

The rubbish survived, but what of the past itself, the past

in which men had managed to live and sometimes with a little pleasure? One of the most poignant scenes in the book is that in which Winston Smith, trying to discover what life was like before the reign of Big Brother, talks to an old prole in a pub. The exchange is unsatisfactory to Smith, since the worker can remember only fragments of disconnected fact and is quite unable to generalize from his memories; but the scene itself is a fine bit of dramatic action, indicating that not only does totalitarian society destroy the past through the obliteration of objective records but that it destroys the memory of the past through a disintegration of individual consciousness. The worker with whom Smith talks remembers that the beer was better before Big Brother (a very important fact) but he cannot really understand Smith's question: "Do you feel that you have more freedom now than you had in those days?" To pose, let alone understand, such a question requires a degree of social continuity, as well as a set of complex assumptions, which Oceania is gradually destroying.

The destruction of social memory becomes a major industry in Oceania, and here of course Orwell was borrowing directly from Stalinism which, as the most "advanced" form of totalitarianism, was infinitely more adept at this job than was fascism. (Hitler burned books, Stalin had them rewritten.) In Oceania the embarrassing piece of paper slides down memory hole—and that is all.

Orwell is similarly acute in noticing the relationship between the totalitarian state and what passes for culture. Novels are produced by machine; the state anticipates all wants, from "cleansed" versions of Byron to pornographic magazines; that vast modern industry which we call "popular culture" has become an important state function. Meanwhile, the language is stripped of words that suggest refinements of attitude or gradations of sensibility.

And with feeling as with language. Oceania seeks to blot out spontaneous affection because it assumes, with good reason, that whatever is uncalculated is subversive. Smith thinks to himself:

It would not have occurred to [his mother] that an action which is ineffectual thereby becomes meaningless. If you loved someone, you loved him, and when you had nothing else to give, you still gave him love. When the last of the chocolate was gone, his mother had clasped the children in her arms. It was no use, it changed nothing, it did not produce more chocolate, it did not avert the child's death or her own; but it seemed natural for her to do it.

IV

At only a few points can one question Orwell's vision of totalitarianism, and even these involve highly problematic matters. If they are errors at all, it is only to the extent that they drive valid observations too hard: Orwell's totalitarian society is at times more *total* than we can presently imagine.

One such problem has to do with the relation between the state and "human nature." Granted that human nature is itself a cultural concept with a history of change behind it; granted that the pressures of fear and force can produce extreme variations in human conduct. There yet remains the question: to what extent can a terrorist regime suppress or radically alter the fundamental impulses of man? Is there a constant in human nature which no amount of terror or propaganda can destroy?

In Oceania the sexual impulse, while not destroyed, has been remarkably weakened among the members of the Outer Party. For the faithful, sexual energy is transformed into political hysteria. There is a harrowing passage in which Smith remembers his sexual relations with his former wife, a loyal party member who would submit herself once a week, as if for an ordeal and resisting even while insisting, in order to procreate for the party. The only thing she did not feel was pleasure.

Orwell puts the matter with some care:

The aim of the Party was not merely to prevent men and women from forming loyalties which it might not be able to control. Its real, undeclared purpose was to remove all pleasure from the sexual act. Not love so much as eroticism was the enemy, inside marriage as well as outside it . . . The only recognized purpose of marriage was to beget children for the service of the Party. Sexual intercourse was to be looked on as a slightly disgusting minor operation, like having an enema . . . The Party was trying to kill the sex instinct, or, if it could not be killed, then to distort it and dirty it . . . And so far as the women were concerned, the Party's efforts were largely successful.

That Orwell has here come upon an important tendency in modern life, that the totalitarian state is inherently an enemy of erotic freedom, seems to me indisputable. And we know from the past that the sexual impulse can be heavily suppressed. In Puritan communities, for example, sex was regarded with great suspicion, and it is not hard to imagine that even in marriage the act of love might bring the Puritans very little pleasure. But it should be remembered that in Puritan communities hostility toward sex was interwoven with a powerful faith: men mortified themselves in behalf of God. By contrast, Oceania looks upon faith not merely as suspect but downright dangerous, for its rulers prefer mechanical assent to intellectual fervor or zealous belief. (They have probably read enough history to know that in the Protestant era enthusiasm had a way of turning into individualism.)

Given these circumstances, is it plausible that the Outer Party members would be able to discard erotic pleasure so completely? Is this not cutting too close to the limit of indestructible human needs? I should think that in a society so pervaded by boredom and grayness as Oceania is, there would be a pressing hunger for erotic adventure, to say nothing of experiments in perversion.

A totalitarian society can force people to do many things that violate their social and physical desires; it may even teach them to receive pain with quiet resignation; but I doubt that it can break down the fundamental, if sometimes ambiguous, distinction between pleasure and pain. Man's biological make-up requires him to obtain food, and, with less regularity or insistence, sex; and while society can do a great deal—it has—to dim the pleasures of sex and reduce the desire for food, it seems reasonable to assume that even when consciousness has been blitzed, the "animal drives" of man cannot be violated as thoroughly as Orwell suggests. In the long run, these drives may prove to be one of the most enduring forces of resistance to the totalitarian state.

Does not Orwell imply something of the sort when he shows Winston Smith turning to individual reflection and Julia to private pleasure? What is the source of their rebellion if not the "innate" resistance of their minds and bodies to the destructive pressures of Oceania? It is clear that they are no more intelligent or sensitive—certainly no more heroic—than most Outer Party members. And if their needs as human beings force these two quite ordinary people to rebellion, may not the same thing happen to others?

A related problem concerns Orwell's treatment of the workers in Oceania. The proles, just because they are at the bottom of the heap and perform routine tasks of work, get off rather better than members of the Outer Party: they are granted more privacy, the telescreen does not bawl instructions at them nor watch their every motion, and the secret police seldom troubles them, except to wipe out a talented or independent worker. Presumably Orwell would justify this by saying that the state need no longer fear the workers, so demoralized have they become as individuals and so powerless as a class. That such a situation might arise in the future it would be foolhardy to deny, and in any case Orwell is deliberately pushing things to a dramatic extreme; but we should also notice that nothing of the kind has yet happened, neither the Nazis nor the Stalinists having ever relaxed their control or surveillance of the workers to any significant extent. Orwell has here made the mistake of taking more than "one step" and thereby breaking the tie between the world we know and the world he has imagined.

But his treatment of the proles can be questioned on more fundamental grounds. The totalitarian state can afford no luxury, allow no exception; it cannot tolerate the existence of any group beyond the perimeter of its control; it can never become so secure as to lapse into indifference. Scouring every corner of society for rebels it knows do not exist, the totalitarian state cannot come to rest for any prolonged period of time. To do so would be to risk disintegration. It must always tend toward a condition of self-agitation, shaking and reshaking its members, testing and retesting them in order to insure its power. And since, as Winston Smith concludes, the proles remain one of the few possible sources of revolt, it can hardly seem plausible that Oceania would permit them even the relative freedom Orwell describes.

Finally, there is Orwell's extremely interesting though questionable view of the dynamics of power in a totalitarian state. As he portrays the party oligarchy in Oceania, it is the first ruling class of modern times to dispense with ideology. It makes no claim to be ruling in behalf of humanity, the workers, the nation or anyone but itself; it rejects as naive the rationale of the Grand Inquisitor that he oppresses the ignorant to accomplish their salvation. O'Brien, the representative of the Inner Party, says: "The Party seeks power entirely for its own sake. We are not interested in the good of the others; we are interested solely in power." The Stalinists and Nazis, he adds, had approached this view of power, but only in Oceania has all pretense to serving humanity—that is, all ideology—been discarded.

Social classes have at least one thing in common: an appetite for power. The bourgeoisie sought power, not primarily as an end in itself (whatever that vague phrase might mean), but in order to be free to expand its economic and social activity. The ruling class of the new totalitarian society, especially in Russia, is different, however, from previous ruling classes of our time: it does not think of political power as a means toward a non-political end, as to some extent the bourgeoisie did; it looks upon political power as its essential end. For in a society where there is no private property the distinction between economic and political power becomes invisible.

So far this would seem to bear out Orwell's view. But if the ruling class of the totalitarian state does not conceive of political power as primarily a channel to tangible economic privileges, what *does* political power mean to it?

At least in the West, no modern ruling class has yet been able to dispense with ideology. All have felt an overwhelming need to rationalize their power, to proclaim some admirable objective as a justification for detestable acts. Nor is this mere slyness or hypocrisy; the rulers of a modern society can hardly survive without a certain degree of sincere belief in their own claims. They cling to ideology not merely to win and hold followers, but to give themselves psychological and moral assurance.

Can one imagine a twentieth century ruling class capable of discarding these supports and acknowledging to itself the true nature of its motives? I doubt it. Many Russian bureaucrats, in the relaxation of private cynicism, may look upon their Marxist vocabulary as a useful sham; but they must still cling to some vague assumption that somehow their political conduct rests upon ultimate sanctions. Were this not so, the totalitarian ruling class would find it increasingly difficult, perhaps impossible, to sustain its morale. It would go soft, it would become corrupted in the obvious ways, it would lose the fanaticism that is essential to its survival.

But ideology aside, there remains the enigma of totalitarian power. And it *is* an enigma. Many writers have probed the origins of totalitarianism, the dynamics of its growth, the psychological basis of its appeal, the economic policies it employs when in power. But none of the theorists who study totalitarianism can tell us very much about the "ultimate purpose" of the Nazis or the Stalinists; in the end they come up against the same difficulties as does Winston Smith in *1984* when he says, "I understand HOW: I do not understand WHY."

Toward what end do the rulers of Oceania strive? They want power; they want to enjoy the sense of exercising their power, which means to test their ability to cause those below them to suffer. Yet the question remains, why do they kill millions of people, why do they find pleasure in torturing and humiliating people they know to be innocent? For that matter, why did the Nazis and Stalinists? What is the image of the world they desire, the vision by which they live? I doubt that such questions can presently be answered, and it may be that they are not even genuine problems. A movement in which terror and irrationality play so great a role may finally have no goal beyond terror and irrationality; to search for an ultimate end that can be significantly related to its immediate activity may itself be a rationalist fallacy.

Orwell has been criticized by Isaac Deutscher for succumbing to a "mysticism of cruelty" in explaining the behavior of Oceania's rulers, which means, I suppose, that Orwell does not entirely accept any of the usual socioeconomic theories about the aims of totalitarianism. It happens, however, that neither Mr. Deutscher nor anyone else has yet been able to provide a satisfactory explanation for that systematic excess in destroying human values which is a central trait of totalitarianism. I do not say that the mystery need remain with us forever, since it is possible that in time we shall be able to dissolve it into a series of problems more easily manageable. Meanwhile, however, it seems absurd to attack a writer for acknowledging with rare honesty his sense of helplessness before the "ultimate" meaning of totalitarianism—especially if that writer happens to have given us the most graphic vision of totalitarianism that has yet been composed. For with *1984* we come to the heart of the matter, the whiteness of the whiteness.

v

Even while noting these possible objections to Orwell's book, I have been uneasily aware that they might well be irrelevant—as irrelevant, say, as the objection that no one can be so small as Swift's Lilliputians. What is more, it is extremely important to note that the world of 1984 is *not* totalitarianism as we know it, but totalitarianism after its world triumph. Strictly speaking, the society of Oceania might be called post-totalitarian. But I have let my objections stand simply because it may help the reader see Orwell's book somewhat more clearly if he considers their possible value and decides whether to accept or reject them.

1984 brings us to the end of the line. Beyond this—one feels or hopes—it is impossible to go. In Orwell's book the political themes of the novels that have been discussed in earlier chapters reach their final and terrible flowering, not perhaps in the way that writers like Dostoevsky or Conrad expected but in ways that establish a continuity of vision and value between the nineteenth and twentieth century political novelists.

There are some writers who live most significantly for their own age; they are writers who help redeem their time by forcing it to accept the truth about itself and thereby saving it, perhaps, from the truth about itself. Such writers, it is possible, will not survive their time, for what makes them so valuable and so endearing to their contemporaries— that mixture of desperate topicality and desperate tenderness—is not likely to be a quality conducive to the greatest art. But it should not matter to us, this possibility that in the future Silone or Orwell will not seem as important as they do for many people in our time. We know what they do for us, and we know that no other writers, including far greater ones, can do it.

In later generations 1984 may have little more than "historic interest." If the world of 1984 does come to pass, no one will read it except perhaps the rulers who will reflect upon its extraordinary prescience. If the world of 1984 does not come to pass, people may well feel that this book was merely a symptom of private disturbance, a nightmare. But we know better: we know that the nightmare is ours.

EPILOGUE:
POLITICS AND THE NOVEL
AFTER *POLITICS AND THE NOVEL*

It may be a little too soon to devise comprehensive terms of description and analysis for the political fiction written after the Second World War. But one thing, I believe, can profitably be said about these fictions: they constitute a literature of blockage, a literature of impasse. From radically different intellectual premises and literary approaches, writers as various as Solzhenitsyn and Marquez, Naipaul and Kundera—one can hardly imagine them in the same room—find themselves blocked as both novelists and thinkers. They portray historical moments and situations; they offer sharply critical understandings; but they can find no way out of the political dilemmas with which they end their books, neither in Eastern Europe nor in the third world. It is a bad time in which they are writing, a time when the horizon of expectation, perhaps even of desire, seems very low. A fog of weariness and resignation settles upon their cultures. Solzhenitsyn may resort to prophetic exhortation, Marquez to revolutionary outcry, Kundera to a grating skepticism; but for a dispassionate reader it seems hardly to matter, since right now little changes, things do not move, the world seems dry and stagnant. This moment is not nearly so dreadful, of course, as the one in the late thirties when the dictators took over most of Europe. But it is still pretty bad, and bad insofar as it comes *after* that moment in the late thirties.

By now disenchantment with ideology and utopia is hardly the problem. Except for a few writers like Garcia Marquez who cling to tokens of revolution—and even he, one suspects, not quite with his earlier faith—there seems rather little left about which to have illusions. (That too is a dilemma, perhaps a severe one for writers engaged with political themes: a measured sobriety seems likely to serve life better than it serves literature.)

The emotions of the ex-Communist can no longer animate a serious work of fiction: who can imagine a novel like *Darkness at Noon* being written in the 1980s? Its time has passed, and to value it for the notable work it is we need to command a strong historical sense, which means a capacity to imagine the torments of others, and a modest historical knowledge, which means to possess a few facts about the Moscow trials and the regime that engineered them. Much the same kind of problem is likely to be experienced by young readers encountering for the first time Silone's *Bread and Wine*, though that work is more generous in its vision of human possibility than Koestler's and therefore less likely to suffer from the fading of its immediate subject.

Theoretical systems disintegrate, ideology recedes, Marxism finds an old-age home in American universities. The debates which excite the characters of Dostoevsky and Turgenev, the creeds that move and destroy the characters of Malraux and Koestler: these hardly figure in the political fiction of recent years, except perhaps as the debris of an earlier time. And not only does ideology fade, even the play of serious ideas declines. After great historical upheavals comes a day when people want quiet, retreat, innerness. Solzhenitsyn, at least in an earlier work like *The First Circle*, is one of the few contemporary novelists still passionately caught up with the life of ideas, perhaps because, through no fault of his own, he came to them rather late. But it's hard to imagine a critic saying

about most of the recent novelists who employ political themes
what a contemporary critic said of Dostoevsky: that he *felt
thought*.

Recent political fiction is often marked by a tone of rawness
and demoralization. The Trinidadian V.S. Naipaul and the
Czech Milan Kundera are as different from one another as two
writers could be, but both—the one with nervous irritation,
the other with sardonic playfulness—must meet up with the
reality of historical impasse. They see countries, societies that
are besotted with slogans and deceit, or are rutted in tyranny
and backwardness, and nothing they can write, no matter how
devastating, seems able to change anything.

Political fiction has not flourished in the relative stability of
the Western countries during the decades after the Second
World War. Neither conservative stasis nor social democratic
moderation, both of which may be seen as virtues compared
to the bloody excesses of recent times and other places, are
able to inspire first-rate novels dealing with political themes.
Perhaps we should be grateful for that. Political fiction requires wrenching conflicts, a drama of words and often blood,
roused states of being, or at least a memory of these. And in
the decades after the Second World War, such excitements
have been abundant only in Eastern Europe and parts of the
third world.

It's as if, in these uneasy years, two myths were confronting
one another in a stand-off: the myth of sobering and exhaustion after the debauch of Communism and the myth of revolutionary desperation in the emerging countries as they try to
get out from under Western imperialism. Both of these myths
have their energizing powers for novelists and both have
enabled the making of fine works of fiction; but both also bring
writers up against the hurt of blockage. Having scourged the
falsities of "socialist" countries without socialism and exposed
the falsities of "liberated" countries without liberation, writers
like Kundera and George Konrad, Naipaul and Mario Vargas
Llosa must ask themselves: what next? what possibilities remain in their familiar subject matter?

Novelists committed to political themes do not have to

arrive at political solutions: it is usually better that they not try to. But there is, I think, a strong psychological and even moral need among both writers and readers of novels—which is one reason novels are not, in any strict sense, tragedies—to feel that the rendered situation may not be utterly intractable; that, sooner or later, there may be a slight motion of change. But what if, in all honesty, the writer sees no such possibility? What if, locked into the unfreedom of his Eastern European country or the wretchedness of his third world nation, he can find no way out? How much will he then be able to do with his irony and anger, his farce and fury? Will there be a point at which he will find himself acknowledging the impotence of words?

These are not questions we need answer, or pretend to be able to answer. For writers they may in fact be beginnings, not ends. An historical impasse should not be airily dismissed through high literary chatter about "the imagination transcending etc." There are realities the imagination cannot transcend and should not try to. The writer can only struggle, through the sobrieties of realism or the artifice of antirealism, hoping to cope with or get round, or best of all, engage once again the urgencies of his moment. Many realities sooner or later loom before us as impasse, and all writers look for ways to scale walls or slip past barbed wires. Critics ought not to be in a hurry to tell them they can't do it.

Here, then, are a few notes—the merest notes—on the stratagems a few recent novelists have employed in confronting the experience of impasse, first of all political but sometimes, in consequence, also literary.

Nadine Gordimer—Revolution Yes, But . . .

There remain in the world a few situations in which the myth of revolution as pure and heroic liberation can retain its hold on the novelist's imagination. But not without a good many qualifications and hesitations.

By inclination and training a novelist of sensibility, Nadine Gordimer writes as a liberal who has apparently begun to wonder whether liberalism is adequate to the anguish of South Africa and whether revolutionary measures must be anticipated and perhaps acquiesced in. Presenting herself as a cultivated middle-class white, she identifies with the outcry of the blacks even as she realizes she cannot speak for and, in any close way, about them. If it is still possible anywhere in the world to think of politics in absolute moral terms, as a blunt counterposition of good and evil, that place is South Africa. The stark circumstances of that country lend force and passion to the work of such writers as Gordimer, J.M. Coetzee, and André Brink, all of whom are haunted—but thereby also enabled—by a great commanding subject. Yet this subject can also prove to be a tyranny: narrow, sterile, confining. Art can be crushed by the sheer moral weight of certain subjects, and these gifted South African writers find themselves gasping for a bit of imaginative space, some portion of freedom from the subject that seems inescapable. What lends their writing a particularly somber cast is an awareness, be it spoken or not, that in circumstances where evil appears to be so complete, a triumph of good might end in a new kind of evil—and that, nevertheless, it remains a moral imperative to accept that triumph. The position has its discomforts.

In *Burger's Daughter*, her most distinguished work, Nadine Gordimer focuses upon a small group of South African whites, in condition middle-class and in opinion Communist, who at risk to their lives and liberty have thrown themselves into the movement for black liberation. This enables Gordimer to negotiate a tentative, nervous entry into the outer precincts of black rebellion and a much more confident entry into the circle of Lionel Burger, a physician who is also a leader of the South African Communist Party. Soon after the novel's opening, Burger is arrested by the government and sentenced in court to life imprisonment.

It is, I think, an extraordinary feat this late in the century to make a Communist leader into a sympathetic, even noble figure without succumbing to either cant or sentimentality. Gordimer manages this not through a full-faced portrayal—she is novelistically shrewd enough to keep a certain distance from

Burger—but through a series of narrative skirmishes which complicate and perhaps even call into question her narrative of revolutionary heroism. It is hard to imagine a novelist managing so positive a response to a Communist leader anywhere else in the world. But the fate of Lionel Burger can still move us because in South Africa, for whatever reasons and with whatever ultimate consequences, the Communists have really suffered in behalf of black liberation. Gordimer, however, is too intelligent to stop there. She finds ways to bring in the Moscow trials, the Prague spring, and Burger's part in expelling a deviant comrade from the party, so that the Burger shown as a selfless and heroic man is also shown to be a faithful agent of Stalinism. Precisely insofar as she registers these complications does Gordimer enable credence for her version of Burger.

He is rarely seen directly. It's as if Gordimer refuses fully to yield herself to the pathos of his fate even as she is using all of her literary resources to make us respond to that fate. A series of secondary characters registers a variety of feelings about him—some influence of Henry James's techniques may be visible here. Burger's comrades adore him. An intransigent black nationalist, indifferent as a matter of principle to Burger the individual, is quite ready to scoff at him as a mere "useful" white. A young white intellectual, prematurely world-weary, keeps probing Burger's story for skeptical depreciations. And Burger's daughter Rosa, through whose intelligence much of the story is strained, opens up old and painful memories: what it was like to have lived as a child in a home totally dedicated to politics, what it was like to have it assumed that the daughter would necessarily follow in the footsteps of the father.

Rosa rebels a little by fleeing to the civilized assurances of Western Europe, as if the act of "finding herself" must mean for a time ceasing to be her father's daughter. At this point the book turns, for several chapters, into something close to a novel of sensibility; yet it's precisely this "digression," while not always absorbing in its own right, that helps to sustain that larger portion of the novel which rests, however uncomfortably, on the myth of revolutionary heroism. Rosa now comes to believe that her father and his friends had "made a Communism for 'local conditions' . . . a connection with blacks that was completely personal. In this way, their Communism was the antithesis of anti-individualism." Gordimer neither indicates her own acceptance of this judgement nor presses her readers to accept it; for the purposes of fictional credibility, it is enough that we suppose it a plausible or likely judgment by Burger's daughter.

Though not very political and certainly not a Communist, Rosa returns to join the black liberation struggle, becoming a prisoner like her father. The immediate task, apparently, must overwhelm all doubts and complicating perceptions, and thereby the revolutionary myth does achieve an equivocal sort of vindication. With what result? We can hardly be sure, since it is neither the politics of revolution nor its mere rejection which dominates this novel, it is the sense of politics as a terrible force beyond the reach of the rationality we like to suppose in control.

Latin Americans: Fable and Farce

A bristling array of talents, styles and opinions, so that all generalities must be suspect, especially those from the north. Yet also, behind the gaudy facades of Latin American fiction, a certain poverty of theme, a sad recurrence of situation and figures. One often feels that this fiction, brilliant in its formal and linguistic virtuosity, is doomed to imprisonment by its own obsessions, doomed to the repetition of grandiose historical rhythms that must sooner or later fall into despair.

The societies we glimpse in the fiction of writers like Gabriel Garcia Marquez and Alejo Carpentier draw upon a bizarre clasp of contraries: brave assertions of native culture and gross hungers for alien ways, rich spontaneous sensuality and numbed social resignation, high rationalist thought and provincial superstition, surrealist poetics and foul privies. Centuries far apart from one another are pressed into a false unity. A theorist might mention "the law of uneven development"; an unclouded eye might notice the interpenetration of primitivism and decadence. But this must be commonplace for Latin American writers, the tired paradoxes on which they grew up; their need as writers is to go beyond such cataloging of plight. For the most part they deal with the paradoxes of their cultures either through a rhetoric of expansion or an antirhetoric of contraction—which is to say, through fable or farce.

The recognition that their cultures are hemmed in by severe limitations—options without much choice—seems to draw these writers away from conventional realism and toward the "imaginative transcendence" of a quasi-surrealism, or what critics have called "magical realism." Historical incapacity is to be compensated for by imagination, sometimes mere fancy.

Farce spreads like a stain through Jorge Ibarguengoitia's *The Lightning of August,* a burlesque of Mexican revolution in which the feuding numbskull generals resemble nothing so much as the Keystone Kops. They bomb the wrong towns, execute the wrong captives, insult the wrong politicians. Ideas play no part here: all is stripped to a brutal farce of gold and knives. It's not hard to see how such a book might seem a welcome relief to Mexicans fed up with the solemnities of their national mythology. But cathartic as farce may be, it cannot encompass the Latin American experience: there is too much blood and hunger, and there are also some dreams of decency. Only when farce serves as a secondary motif for something other than itself, which here may mean a secondary motif for historical fable, does the futility of all those coups, dictators and pronunciamentos take on a kind of skeletal grandeur.

In Garcia Marquez's brilliant *One Hundred Years of Solitude* the elemental and mythic cycles of life in a Central American country—the haughty decorums and cruel sensualities by which people in the town of Macondo order their existence and relieve its barrenness—become the stuff which the wretched politics of the country cannot quite destroy. Garcia Marquez is intent upon salvaging what memory gradually forfeits and perhaps only fable can regain: the true subhistorical "history" of his people. How did they live through the times of civil war, apart from or beyond it?

By itself alone the fabulous narrative of the rise and fall of the Buendia family from the nineteenth into the twentieth century, despite all its wild humor and hyperbole, might come to seem a piece of evasion, almost a Central American operetta with Zorba-like tales of sexual prowess, personal willfulness, magical transformation. What gives the book its ration of ferocity, its grittiness of tone, is the recurrent intrusion of politics into the life of Macondo, politics not as ideology or thought (hardly Garcia Marquez's strong point) but as recurrent outbursts or rituals of violence. Colonel Aurelio Buendia, leader of thirty-two failed revolts, a brave and (as far as we can tell) mindless anarcho-rebel, is a figure of some pathos, but also of some farcicality, like a comic who always finds the banana peel on which to slip. Politics in *One Hundred Years of Solitude* becomes a supportive undercurrent or subtheme, the indispensible intrusion of a sterile history in a setting presented as fabulous in order to "transcend" the sterility. The matriarch who dominates a good part of the novel feels, at one crucial moment, that "time was not passing . . . but that it was turning in a circle."

That circle's turning is evoked in Alejo Carpentier's *Reasons of State*, a sardonic picture of the Latin American dictator whose strength draws upon the weakness of his country's social classes and its inability to achieve a stable political culture based on either alien or indigenous models. The dictator is an ignorant barbarian but also a shrewd mimic with an "infallible instinct of acquiring information at second hand." He knows nothing, yet can recite the names and titles of advanced European culture. He recognizes that he is "hated, abhorred by the mass of the people," yet skillfully exploits their fondness for exalted speech. He has no trouble in suppressing rebellious generals; he has a little trouble in coping with Dr. Luis Leoncio Martinez, the "austere professor of philosophy and translator of Plotinus" who advocates "a constitutional and democratic order" along European lines; but he is quite bewildered by the nameless "Student" who tries to organize the workers in behalf of revolution. The Student— N.B., not the Worker—appears to Carpentier an agent capable of breaking the cycle of political futility; but had he cast upon the new revolutionary dictatorships the critical eye he had turned upon the old caudillo dictatorships, he would have seen that the cycle has not been broken. Tomorrow the incorruptible Student will appear as the implacable dictator.

These novels yield a rich gathering of metaphor, hyperbole, and mocking eloquence, so bewitching to North American readers brought up on minimalist deprivations that they can easily forget how a style of high rhetoric may become as conventional as a style of sparse understatement. Garcia Marquez intends his language, like his fable, to serve as a pledge of commitment to obscure people who manage somehow to endure and to protect themselves from the depredations of politics, but finally his rhetoric may serve the very end it has been designed to oppose. It becomes, so to say, the skin of helplessness, of that despair which assails all thoughtful people in Latin America. Affirming defiance, it reflects weakness. As a character in Carpenter's novel remarks: "We are too partial to unbridled eloquence, pathos, platform pomposity, resounding with romantic braggadocio."

Once these writers acknowledge the reality of impasse, they sometimes turn to a hard, lean style, as if to bow before the sovereignity of fact and discount their own gifts for enchantment. In a splendid early work, *No One Writes to the Colonel*, Garcia Marquez employs this style to portray an aging survivor of the revolts led by Colonel Aureliano Buendia. This intrepid old warrior waits for a pension that never comes and in the end, when his wife asks what they will eat, he answers with an ultimate lucidity: "Shit."

Milan Kundera and the Jokes of History

"Spare me your Stalinism," replied Milan Kundera to an interviewer who in all innocence had called Kundera's novel *The Joke* "a major indictment of Stalinism." No, added Kundera, "*The Joke* is a love story." Another time he insisted rather testily that a political reading of his fiction must be a "bad reading."

Now consider the book Kundera calls "a love story:" It starts with an incident in the 1950s when the Prague student Ludvik, a staunch Communist whose faith is flawed only by a residual sense of humor, mails his zealous girlfriend a postcard reading: "Optimism is the opium of the people! A healthy atmosphere stinks of stupidity! Long live Trotsky!" Betrayed by a friend, Ludvik has to spend several years laboring in the mines as a "correction" for his sins. The remainder of the novel, including a distasteful scene in which Ludvik gains revenge by seducing the wife of the comrade who had denounced him, takes its motives and energies from this initial "joke"—an act the Communist authorities rightly see as political, no matter what Ludvik's intentions.

How, then, is it possible to deny that in this novel, as in several others by Kundera, politics shapes and misshapes the depicted events, or to put it somewhat differently, politics is the force against which the characters butt their heads trying to find a bit of living space for themselves? Since no one has ever supposed Kundera to be obtuse, one must suspect that in calling *The Joke* a love story he is striking a pose, as a sort of provocation or even perversity.

It's not hard to understand, of course, why a writer should dislike being categorized. To be typecast as a "dissident" or "political" novelist is to suffer insinuations of narrowness. For Kundera politics has meant living under a sodden, oppressive regime and being subject to ideological arm-twisting and the kitsch of its "progressive" propaganda. Little in his experience could sustain an Aristotelian notion of politics as the distinctly human activity through which citizens regulate their shared life. Kundera implies that his work merits, as of course it does, attention for its literary elements and that he should not be fixed as a writer captive to his time, place, and situation.

But in some measure, alas, he is captive. He struggles against that condition, mobilizing all his gifts to send out signals of freedom. He succeeds, in part. But his situation as a novelist born and raised in Czechoslovakia holds him in its grip. While by no means a mere helpless victim, neither is he quite the free spirit he wishes and no doubt deserves to be. The problem is known as history.

In such fictions as *The Joke, Laughable Loves,* and *The Book of Laughter and Forgetting* Kundera has undertaken a project with few parallels in modern literature. He strives to evoke the "feel" of life in a society eaten away by a profound demoralization, a kind of sickness with itself. No other writer has so sharply drawn a Communist society in its phase of decadence and so pitilessly shown the moral and psychological costs this decadence exacts. The fanaticism of the early fifties is gone, the ideology of Stalinism lies shattered, the claims of Marxism are the merest pretense. Nobody believes any longer what everyone must say, and everyone knows that nobody believes. Yet the power of the State remains intact, and behind it looms the Great Protector.

A slack nihilism pervades Kundera's world. People are oppressed, people are sad, yet if they keep quiet they will not suffer overt terror. This leaves them sufficient time and opportunity to measure their common humiliation. Some of them develop a hatred for language itself, since in such circumstances language becomes a falsity, the container for that kitsch—"the translation of the stupidity of received ideas into the language of beauty and feeling"—which Kundera regards as the essence of Communist speech, though also abundant enough in the West.

Still, people must find relief and Kundera's characters look for it in personal relations. They bury themselves in one another. They do this programatically—a decision without choice. It is at this point in his fiction that Kundera is at his strongest but also his most problematic. He knows, as his characters occasionally sense, that the falsities pervading public life have a way of seeping into the private relations to which people turn for shelter. The very idea of an "internal emigration" comes to seem dubious, almost a kind of utopia. Love requires speech, and speech becomes devalued. Love depends on candor and good faith, and these have become rare. What Kundera's characters often turn to is not love but sex and violence, or sex as violence, all possible without speech and undertaken without warmth. Sex may seem a momentary escape, an elemental act beyond social controls, but insofar as Kundera's characters suppose this to be so, they are mistaken. Soon this mistake opens the way for the routines of farce, which in turn leave everyone stripped and empty. "No, ladies and gentlemen," writes Kundera at the end of a story, "a man lives a sad life when he cannot take anything or anyone seriously." It's hard to know exactly which tone of voice Kundera would attach to this sentence, but no matter which it may be the result is terrible.

Turning bad, erotic experience becomes at times a sadistic game, at times a pointless fumbling. Is this to be seen wholly as a reflex of the torn lives Kundera's characters must lead or does it also, in some surreptitious way, turn upon the writer's own sensibility? Novelists who portray degradation find it hard wholly to escape its stain. Sometimes the trouble in Kundera's work seems a mere adolescent superciliousness in the narrating of sexual adventure. More bothersome is a seemingly unplanned vindictiveness which he betrays in the treatment of sexual relations. The scene in *The Joke* where Ludvik humiliates the wife of the man who has betrayed him is unnerving, with Kundera complicit in both action and voice.

Perhaps Kundera is himself, as a writer, subject to those demanding pressures which beset and undo his characters. Perhaps a merely "healthy" writer could not "catch" that disorder of conduct, that breakdown of morale, which Kundera so vividly portrays against the background of a Communist society in its post-ideological phase. Yet there are a number of fictions by Kundera where one does not feel such qualms, for example the story "Litost" in *The Book of Laughter and Forgetting*—a sardonic imagining from afar of Czech writers in their cups. Here the mixture of farce and sorrows works exactly right, without a false note.

At such times Kundera is a novelist of great resourcefulness, breaking apart conventions long attached to the novel, especially the realistic nineteenth-century kind, and returning to the verbal improvizations, the union of mimetic illusion and its deliberate suspension which he loves in Sterne and Diderot.

This is the ground of his pride, the artificer's pride, and the warrant for his claim to freedom. He resists the politics of repression with an imagination constantly geared to new tricks. And surely he would be delighted, if he knew it, with Benjamin Whorf's remark that "language is the best show man puts on."*

Kundera writes novels that tell love stories (often really antilove stories), provide meditations on a folk culture increasingly contaminated by kitsch, trace the pratfalls of characters thrust into farcical humiliations; but a good part of his work is saturated with politics, impossible to understand in its peculiar urgency without some sense of politics. Like his Ludvik, Kundera is trapped by his time. And that may be the most rotten of the jokes history has played on him, with farce the merest shade away from the tragic.

Naipaul—the "Half-Made" World

"Fine, witty, piercing, almost unbearable in its cruelty"— so a character in an early Naipaul novel describes "an anonymous satiric tale" about a "revolutionary regime" in the Caribbean. So might Naipaul's novels be described themselves, at times by bitter enemies who say he maligns the poor young struggling nations of the Third World and at other times by uneasy admirers who believe he draws accurate if stringent portraits of demagogic fecklessness in those nations.

I am among the uneasy admirers. Uneasy because of his surplus of disgust and paucity of tenderness, but an admirer because he writes with a strict refusal of romantic moonshine about the moral charms of primitives or the virtues of bloodstained dictators. Although he has attached himself by decision to the styles and values of English liberalism, he still sees things from the margin, as a son of Hindu parents raised in

*Benjamin Lee Whorf, *Language, Thought, Reality: Selected Writings*, ed. John B. Carroll (Cambridge, Mass.: The MIT Press, 1982), p. 25

Trinidad. He is a scourge of our disenchanted age, as free of colonialist bias as of infatuation with Third World delusions. Tough-minded about the sleaziness of much contemporary history, Naipaul lacerates his characters—sometimes himself—with assaults upon the misused rhetoric of Third World politics, often the leavings of Paris and Moscow, the "sinister mimicry" with which the south "twists the revolutionary jargon of the north."

"We used borrowed phrases which were part of our escape from thought, from that reality we wanted people to see but could ourselves scarcely face." So speaks the narrator of *The Mimic Men*, an early fiction about a failed "revolutionary" from the Caribbean. And the sad truth, hinted at in Naipaul's novels but openly stated in his journalism, may be that some of these Third World nations have no "phrases" of their own but must continue to stumble along as best they can on what they pick up here and there. Naipaul's notion of "half-made" societies—those that have never fulfilled themselves or achieved a settled personality—is at the base of much of his fiction. One can of course hope that he is wrong or that he overstates a case which is valid for the moment, but there must lurk the fear that he is right. For what Naipaul makes us question is that assumption of "progress" which suggests that finally, somehow, in the long run, things will work out for even the most backward and wretched nations. He does this, too often, with a manner that is deliberately provocative, a sort of grating insistence, which may cause one to wonder at his own feelings and motives. Yet only a fool or an ideologue will dismiss what he says and shows.

There was a time when Naipaul did come rather close to being the "lovable" performer that Westerners have often looked for in colonial writers. His long Dickensian novel *A House for Mr. Biswas*, depicting Indian life in the exile of Port of Spain, has many touches of humor and kindliness. But since publishing that book in 1961 Naipaul has grown increasingly astringent, and in his more recent fictions set in the Caribbean and Africa he no longer troubles either to perform or to please. He is now in the grip of a harsh vision of what happens in those unfortunate countries that have just toppled out of a tribal past or freed themselves from colonial rule, but cannot reach the uncertain blessings of modernity. He is obsessed, exasperated, enraged with the shallowness of pro-claimed liberations—"dictatorships of the proletariat" in coun-tries that have no proletariat, religious fanaticisms that dwindle into butchery, great building projects that end as rubble, the pathos of a Fanonist rhetoric that masks the blackjacks of new tyrants. And his aim is deadly: the bureaucrat with a fourth-grade education who "runs" economies, the agitator without a thought in his head, the dictator ("Big Man" in *A Bend in the River*) for whom power is registered by arbitrary wilfulness. Naipaul's fiercest thrusts, often superbly wicked, are directed against white intellectuals who dress up the African dictator's three-hour speeches with verbal ornaments from Paris. In both *Guerillas* and *A Bend in the River* Naipaul dissects the vainglory of this type, shifting readily from liberationist pro-nunciamentos to bending the knee before the "liberators."

Control—control of his feelings, control of his language—is Naipaul's main problem as a novelist. In his rage against the thugs and disdain for the playboys of "revolution" he can overreach himself, so that in his decidedly nasty *Guerillas* he grinds away in a vindicative spirit, allowing polemical fury to overcome novelistic tact.

But in his most recent novel, *A Bend in the River*, there is both acute detail and a new, if still mild, note of tolerance, even sympathy. The African country that forms the novel's locale, a blend apparently of Zaire and Uganda, has entered modern history or at least a parody of it. Impressive buildings go up, for no clear purpose; local toughs are bundled into the army; young people are sent off to universities; the population endures windy orations by the Big Man; and Raymond, the Parisian intellectual, celebrates the dictator's ramblings as an attempt "to give sanctity to the bush of Africa." For the blacks in the bush, for the Indians on the coast, even for the quaver-ing elite on top, everything is unsettled, dependent on the whim of the Big Man. Perhaps it's a country, but it's not a coherent society. The fading of the tribes, the feebleness of all social classes in the towns, the jitteriness of the local intelligentsia (the "mimic men"), all lead to the army being the single source of power, and within and over the army, Big Man.

There are signs of a new patience in *A Bend in the River*. Naipaul knows that in the Big Man's country, human effort must burn out into waste, while ideas shrink to mere covers for power. But the Indian narrator finds in himself a moral obligation to wait and avoid passing quick judgment. And the young black Ferdinand who has come out of the bush to become commissioner of the town, speaks with a new grasp of the terribleness behind all the Big Man's talk.

Beyond this Naipaul can offer no intimations of hope or signals of direction. He has reached an impasse: can there be any way out for this country overwhelmed by disasters? Can there be any further development of a fiction that corrodes the very substance on which it rests?

There is a literary–moral problem here that for the moment may be beyond solution. A writer has to be faithful to what he sees, and few see as sharply as Naipaul; yet one may wonder whether, in some final reckoning, a serious novelist can simply allow the wretchedness of his depicted scene to become the limit of his vision. Such novelists as Dostoevsky, Conrad, and Turgenev, also dealing with painful aspects of political life, struggled to "surmount" or "transcend" them. Naipaul seems right now to be a writer beleaguered by his own truths, unable to get past them. That is surely an honorable difficulty, far better than indulging in sentimental or ideological uplift; but it exacts a price.

Perhaps, given the moment in which he lives and the subject that grips him, Naipaul has no choice. Perhaps we ought simply to be content that in his austere and brilliant style he holds fast to the bitterness before his eyes. But it might be remembered that a little charity can also form part of understanding.

*　　*　　*

Solzhenitsyn and the Russian Intelligentsia

There is a sense, an unhappy sense, in which every word Solzhenitsyn has written is political. That is the price a writer pays for living in, or being an exile from, a totalitarian country. It is a high price, blocking him from many human enterprises and literary possibilities, and forcing him, whether he wishes it or not, constantly to confront the hovering leviathan. Solzhenitsyn's first book, the short novel *One Day in the Life of Ivan Denisovich,* seems largely devoid of ideological content: it could have been written by an anti-Stalinist Communist, which is probably what its author then was. Solzhenitsyn's intent seems to have been close to that of the nineteenth-century European realists: to render a "world," that of the Siberian camps, with mimetic transparency. Modest in scope, this aim is ambitious in character, since the writing of such a fiction depends on the writer's command of truth or at least actuality. Actuality most of all, with the writer counterposing the vital substance of day-to-day existence, what "actually happens," to all systems of perception and belief. Georg Lukacs was very keen in comparing this short novel with the short novels of Conrad and Hemingway, for they too wished to counterpose a grasped actuality—the heart of darkness, the expatriation in Paris—to received systems of perception and belief.

Yet, as everyone immediately understood, *One Day* is devastating in what it shows and implies. This simple story filtered through the mind of a simple peasant forces a society to recognize that something ghastly, indeed unforgivable has happened to it. Yet there is little, if any, explicit politics in the book; almost nothing is discussed; Solzhenitsyn is here essentially faithful to the Flaubertian line of modern fiction.

For so passionate a writer this could not remain tolerable for very long. In his next two novels, thus far his major ones—*The First Circle* and *The Cancer Ward*—Solzhenitsyn turns to open speech, the thrust of debate, releasing all that has been held in for decades. There is a poignant moment in *The Cancer Ward* when a guilt-ridden ex-Stalinist, Shulubin, enunciates his creed of "ethical socialism," apparently speaking for the Solzhenitsyn who wrote the novel, though not of course for the later, messianic Solzhenitsyn. "Did you think of this during these twenty-five years when you were bowing low and renouncing your beliefs?" Shulubin is asked. "Yes, I did," he answers, "I renounced everything and kept on thinking. I stuffed the books into the stove and I kept thinking. Why not? Haven't I earned the right to a few thoughts through my sufferings, my betrayal?"

A "few thoughts"—they are the salvage of a century—form the heart of *The First Circle*, Solzhenitsyn's most impressive fiction and, in my judgment, the greatest imaginative work of recent years to deal with the life of politics.

Reading *The First Circle* we enter a world in which men suffer because they think and manifest their humanity by an insistence upon thinking for themselves. The idea of human culture as *plenitude*, which for Solzhenitsyn stirs images of the Russian culture of Dostoevsky and Tolstoy, becomes the tacit premise of *The First Circle*. To reach back, as if by program, to the largesse of Tolstoy and the penetration of Dostoevsky means of course to acknowledge tacitly that these qualities cannot now be realized—but also that a conscious effort is being made, through a work of the imagination, to heal the rupture in Russian cultural tradition that was caused by years of political terror.

Solzhenitsyn's novels help to persuade us, at least as much as any novels can, that the claims made by certain writers that the totalitarian states have succeeded in transforming not only public speech but also private minds, are not wholly or perhaps even largely true. In the laboratory–prison of *The First Circle*, filled with scientists and intellectuals, there is a remarkable freedom and range of opinions, quite what one associates with the Russian cultural tradition at its best. The novel comes to seem like a gathering of long-suppressed voices, from Rubin, the lovable fool still entranced with the system that has locked him up, to Kondrashev, the painter of transcendental inclinations.

The inmates of this laboratory–prison are treated better than the prisoners in Siberian camps, but they remain captives forced to do shameful tasks for their captors. They come to resemble, in their extreme situation, the larger society of post-Stalinist Russia, no longer quite terrorized but by no means free. Perhaps more important, they testify to the survival of Russian culture and provide, thereby, a possible glimpse of how it might again flourish were freedom possible. Solzhenitsyn does not of course, as a novelist, put things so abstractly. He has done the novelist's job of work: he has created a group of vibrant figures clearly set apart from himself, men individualized in voice and manner and endowed with strength, intelligence, and personal flavor. The confinement in Stalin's laboratory–prison is matched by activity of minds, and while we can, if we care to, infer Solzhenitsyn's own biases, he writes here with a generosity of feeling such as will seldom be evident in his later work. What he shows in *The First Circle* is something the novelist, but especially the novelist of politics, cannot afford to lose: a belief in the integrity of *other minds*. Following the mental journeys of characters such as Nerzhin, Rubin, Sologdin and many others, we respond not so much to the rightness of one or another opinion but to the sturdiness of their bearing, the honesty with which they speak their convictions.

The prisoners in *The First Circle* are men of thought and articulateness, full of individual passions and eccentricities. Learning the lesson of Dostoevsky, who in *The Possessed* makes his most ridiculous character, the old liberal Stepan Trofimovich, also his most lovable one, Solzhenitsyn creates in Rubin an equally ridiculous and lovable character, the still-faithful Communist who maintains his ties with the other prisoners simply because he cannot deny in himself a need for fraternity. At the opposite extreme in the laboratory–prison stands Sologdin, a man devoted entirely to the disciplining of the will, though full of humor in the doing of it, a brilliant figure who believes in "unique personalities" rather than any system of ideas. And at the center of the book is the character who may be taken as Solzhenitsyn's surrogate, at least for the time he wrote *The First Circle:* a "positive hero" rich in flaws, a humanist who draws a line beyond which he will not voluntarily go, a seeker who questions all the solutions of his friends, a skeptic whose journey leads toward dissatisfaction with skepticism. Nerzhin tells the ever-credulous Rubin that skepticism may represent "only a shed by the roadside where I can sit out the bad weather. But skepticism is a way of freeing the dogmatic mind and that's where its value lies." The fiercely intolerant Solzhenitsyn of later years might consider these lines again.

When Nerzhin is sent off to Siberia, he gives his cherished copy of Yessenin's poems to the janitor Spiridon, who in *The First Circle* appears as a descendant of Tolstoy's saintly plebeian, Platon Karataev. What Spiridon has given Nerzhin in turn is a memorable distinction between the guilty and the innocent: "sheepdogs are right and cannibals are wrong."

This seems about as far as the Solzhenitsyn on *The First Circle* and the smaller, gentler *The Cancer Ward* can go. While his marvelous demonstration that the Russian intelligentsia has spiritually survived the Stalinist terror is of capital importance politically, it still cannot offer any way out of the reality of totalitarian power. The figures in the laboratory–prison share this in common: that each is caught in the same trap of helplessness, none has any usable way of bringing about a change, all must live with the thought that the condition of impasse will have to be endured for a long time to come. Now, in any other novel, even in a novel dealing with politics, this might not matter very much—after all, we do not look to the other writers I have glanced at in these notes for solutions to the political problems that engage them. But it does, somehow, matter with regard to Solzhenitsyn's work. He writes out of such a powerful sense of apocalyptic urgency that he raises in his readers the (no doubt unwarranted) expectation that at the end some blinding light, some solution of wonder, will present itself. None does and none can. But this thwarted expectation must surely be one reason Solzhenitsyn would soon abandon the liberalism and tolerance which shine through *The First Circle* and *The Cancer Ward* and turn to the quasi-prophetic Christian and harshly authoritarian "Great

Russian" stances of his later work. Those who see no path on earth will, in desperation, look for ways of surmounting or "transcending."

The intense political consciousness of the Solzhenitsyn who wrote *The First Circle* leads him to, or forces upon him, the conclusion that there is no political answer—not, at least, in the present historical moment. The politics of the book becomes then an act of symbolic consciousness, and that explains why Solzhenitsyn, like Pasternak and Vassily Grossman, cares so much about creating a version of the ninteenth-century Russian novel. *The First Circle* rests on a persuasion that such a return to the largesse of Tolstoy may constitute a revolutionary act of the spirit, a struggle to regain the image of freedom. Solzhenitsyn at this point in his career seems to have reached the "instinctive" conclusion that in a totalitarian or authoritarian society the writer's central hope is to preserve fundamental supports of moral existence, direct intuitions of human fraternity. A writer seized by such a vision—which must be regarded as "religious" in urgency and depth, and may well lead to more familiar religious persuasions—is not likely to be attracted to modernist innovations in literary method. His effort to reestablish the capaciousness of the nineteenth-century Russian novel is an effort to attach himself to the spirit of freedom which characterized it at its frequent best.

There is no conclusion. We are charting paths here which twist and turn each day, and sometimes come to a halt in the pain of impasse. So it seems at the moment; in the far, and perhaps even the near, future it may all change. One can only hope so, looking for what the historian Gershom Scholem has called "a plastic hour," that moment in the life of mankind when new possibilities suddenly come to light.

I.H.
October, 1986

0011